# Maximize Your Benefits

## A Guide for All Employees

## Neil Downing, CFP

DEARBORN™
A **Kaplan Professional** Company

# Dedication

For my wife, Vicki-Ann, and the children with whom God has blessed us: James, Andrew, and Caitlin.

Associate Publisher: Cynthia A. Zigmund
Senior Managing Editor: Jack Kiburz
Interior Design: Lucy Jenkins
Cover Design: Salvatore Concialdi
Typesetting: the dotted i

Published by Dearborn, a Kaplan Professional Company

Printed in the United States of America

00 01 02   10 9 8 7 6 5 4 3 2 1

**Library of Congress Cataloging-in-Publication Data**
Downing, Neil.
    Maximize your benefits : a guide for all employees / Neil Downing.
        p.   cm.
    Includes bibliographical references and index.
    ISBN 0-7931-3700-4 (pbk.)
    1. Employee fringe benefits—United States.   I. Title.
HD4928.N62 U6277 2000
331.25'5'0973—dc21                                           00-025232

# Advance Praise for *Maximize Your Benefits*

"It's a shame that most employees do not take full advantage of the many benefits their employers offer. By reading Neil Downing's book, you will be sure to maximize every benefit that you are entitled to. He not only explains all the traditional benefit plans, but also all of the latest options including Medical Savings Accounts, SIMPLE plans, Roth IRAs, cash balance pensions, Preferred Provider Organizations, stock option plans, and much more. Read this book and reap the most from your benefits!"

—Jordan E. Goodman, Author, *Everyone's Money Book*

"Planning frequently gets a bad rap in this age of high-tech free-form innovation, but when it comes to financial security and employee benefits there is no substitute for planning. *Maximize Your Benefits* paints a beautiful picture of how planning can essentially give you a raise without having to ask—and a better prospect of long-term financial security. In short, this is a book that will pay for itself a thousand times."

—Dallas L. Salisbury, President & CEO, Employee Benefit Research Institute

"This is a must-read for every worker in the U.S. Neil has taken the myriad of employee benefits and translated them into English for his readers. Workers need to understand their benefits so that they can make educated choices when changing jobs."

—Dee Lee, CFP, Harvard Financial Educators, and Author, *Let's Talk Money* and *The Complete Idiot's Guide to 401(K) Plans*

"I have found over the years that many individuals who work for companies that have excellent benefit programs fail to appreciate what they have until they lose these benefits. Frequently, this occurs when they leave and start a new business. Attempting to replace these benefits usually is a shocking experience. Neil Downing's extensive treatment of this important subject will clearly help readers to understand the value of the benefits that are so commonly taken for granted."

—Ted Benna, President, 401(k) Association

"Neil Downing, with his book *Maximize Your Benefits,* has put together the definitive 'one-stop source' for everything you need to know about the often-confusing, but extremely important world of employee benefits."

—Charles B. Carlson, CFA, Author, *Eight Steps to Seven Figures*

"Well organized, clearly explained, this book will help people do what the title says. Instead of trying to piece it all together yourself, Neil's thorough research helps you get to the important questions quickly. This book already has me reevaluating some of the benefits that I offer to my workforce. Finally, it is a guide that presents explanations, promises, and problems associated with various benefit options."

—Daniel J. Pederson, Author, *Savings Bonds: When to Hold, When to Fold*, and President, The Savings Bond Informer, Inc.

# Contents

# Preface

Twenty years ago I left a full-time newspaper job *with* benefits for a part-time newspaper job *without* benefits. Some of my friends and coworkers thought I was crazy. True, the full-time job paid poorly and offered only the skimpiest benefits package, but at least it provided some benefits; the new job offered none.

Why switch? The new job paid a lot by comparison. More importantly, it offered an opportunity for advancement. I took the new job, and within a few months I was hired full-time. The gamble paid off.

In the interim, however, I was often reminded about the vital role that employee benefits play in a worker's everyday life. The lesson was driven home to me repeatedly: every time I had to write a check to pay for my individual health insurance policy, every time I read about the advantages of company-sponsored retirement plans, every time a coworker talked about taking a sick day with pay.

Having no benefits also motivated me to work harder to try to secure full-time employment, with its promise of a complete and well-rounded benefits package.

## Taking Your Benefits for Granted

It's easy to take your benefits for granted. You get a brochure or handbook from work, then stow it in a filing cabinet or on a bookshelf and forget about it.

That's a mistake, because your benefits package is just as important as your pay. In some respects, it's even more important.

Benefits can play a key role in helping you determine when and whether to buy a house; whether to start a family or add to your family; whether you'll need to save on your own for retirement or save more for retirement; and whether to look for another job that offers a better range of benefits that are better suited to your needs.

Understanding how employee benefits work and how to make the most of your benefits is more important today than ever before because of the revolution that's going on in the American workplace. Employers who once took full responsibility for workers' benefits, arranging for cradle-to-grave coverage, have gradually shifted the burden to the employees themselves.

Workers now have more freedom to choose, but they also face a dizzying and complex array of choices:

- Should you pick a traditional health insurance plan or an HMO?
- How much should you contribute to your 401(k) retirement savings plan, and how should the money be invested?
- Should you take part in your company's cafeteria plan? How much will it cost you?
- Should you take advantage of a flexible spending account? What could you lose if you don't?
- Should you cash in your company stock options? What would be the income tax consequences?

## A Clear Road Map

Employers are reluctant to offer advice, fearing liability. Where can you turn?

This book offers a clear road map to consumers who are grappling with dozens of alternatives in their existing benefits packages. It goes well beyond the standard benefits brochure or booklet your employer gives you, showing exactly how benefits work, the advantages and disadvantages of each, and how to use your benefits package more effectively.

It is also essential reading for those who are seeking ammunition as they try to improve their benefits plans, and for job seekers trying to evaluate benefits plans offered by prospective employers.

### Health Insurance

Part 1 focuses on what may well be the most important employee benefit to you and your family—employer-sponsored health insurance.

This section explains in plain language not only how all the various health plans work, but also how to choose a plan using two key measures: cost and the range and quality of health care you can expect to receive.

You'll also find help on the complex decisions many workers face when discerning how best to use cafeteria plans, flexible spending accounts and medical savings accounts.

This section also spells out exactly what rights you have for continuing your health insurance coverage when you leave your job or if you're laid off.

## Retirement Plans

Part 2 examines what is probably the second most important feature of an employee benefits package: retirement savings plans. You'll see what pensions are, how they work, and which offer the best deals for you.

Part 2 also highlights the explosive growth and popularity of 401(k) retirement savings plans. You'll find out not only how to put money in and how to invest it wisely, but also how and when you can take your money out—in the form of loans, hardship withdrawals, rollovers, and transfers—and the different tax consequences that can apply to each. You'll also see why a 401(k) plan may not be your best choice to save for long-range goals.

In addition, Part 2 shows what makes traditional pension plans so appealing, why these plans are so little understood, and why they're being targeted for elimination by some employers, who want to replace them with controversial cash balance plans. Small-business retirement plans—including the hot new SIMPLE plan and the popular SEP plans—are also covered, as are some less well-known, but important, retirement savings vehicles for nonprofit and government workers—the 403(b) and 457 plans.

Part 2 also shows the tax consequences of transferring pension benefits from one job to another, how to keep track of your pension benefits when employers aren't forthcoming, and what to do with your pension balance when you lose your job. You'll also get guidance on searching for lost pension benefits.

## The Wider Range of Benefits

The chapters in Part 3 examine the wide range of other benefits available in the workplace today, including company-sponsored stock option plans; life insurance, disability insurance, and long-term care insurance programs; educational assistance plans; adoption benefit programs; and childcare and dependent-care plans.

This isn't a textbook written for human resources specialists; it's an easy-to-read consumer guide. Don't read it all at once; it's meant to be a handy reference tool, a faithful companion that can accompany you from one job to another, from your early working years straight on through retirement.

*Maximize Your Benefits* doesn't just explain how benefits work; it also adds value by offering ways you can make the most of your benefits package. And it helps you monitor your plans to ensure that you're getting what you're promised.

Enjoy!

# Acknowledgments

I am grateful to Arnold S. Johnson, chief executive officer, and Thomas G. Anderson, president, of Universal Pensions Inc. (UPI), of Brainerd, Minnesota, and to the entire UPI team, including Pam O'Rourke, Mike O'Brien, Keith Stunek, Mike Rahn, Roger Geraets, and Karleen Schmidt.

Thanks also to Dallas Salisbury and the staff at the Employee Benefit Research Institute; Jeanne Medeiros, regional coordinator of the New England Pension Assistance Project; Ed Slott, CPA, editor of *Ed Slott's IRA Advisor* newsletter; Barbara C. Shuckra; Jordan E. Goodman, founder and president of Amherst Enterprises and "The Money Answers" consumer information group; Mark Luscombe, Nicholas Kaster, Leslie Bonacum, Mary Dale Walters, Irene E. Tatara, and the staff at CCH Inc.; and Missy Krasner and the staff at the Henry J. Kaiser Family Foundation.

I am also grateful to Daniel J. Pederson, president of The Savings Bond Informer; Ed Carberry at the National Center for Employee Ownership; Dana Gagne, CFP; Patricia A. Thompson, CPA, CFP; Robert E. Cusack Jr.; and Robert J. Glovsky and the faculty, staff, and students of the Boston University Program for Financial Planners.

I also appreciate the support and commitment to excellence of the officers, directors, and staff of the *Providence Journal*, including Howard G. Sutton, publisher, president, and CEO; Joel P. Rawson, senior vice president and executive editor; and Carol J. Young, Thomas E. Heslin, Peter Phipps, John Kostrzewa, and the rest of the *Journal* team.

I am particularly indebted to readers of the "MoneyLine" column throughout the country, whose questions and comments inspired sections of this book; and most of all, to Cynthia Zigmund, associate publisher at Dearborn Trade, for her guidance, faith, and support, and to the rest of the Dearborn team.

# *HEALTH INSURANCE*

Most Americans pay for their health care through health insurance, and most get that insurance through the workplace—through their own job, or the job of a family member.

Unfortunately, radical changes are taking place in the world of health insurance. At one time, you could pick your own primary doctor or visit a specialist of your choosing, and your company's health insurance would pay the bill. That was the health care "prescription" for millions of workers and their families. Today, that prescription has all but expired and has been replaced with a mind-boggling array of rules and restrictions.

The following chapters on health insurance will help guide you through the maze. You'll read what types of health care plans are available through employee benefits packages, how the different plans work, and how you can make them work for you to fit your needs.

You'll read how to make a choice among health plans based not just on cost but also on quality. In addition, you'll find a plain-language guide to your rights to continued coverage under an employer-sponsored health plan, whether you quit your job, get laid off, or take a leave of absence.

Bear in mind that our nation's health insurance system is far from perfect. Even though employer-sponsored health insurance is widely available, some firms don't offer it, mainly because it has become such an expensive benefit. In addition, even at firms that offer health insurance as a benefit, some workers don't have coverage—either because of the way the plans are set up or because eligible workers simply can't afford it.

Even for those workers who are enrolled in their employer's group health insurance plan, coverage can be skimpy, offering only the most basic benefits; workers are on their own for everything that's not covered.

The following chapters aren't intended to suggest that America's health insurance and health care system is faultless. There are lots of problems—big problems—and the system seems to lurch from one crisis to another, year after year. Still, the system that's in place is the only one available. The chapters in Part 1 are intended to help you understand how the system operates and how to make it work for you and your family.

# Health Insurance Today

Health insurance is the mother of all employee benefits. It's the reason some people choose one job over another. It's the reason some people keep a job instead of moving to another.

Why? Whether you're rich or poor, single or married, male or female, in good health or in bad, you need health insurance. It serves as a kind of safety net, there to catch you—and your family—when you need health care. It may not pay for all of your health care expenses, but it usually covers the lion's share of them. Without health insurance, you could face financial ruin: even treatment for a fairly minor illness or injury can cost thousands of dollars.

With some other types of insurance, such as life insurance and disability insurance, you may never wind up filing a claim. In other words, you may never see an actual payoff (although you do get lots of peace of mind). With health insurance, however, you typically see a payoff every time you visit a doctor, hospital, or other health care provider.

## Who Has Coverage?

If you're lucky enough to have health insurance, odds are you're like most Americans: you have it through your job or the job of a family member. Health insurance is a common employee benefit, and it is vitally important to millions of Americans. It is so important that, year after year, Congress continues to give better tax breaks for health insurance than for any other employee benefit.

Think of it: Your employer gets to claim a federal income tax deduction for the money it spends to provide you with health insurance. The value of the benefits you receive through your company-sponsored health plan are tax-free to you. If you spend money yourself to pay for health insurance and medical expenses, you may be able to claim a federal income tax deduction, too.

**Figure 1.1**    Sources of Health Coverage

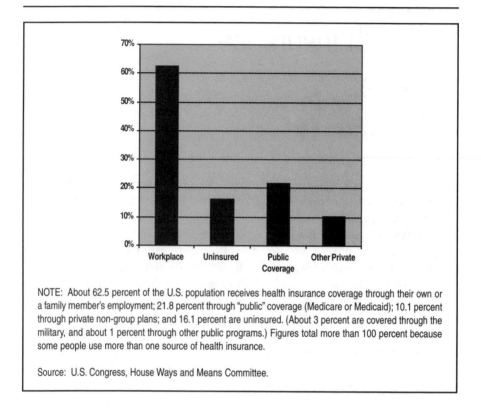

NOTE:  About 62.5 percent of the U.S. population receives health insurance coverage through their own or a family member's employment; 21.8 percent through "public" coverage (Medicare or Medicaid); 10.1 percent through private non-group plans; and 16.1 percent are uninsured. (About 3 percent are covered through the military, and about 1 percent through other public programs.) Figures total more than 100 percent because some people use more than one source of health insurance.

Source:  U.S. Congress, House Ways and Means Committee.

## Tax Breaks and Benefits

The tax breaks are no small matter. Consider the big picture: By giving preferential tax treatment to health insurance in the workplace, the U.S. government in 1999 passed up a chance to rake in more than $60 billion in federal tax revenue, according to an estimate by the U.S. Congress Joint Committee on Taxation.

That's more, by far, than for any other employee benefit—including pensions, group term life insurance, company-provided childcare, employer-paid educational assistance, and other benefits. By 2002, the amount of the tax break is expected to grow to more than $73 billion, according to a committee forecast.

Even when Congress looks to expand government revenues, it largely leaves health insurance benefits alone. In recent years, in fact, Congress has considered broadening its favorable treatment of health insurance by letting more people qualify for a tax deduction for the money they spend on medical insurance premiums and medical care.

**Figure 1.2** Tax Breaks for Health Insurance

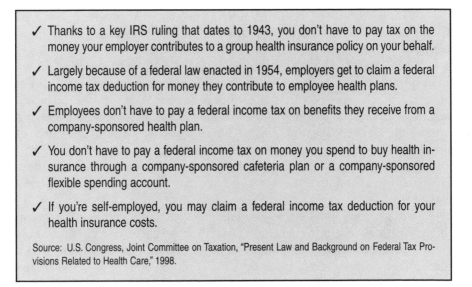

✓ Thanks to a key IRS ruling that dates to 1943, you don't have to pay tax on the money your employer contributes to a group health insurance policy on your behalf.

✓ Largely because of a federal law enacted in 1954, employers get to claim a federal income tax deduction for money they contribute to employee health plans.

✓ Employees don't have to pay a federal income tax on benefits they receive from a company-sponsored health plan.

✓ You don't have to pay a federal income tax on money you spend to buy health insurance through a company-sponsored cafeteria plan or a company-sponsored flexible spending account.

✓ If you're self-employed, you may claim a federal income tax deduction for your health insurance costs.

Source: U.S. Congress, Joint Committee on Taxation, "Present Law and Background on Federal Tax Provisions Related to Health Care," 1998.

What's the big deal? Congress understands how meaningful health insurance is to workers—and to employers. Before World War II, few Americans had health insurance, and most policies covered only hospital room and board and related services, according to a report by the nonprofit Employee Benefit Research Institute in Washington.

**Figure 1.3** Health Care Spending

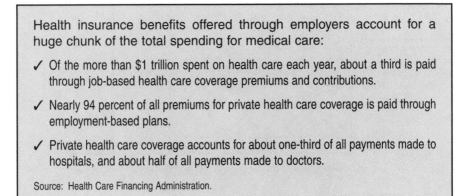

Health insurance benefits offered through employers account for a huge chunk of the total spending for medical care:

✓ Of the more than $1 trillion spent on health care each year, about a third is paid through job-based health care coverage premiums and contributions.

✓ Nearly 94 percent of all premiums for private health care coverage is paid through employment-based plans.

✓ Private health care coverage accounts for about one-third of all payments made to hospitals, and about half of all payments made to doctors.

Source: Health Care Financing Administration.

# How Health Insurance Is Evolving

During World War II, the number of people with coverage increased sharply, partly because wages were frozen, but health benefits were not (nor were they subject to income tax or Social Security taxes).

Since then, health insurance coverage in the workplace has grown sharply, and the number of services covered—and options for health care—have grown. The numbers are staggering: Today, employer-sponsored health insurance covers more than 168 million Americans, according to a 1999 report by the House Ways and Means Committee. That's nearly two-thirds of the country's total population of nearly 270 million.

You don't need statistics to understand how big health insurance benefits are to you. You do, however, need to know all you can about this crucial benefit.

Perhaps your job is secure and you're happy with your health plan. In today's rapidly changing business world, however, your circumstances could change in a heartbeat. Your company could tighten its belt to prepare for a public stock offering. Your company could be bought out. Your hours could be cut, your workload increased, your benefits reduced. You could face a layoff, a buyout, or an early retirement offer. You may suddenly find yourself searching for a new job, one with a good health plan, and wondering where to turn for health coverage if you're between jobs.

The possibilities are endless. It's essential, therefore, to know how employer-sponsored health insurance operates, and how it can work for you.

**Figure 1.4**   Nine of Ten Americans with Private Health Insurance Have It through Work

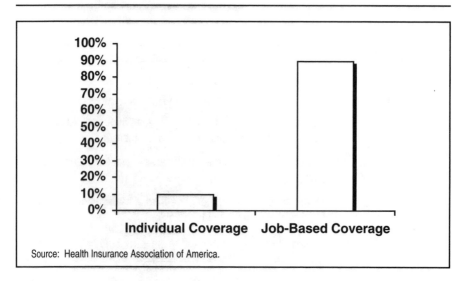

Source: Health Insurance Association of America.

**Figure 1.5**   More Workers in Managed Care Plans Than in Traditional Plans

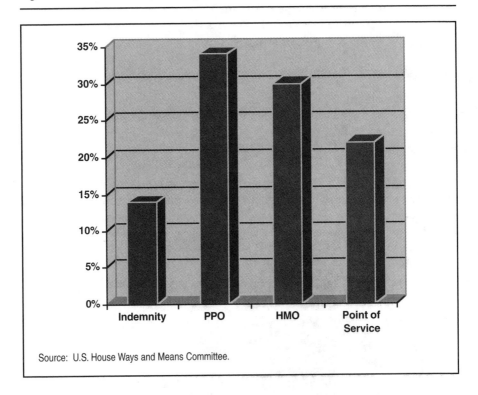

Source: U.S. House Ways and Means Committee.

It's also important to understand your rights, and to have some idea of the enormous changes in recent years that have strengthened your rights—and responsibilities—under the law.

## A Changing World

Had you fallen asleep in the late 1980s and awakened a decade later, you would have been stunned by the change in the health care landscape. In 1988, about 71 percent of employees enrolled in health plans took part in a traditional "indemnity" plan, or fee-for-service plan. It typically worked this way: You paid a certain amount of your annual health care expenses, known as your "deductible." After that, your company plan paid the rest (subject to certain other limits). You chose your doctor, your hospital, your pharmacy. In short, you were in charge of deciding who provided your care; your company's insurance plan essentially took care paying for it.

By 1998, however, only 14 percent of covered employees were enrolled in traditional indemnity plans, while 86 percent took part in managed care plans, according to a 1999 report by the House Ways and Means Committee.

These managed care plans have created a host of new catch-phrases in the health care marketplace: the health maintenance organization (HMO), the preferred provider organization (PPO), and the point-of-service plan (POS).

## A Matter of Choice

What it all amounts to is a massive change in how company-sponsored health plans are run. For you, a big part of the change has to do with choice. With traditional indemnity plans, you choose who will provide your care; with managed care plans, you typically have less choice.

Also, your share of health care costs has risen. Advanced technology, new drugs and treatments, expanded coverage, and other factors have combined to increase the overall cost of health insurance, according to a report by the federal government's Bureau of Labor Statistics. Employers have had to pay a lot more—about $263 billion in 1996, up from just $61 billion in 1980, according to one study—and they've asked workers to pay a greater and greater share of the cost.

To understand exactly how all this works, you must first know a bit about how each type of plan works.

# Traditional Plans

If you're new to the job market or you're just entering it, you may never have heard of the traditional indemnity plan. Nevertheless, it wasn't long ago that this was the main type of health insurance for many workers. Indemnity plans still exist, but they're not nearly as common as they were before. In fact, some experts on employee benefits call the traditional plan a dinosaur.

Still, it's important to know what an indemnity plan is. Even if you're not currently covered by such a plan, you or a loved one may be some day. By understanding how traditional plans work, you can also get a better feel for the finer points of how other plans work.

In a nutshell, here's how the traditional plan, or fee-for-service plan, operates: Your employer signs a contract with an insurance company—a commercial insurer like Blue Cross and Blue Shield, for example. The insurer agrees to cover health care costs for you and other workers. When you have a bill, the insurer pays it. This is why these plans are sometimes called fee-for-service plans: When you need health care from a doctor, a clinic, or a hospital, the insurance company picks up the tab for the service. Either the health care provider bills your company's insurance plan directly, or you pay and get reimbursed by the insurer later on.

**Figure 1.6**   Enrollment in Traditional Plans

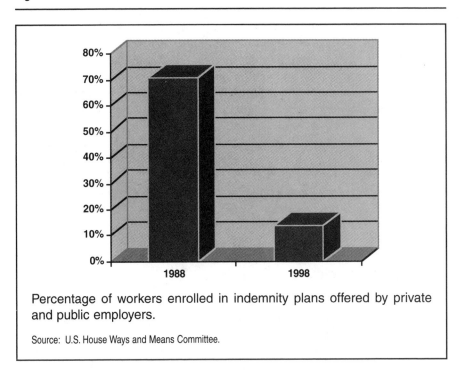

Percentage of workers enrolled in indemnity plans offered by private and public employers.

Source: U.S. House Ways and Means Committee.

These plans typically give you a lot of freedom because they generally let you decide which doctor, hospital, or other health care provider you'll use. The freedom can be costly, however—to all parties involved, including you and your employer. Administrative expenses are just a part of this cost. In addition, some people may take advantage of their freedom by ringing up big health care bills. To control expenses, and to make employees more aware of the cost of health care, traditional health plans have gradually increased the share of expenses that the consumer pays—in a lot of different ways.

You typically must keep track of your costs, so there's paperwork involved. There can also be different types of fees at different stages, so there's money to consider, too. Here's a rundown on some of the key expenses.

**Premiums.**  The amount of money your employer must pay to the insurance company for coverage is known as the premium. In some cases, employers pay the entire premium. In most cases, however, employees kick in a portion, usually through payroll deduction. The amount varies depending on the plan.

**Deductibles.**  Although you probably must pay part of the cost of your health insurance by sharing the cost of the premiums, the actual coverage may not kick in immediately. Your plan may require you to spend some money out of pocket to cover the first health care expenses you incur in any given year. This amount is known as the deductible, and it typically works the same as deductibles do for your car or homeowners insurance policy. For instance, your employer's plan may reimburse you for health care expenses in a given year only after you've paid the first $200 in expenses out of your own pocket. The amount of the deductible varies; it can be as high as $500 or more. A plan may require each member of your family to meet a deductible, or it may levy an overall amount as a family deductible.

**Coinsurance.** Even after you've paid your portion of the plan's premium, and even after you've met your deductible, your plan still may not cover all your expenses. You may have to pay a share of them. This is known as coinsurance. A typical plan will require you to pay 20 percent of your health care expenses; the plan will pay the rest.

## The Cost of Traditional Plans

As you can see, traditional health insurance plans can get complicated—and costly for you. Suppose, for example, that your plan runs on a calendar year, requires you to meet an annual $200 deductible, and also has a coinsurance provision that requires you to pay 20 percent of your medical expenses.

In January, you suffer a serious injury while skating and require back surgery, ringing up $3,600 in doctor, hospital, and related expenses. In this example, you must pay the first $200 out of pocket to meet your deductible. Of the remaining $3,400 in expenses, the plan pays 80 percent ($2,720), and you pay 20 percent ($680) because of your coinsurance requirement. Your out-of-pocket expenses in this example total $880.

## Out-of-Pocket Limits

For other health care costs during the year, your deductible has already been met in the above example. But what of the remaining expenses? Because of coinsurance, you could face some huge bills if you or a family member has a serious injury or illness. For this reason, many plans limit the amount you'll have to shell out. Once you reach the out-of-pocket limit, the plan picks up 100 percent of your expenses.

The limit varies depending on the plan. Once you know what it is, however, you can get a pretty good idea of how much your maximum out-of-pocket expenses might be for a given year. If you like to plan ahead, when you draw up a budget for the coming year, this can help you forecast the most you'll pay on health care costs.

For instance, suppose your plan has a $200 deductible and a coinsurance clause that makes you pay 20 percent of the next $5,000 in expenses for the year. The most you might wind up paying out of your own pocket is $1,200. Why? In this example, after you pay the $200 deductible, you must pay 20 percent of the next $5,000 in medical expenses, or $1,000. That brings you to a total of $1,200.

### Lifetime Limits

The limit on out-of-pocket payments can leave insurance companies on the hook for potentially huge expenses. As a result, most plans place an overall limit on how much they'll pay for your health care expenses—just as an insurer may limit the amount it'll pay under your auto or homeowners insurance policy. Here, too, the limit varies, but it's usually set so high that most workers will never reach it—perhaps $1 million over a worker's lifetime.

If you're covered under one of these plans, check your health care booklet or brochure to see exactly what the plan provides and what it will and won't cover. (Your employer must give you a copy of what is technically known as the "summary plan description.")

### Limits within Plans

Some plans impose a variety of limits on what they will pay after you meet the deductibles and other out-of-pocket costs. For example, under the section that outlines coverage for hospitalization, your plan may cover most inpatient hospital expenses, including room and board, but only some outpatient expenses.

Keep in mind, too, that your health plan may provide only basic medical coverage; you may have to get coverage for dental or vision care under a separate policy. These and other benefits may be available at work through a "cafeteria" benefit plan, or you may be able to pay for them on a pre-tax basis by using a flexible spending account at work. These arrangements are outlined in Chapter 5.

### Managed Care

Because traditional health insurance plans have become expensive, employers have taken measures to try to control costs. If you participate in a traditional health plan at work nowadays, odds are your plan has one or more of the following features. If you haven't had to deal with them yet, you probably will someday soon. Here's a snapshot of what these features are and how they work:

- Employers are requiring employees to begin sharing health care costs or to increase the share they already pay. You may have to begin paying a deductible, or pay a higher deductible than you did before. You may have to begin covering health care costs through a coinsurance clause, or cover a greater portion of these costs than you did before.
- You may face what is called "utilization review." For instance, you may have to get a second opinion before you have a certain type of surgery. You may have to go through various tests before you can be admitted to a hospital. Before, during, and after your hospitalization, you may have to keep in touch with your insurance company or its representative to provide updates on your status.
- Your plan may offer financial and other incentives to get you to use lower-cost alternatives for your health care, such as walk-in clinics, day-surgery centers and surgi-centers, extended-care facilities, home health care, and hospice care.
- Your employer may encourage you to enroll in wellness programs offered in or near your workplace. These may include fitness centers, stop-smoking programs, and programs that monitor your weight, blood pressure, and cholesterol levels.

### In a Nutshell . . .

Traditional group health plans typically offer you the most freedom to choose the doctors, hospitals, and other health care providers you want. These plans are generally also the most costly to workers, who typically must pay premiums, deductibles, coinsurance, and other charges. In addition, these plans could become more costly in the future because of "adverse selection": other plans, such as HMOs, are typically more appealing to younger, healthier workers; traditional plans can be more attractive to older workers with more health problems, raising the cost of these plans.

# Health Maintenance Organizations (HMOs)

Millions of Americans spell health care with three letters: HMO. Although the first health maintenance organization was established as far back as 1929, and a federal law that encouraged the formation of more HMOs was enacted in 1973, HMOs did not come to the forefront until the 1980s, when health care expenses were soaring and employers were grasping for ways to cut their costs.

**Figure 1.7**    Enrollment in HMOs

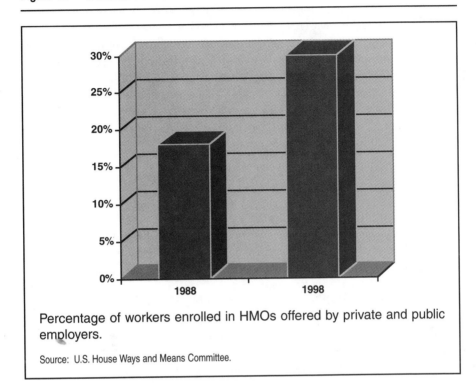

Percentage of workers enrolled in HMOs offered by private and public employers.

Source: U.S. House Ways and Means Committee.

Today, there are about 650 HMO plans nationwide, and enrollment has increased sharply, from about 36 million in 1990 to about 68 million in 1997, according to a congressional report. In other words, about one in four Americans is enrolled in an HMO—most of them through employer-sponsored plans.

What made HMOs attractive in the 1980s still gives them appeal today. The employer pays the HMO a fixed amount up front, and the HMO provides the workforce with comprehensive health coverage. Instead of hiring a traditional insurance company to act as the intermediary between the employee and a variety of doctors, hospitals, and other health care providers, the employer just hires an HMO, which provides a kind of one-stop shopping for just about all of an employee's health care needs. In other words, an HMO doesn't just act as the administrator; it also delivers the health care services.

## Preventive Care

An HMO also offers another feature that appeals to cost-conscious employers: preventive care. Why? The employer typically pays the HMO a fixed fee. The HMO therefore typically has only so many dollars to spend on an employee (and his or her family) for a given year.

As a result, the HMO has an incentive to keep costs down, and one way to do this is to give people regular check-ups in order to get involved early on before a minor ailment flares into a serious—and costly—condition.

With HMOs, you typically don't have to pay deductibles or fill out any lengthy claims forms. You probably will, however, have to pay for a portion of the premiums, usually through payroll deduction. You may also have to make a small payment, called a "copayment," for each service you use—perhaps $10 to $20 for a doctor's visit, for example.

## The Gatekeeper

You also typically get assigned a primary-care doctor, who serves as a kind of gatekeeper, deciding when, and if, you should get specialized—and potentially more expensive—treatment. You're still free to use doctors, specialists, hospitals, or other providers outside of your HMO's umbrella. You'll just pay for these services yourself.

Just as there are different types of health care plans, there are different types of HMOs. Some operate their own central office, or a network of offices, which you visit for just about all your health care needs, including general doctor's appointments, lab tests, therapy, and so on. Other HMOs hire one or more medical groups to provide these services. Some HMOs use a combination of options.

## Less Choice, More Care?

In an HMO, you may wind up with less choice—less freedom to choose among independent doctors, laboratories, and other health care providers. On the other hand, you may also wind up getting more care for less cost. Although you may have to shell out a relatively small amount of money for a doctor's visit or a prescription, for example, you typically won't face the paperwork, expenses, and other potential problems that you may encounter with a traditional fee-for-service indemnity plan.

## In a Nutshell . . .

Workers usually pay less with an HMO than with a traditional plan. You typically must pay premiums, but not deductibles or coinsurance. Also, most HMOs offer comprehensive care, emphasizing preventive care and encouraging the use of outpatient health services instead of in-hospital treatment when possible. In exchange, however, your choices are sharply limited: you typically must use only the doctors, hospitals, and other providers that are part of the HMO, and you usually won't get reimbursed if you use others (except in case of emergency).

## Preferred Provider Organizations (PPOs)

Millions of other workers and their families spell health care with three other letters: PPO, which stands for preferred provider organization. Enrollment in PPOs has swelled from about 38 million in 1990 to about 98 million in 1996, according to a congressional report.

In effect, a PPO acts as an intermediary, unlike an HMO, which typically provides care directly to patients. The PPO hires certain doctors, labs, hospitals, and other health care providers, usually at a fixed price. The plan steers you toward these doctors and other providers. You don't have to use them, but you'll generally wind up paying more if you don't.

**Figure 1.8**   Enrollment in PPOs

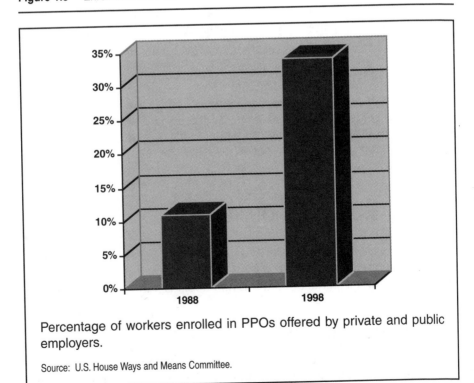

Percentage of workers enrolled in PPOs offered by private and public employers.

Source: U.S. House Ways and Means Committee.

The idea is to offer you an incentive to stick with the doctors, hospitals, and other health care providers that have contracts with your PPO.

What's in it for the doctors, hospitals, and other outfits that sign a contract with a PPO? They may agree to charge a slightly lower price for their services. In return, however, they may get their claims processed more quickly, and they may also get a larger, more steady stream of patients (some of whom may be lured away from HMOs).

### More Freedom

What's in it for you? In general, you get a bit more freedom to choose your health care provider than you would with an HMO, but a bit less freedom of choice than you would with a traditional plan. Using a PPO may also be less costly for you than using a traditional plan.

PPOs differ from HMOs in several ways. One key difference is that in a PPO, a visit to a specialist generally doesn't require a referral from your primary-care doctor. Another difference involves payments. A PPO typically charges on a fee-for-service basis, similar to traditional indemnity-style plans. As a result, you may wind up paying a deductible as well as a share of the premiums, and some PPOs require you to make copayments. Like an HMO, a PPO closely monitors care to try to ensure that it's efficient as well as effective.

### In a Nutshell . . .

Workers typically face lower costs with a PPO than with a traditional plan. You also typically get more choice of doctors and other providers than you would from a traditional HMO. However, you may have to pay substantially more if you use a doctor or other provider who isn't on the plan's list of preferred providers.

# Point-of-Service (POS) Plans

A point-of-service, or POS, plan is generally regarded as a form of HMO, but in practice it's neither a traditional plan nor a standard HMO. Instead, it includes elements of both traditional plans and HMOs.

### Cost Based on Network

A POS plan typically applies one set of rules when you use its network of doctors and other health care providers, and another set of rules if you use doctors and other providers outside the plan's network.

**Figure 1.9**    Enrollment in POS Plans

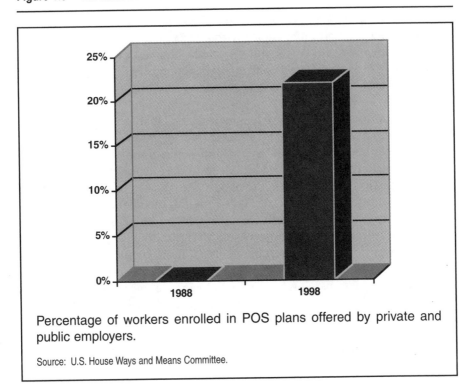

Percentage of workers enrolled in POS plans offered by private and public employers.

Source: U.S. House Ways and Means Committee.

When you use the POS plan's network, you generally face the same sort of rules you would if you used an HMO: little or nothing in the way of a deductible, and perhaps a small copayment when you visit a doctor, for example.

When you go outside the network, you generally face the same rules you would if you used a traditional plan: higher deductibles and higher copayments. In this respect, a POS plan is similar to a PPO. A POS plan, however, may have more managed care elements than a PPO, including a gatekeeper who monitors care and patient choices.

### Rapid Growth

POS plans are the newest in the field, and they are growing quickly. In 1988, few, if any, people were enrolled in such plans, according to a congressional report. By 1998, 22 percent of workers took part in POS plans, the report said.

POS plans can be especially appealing if you or a family member wants to stick with a certain doctor or other health care provider who isn't in the plan's network.

## In a Nutshell . . .

In general, workers pay less with a POS plan than with a traditional plan. You also get a bit more choice with a POS plan than you would with an HMO. However, you'll probably pay more—maybe a lot more—for that freedom; a POS plan may levy sharply higher charges, in the form of higher deductibles and coinsurance, if you use doctors and other providers outside of the plan's network.

Keep in mind that this is only a general explanation of how the major types of health plans work. In the real world, the lines aren't as sharply drawn. A traditional plan, for example, may include some of the managed care features you're likely to see in an HMO. A 1998 report by the President's Advisory Commission on Consumer Protection and Quality in the Health Care Industry found that 80 percent of HMOs require members to get prior approval before seeking emergency care, unless the condition is life-threatening (or state or federal laws say otherwise). Many traditional plans have also adopted such practices, the report found. In addition, people who use doctors or other health care providers outside of the network offered by a POS plan may find themselves using what amounts to a more traditional plan.

The point is that the lines have blurred. Each health insurance plan doesn't fit neatly into a little box; the world of health care is changing, and health insurance is changing too. The truth is that most health insurance plans today are, at least in some respects, managed care plans, no matter what they're technically called.

# The Growth of Self-Funded Plans

In addition, many companies have taken a much greater role in the way their health care plans are paid for and the way in which services are delivered.

For example, there's been an explosion in the number of so-called self-funded plans in the marketplace. Under these arrangements, a company gets to hold on to the money it would otherwise pay in insurance premiums. These plans may also give a company more control over the way a plan is designed and how money is spent. In effect, your employer takes over the role of the health insurance company, handling claims, paperwork, funding, and other areas (although some of this work may be assigned to an intermediary).

In 1979, only about 11 percent of workers in medium and large companies were covered by self-funded plans. By 1997, however, nearly half of workers at medium and large companies were in self-funded plans, according to a 1999 report by the U.S. Bureau of Labor Statistics.

**Figure 1.10** How Health Plans Compare

| Type of Plan | Potential Benefits | Potential Drawbacks |
|---|---|---|
| **Indemnity** (Traditional; fee-for-service) | You choose doctor, hospital, other health care providers. | Your cost could be high for premiums, deductibles, coinsurance; lots of paperwork; check-ups, other preventive care may not be covered. |
| **Health Maintenance Organization (HMO)** | Stresses preventive care; little paperwork; you may pay only premiums, small copayments; care offered through main facility or network. | You may have to use only HMO's doctors; you may have to get approval from your primary-care doctor ("gatekeeper") for specialists, advanced treatments; use of outside providers may be limited or prohibited. |
| **Preferred Provider Organization (PPO)** | Broader—but not unlimited—choice of doctors, other providers; prior approval may not be required for use of specialists; preventive care may be covered; you may have to pay only premiums, copayments. | You'll probably pay a deductible and coinsurance for using doctors, other providers outside PPO network; some paperwork required. |
| **Point-of-Service (POS)** | You may use in-network or out-of-network doctors, other providers; a primary-care doctor may coordinate care; preventive care may be covered; your in-network cost may be lower than out-of-network cost. | Cost for in-network providers similar to HMO, but you may pay far more—in deductibles and other ways—to use out-of-network providers; some paperwork required. |

NOTE: These are only broad outlines; specific plans may apply different rules.

Source: AARP; Employee Benefit Research Institute; U.S. Department of Health and Human Services (Agency for Healthcare Research and Quality).

# Taking Advantage of Your Health Care Plan

No matter what a health plan is called and how it works, it provides an important benefit. If your employer offers one (or more) health plan, and you're eligible, sign up and don't delay. In almost all cases, getting health insurance through your job is easier—and cheaper—than getting it on your own.

Yes, there are lots of individual policies available. The question is, will you qualify? With a company-sponsored plan, you typically won't have to pass a battery of tests or fill out lots of forms before you can enroll. If you're applying for an individual policy in the open market, however, you may have to jump through some hoops, and the insurer may also look closely at your health records before deciding whether you can enroll and how much to charge you.

Will companies continue offering health plans as an employee benefit? No federal law requires companies to offer group health insurance as a benefit. Still, many employers do offer it, not only because it's an important benefit, but also because it's a good way to attract and retain good workers. In fact, many employers offer a choice of health plans. While 35 percent of covered workers have no choice (because their employers offer only one plan), 15 percent of covered workers can choose between two plans, and another 50 percent can pick from a menu of three or more health plans, according to a survey by the Henry J. Kaiser Family Foundation and the Health Research and Educational Trust. (Small firms typically offer just one plan; medium and large firms generally offer two or more.)

## Don't Risk Financial Ruin

If you have the chance to get this benefit, then take advantage of it. Even though you'll probably wind up paying a chunk of the cost, it's usually better than paying for coverage on your own through an individual plan outside the workplace.

It's also far better than going without coverage. Consider this: The most expensive conditions treated in U.S. hospitals were spinal cord injury ($56,800), infant respiratory distress syndrome ($56,600), low birthweight ($50,300), leukemia ($46,700), and heart-valve disorders ($45,300), according to a 1999 study by the U.S. Agency for Healthcare Research and Quality. (The agency looked at average charges for hospital stays in 1996.) Can you risk the potential financial calamity if you or a family member winds up with a serious health problem? If your employer offers health insurance, take it.

You can count yourself lucky, too. About 44 million workers don't have health insurance through their jobs, according to a 1999 report by the Census Bureau. Of these, about 19 million workers were at firms that don't provide health insurance at all; another 9 million or so were at firms that offer coverage to some of the staff, but not to everybody. Altogether, about half of full-time workers with low incomes don't have health insurance at all, according to a 1999 study by the U.S. Census Bureau.

## Points to Keep in Mind

If you're looking for a job and wondering about health insurance coverage, keep these points in mind:

- Union workers are significantly more likely than nonunion workers to have health care coverage through work, according to a survey by the Employee Benefit Research Institute.
- Your chances of getting health coverage are better in some industries than in others, as Figure 1.11 shows. Government workers, for example, are far more likely than retail workers to have health insurance through their jobs.
- Full-time workers stand a better chance of having group health insurance through work than do part-time workers and occasional workers. The chances of being uninsured are twice as high for con-

**Figure 1.11**    Health Insurance by Industry

If you're looking for a job, keep in mind that some industries have a better record than others of offering health insurance benefits:

| Industry | Percent Offering Some Kind of Health Coverage |
|---|---|
| Government | 91% |
| Wholesaling | 74 |
| Mining | 74 |
| Manufacturing | 72 |
| Finance | 71 |
| Health Care | 63 |
| Transportation, Utilities, Communications | 58 |
| Service | 52 |
| Construction | 49 |
| High Technology | 47 |
| Retail | 41 |

Source: U.S. General Accounting Office (1999 report).

tingent workers as for regular employees, according to the Employee Benefit Research Institute.

- People in the South and West are more likely to be uninsured than those in the East and Midwest, government statistics show.

Now you know a bit about what employer-sponsored health plans are and how they operate. How can they best work for you? How much will you wind up paying, and what kind of services can you expect to receive? What quality of care can you expect? Do you have the right to continue coverage if you lose your job or your hours get cut? These topics are the focus of the following three chapters.

## For More Information . . .

- The U.S. Department of Labor enforces federal laws that cover employer-sponsored health plans. As part of an education campaign, the department is trying to get the word out to workers about what they need to know to get the best coverage from their company health plans. Part of the campaign includes three educational brochures: "Top 10 Ways to Make Your Health Benefits Work for You," "Changes in Your Work Status May Affect Your Health Benefits," and "Life Changes Require Health Choices—Know Your Options." For a free copy, call the agency's toll-free publications hotline, at 1-800-998-7542. If you have access to the Internet, you may read or download copies of these and other health-benefits publications at the agency's Web site: <www.dol.gov>.
- The Employee Benefit Research Institute and other groups are sponsoring a nonprofit organization to help consumers better understand, acquire, and use health insurance. The organization's name is Consumer Health Education Council (CHEC). You can reach CHEC at 1-202-659-0670. If you have access to the Internet, check out the CHEC Web site: <www.healthchec.org>.
- The Health Insurance Association of America (HIAA), a trade group in Washington, publishes a brochure, "Guide to Health Insurance," that explains what health plans are available and what type of coverage each offers. To view it, contact the group's Web site: <www.hiaa.org>.
- Insure.com, an online news organization, covers the world of insurance and also offers lots of online materials about group health insurance, all written in plain language. Here's the address: <www.insure.com>.

# Choosing a Plan Based on Cost

If you're thinking about switching to a new health plan, either at your present job or at a new job, you need to make some comparisons. By taking a few steps, you should be able to figure out which plan will best suit you and your family.

In this chapter, you'll find out how to compare plans based on cost. (Chapter 3 looks at how to compare plans based on quality.)

## Employees' Share of Premiums

Cost is a big factor, so big, in fact, that some workers don't take advantage of company-sponsored health insurance even when they have access, according to a study by the U.S. General Accounting Office (GAO). Between 1988 and 1996, the number of workers offered health insurance by their employers grew slightly, from about 72 percent of the workforce to about 75 percent, the study found. During approximately the same period, however, fewer workers chose to accept coverage, for either themselves or their dependents. In 1987, about 88 percent of eligible workers accepted coverage; by 1996, only about 80 percent accepted coverage.

Why? You probably already know, just from looking at your pay stub. Between 1988 and 1996, health insurance premiums increased by an average of about 8 percent a year. What's more, workers have been asked to shoulder a greater and greater share of the cost of health insurance premiums.

### Workers' Share of Costs Is Increasing

In the late 1980s, workers at small and large firms had to pay an average of about 12 percent of the overall cost of health insurance premiums for individual coverage. By 1996, workers at large firms were paying an average of about 22 percent, while workers at small firms were shelling out an even greater share—about 33 percent on average.

**Figure 2.1**   Workers' Share of Health Insurance Premiums (Large Firms)

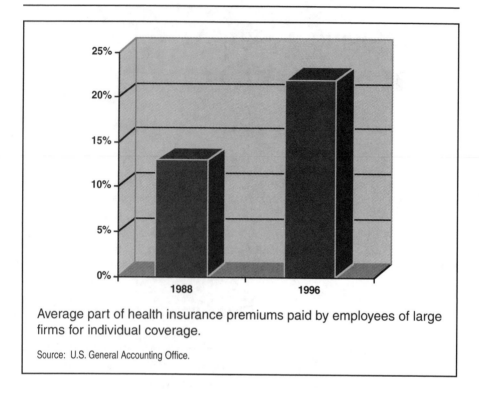

Average part of health insurance premiums paid by employees of large firms for individual coverage.

Source:  U.S. General Accounting Office.

When you combine the effects of both rising premiums and the increase in the share of premiums that workers have had to pay, the result has been staggering: workers have wound up paying 85 percent more for family coverage and 189 percent more for individual coverage, even after making adjustments for inflation, according to the GAO study.

You don't have to be a genius to know that pay increases haven't kept pace. Throughout the 1980s and into the early 1990s, the percentage increase in health care costs far outstripped the increase in wages and salaries, a U.S. Bureau of Labor Statistics report found. From December 1980 to September 1998, health care costs increased nearly 2½ times as much as other benefits costs, and more than 3 times as much as wages and salaries.

The rate of increase wasn't constant: in some years, health insurance costs accelerated steadily; in other years, they rose at a slower pace, the government report found.

In the years when health care costs slowed, it was partly the result of efforts by employers to contain costs—including the shifting of costs to employees. Indeed, the share of workers whose health insurance premiums are wholly paid by employers has declined sharply since 1980.

**Figure 2.2**   Workers' Share of Health Insurance Premiums (Small Firms)

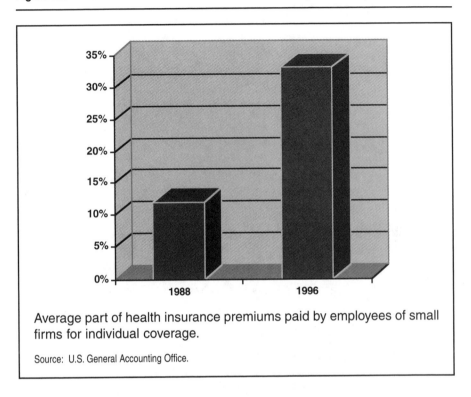

Average part of health insurance premiums paid by employees of small firms for individual coverage.

Source:  U.S. General Accounting Office.

Among full-time workers in medium and large companies who take part in medical care plans, only 31 percent had individual coverage wholly financed by their employer in 1997, down from 72 percent in 1980. During the same period, only 20 percent had family coverage fully paid by their companies, down from 51 percent.

### Design of Plans Has Changed

Companies have taken other steps to try to control costs. They've changed the design of their health plans to increase the employer's control over the type or delivery of health care services. They've imposed deductibles and coinsurance payments. They've scrapped basic coverage for certain types of care. They've also shifted to managed care programs or self-funded health plans.

As a result of all this, most workers have been seeing a bigger and bigger share of their paychecks going toward health insurance, and some workers have simply opted out, choosing instead to go without coverage altogether. (In fact, one 1998 study found that for every 1 percentage point

**Figure 2.3**   Wage Hikes Can't Keep Pace with Jumps in Health Care Costs

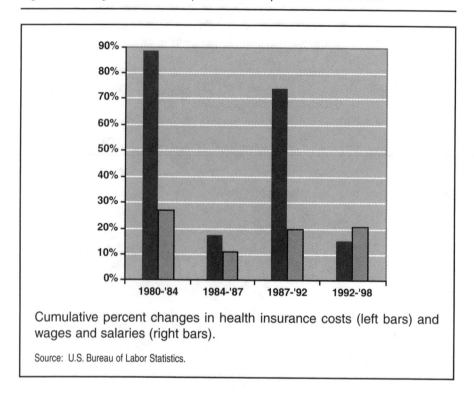

Cumulative percent changes in health insurance costs (left bars) and wages and salaries (right bars).

Source: U.S. Bureau of Labor Statistics.

increase in premiums, about 300,000 people might drop coverage.) That's one reason why the number of people without health insurance—the uninsured—has grown sharply.

Nevertheless, if you have the option to get health insurance through your job, you should. You may have to try squeezing more money out of your family budget to do it. There are other ways to afford coverage, however, especially if you have more than one plan from which to choose.

### Figuring Out the Cost

With the information contained in the booklets that an employer, prospective employer, or health plan gives you, you should be able to figure out the maximum amount each plan will cost you out of pocket in any given year.

You probably won't be able to figure out *exactly* what a particular plan may cost you over a year's time, but you can come up with a pretty good estimate, based on the average of your health care claims in prior years from other plans.

**Figure 2.4**   Fewer Workers Are in Employer-Pay-All Health Plans

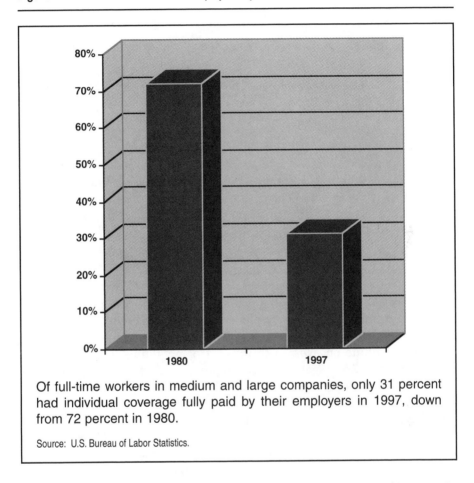

Of full-time workers in medium and large companies, only 31 percent had individual coverage fully paid by their employers in 1997, down from 72 percent in 1980.

Source: U.S. Bureau of Labor Statistics.

Because of managed care, and for other reasons, the rate of increase in health care costs slowed in the mid-1990s. There is evidence, however, that the trend toward higher costs is once again gaining momentum, as health care expenses rise faster than the rate of inflation. This means you have to look carefully at exactly how much you'll have to pay for any plan.

## Comparing Plans Point by Point

Once you have all the materials you need—information from your employer and from each plan, and receipts for medical care from the past one or more years—consider these points in your calculations:

**Figure 2.5**   What Health Insurance Premiums Can Cost

---

Average monthly premiums for group health insurance (including company contribution and employee share of cost) in 1999:

|           | Individual Employee | Employee and Spouse | Family Plan |
|-----------|--------------------|--------------------|-------------|
| Indemnity | $200               | $396               | $529        |
| PPO       | 178                | 374                | 514         |
| POS       | 171                | 349                | 483         |
| HMO       | 161                | 328                | 459         |

Average 1999 per capita premium costs for 213 employers surveyed—mainly large Fortune 1000 companies that, altogether, provide medical benefits to more than 3.1 million employees, retirees, and dependents across the country.

Source: Towers Perrin.

---

**Premiums.** How much will a plan cost you out of your paycheck each month? Remember that some employers still pay the entire premium, but most require you to shoulder some—or all—of the cost. (To see how much workers contribute on average to the cost of premiums for group health plans, see Figure 2.6. To get an idea what premiums cost overall on an annualized basis—including the employer and employee share—see Figure 2.5). Keep in mind, too, that as a general rule, you may have to pay a far greater percentage of the premiums for a family plan than for a plan that covers just you alone. In fact, a 1999 study by the Henry J. Kaiser Family Foundation and the Health Research and Educational Trust found that, on average, a worker pays 16 percent of the premium for a plan that covers only him or her, but 32 percent for a plan that covers the worker and his or her family.

**Deductibles.** Does the plan charge a deductible? Find out how much you will have to pay out of your own pocket before the insurance starts to cover your costs. Some plans have no deductible, but many do. A 1999 report by the U.S. Bureau of Labor Statistics found that more than 90 percent of conventional plans require a deductible; other types of plans often require them, too. Most plans use a fixed dollar amount, but the exact amount varies widely: few have a deductible of less than $100; some set it at $300 or more. A general rule is that you'll pay a lower deductible for individual coverage than for family coverage. In addition, deductibles are generally higher for conventional indemnity plans than for preferred provider organizations (PPOs) and point-of-service (POS) plans, especially if you stay within the plan's network of doctors and other health care providers. Still, there can be

**Figure 2.6** Part of Premiums Paid by Workers

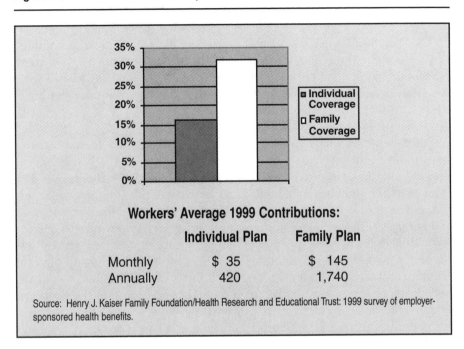

**Workers' Average 1999 Contributions:**

|  | Individual Plan | Family Plan |
|---|---|---|
| Monthly | $ 35 | $ 145 |
| Annually | 420 | 1,740 |

Source: Henry J. Kaiser Family Foundation/Health Research and Educational Trust: 1999 survey of employer-sponsored health benefits.

big differences between plans. For instance, one plan may require you to meet a much higher deductible for individual coverage than another plan will. If you're looking for family coverage, make sure you understand exactly how the deductible will be calculated: will each member of the family have

**Figure 2.7** Average Deductibles

| Type of Plan | Average Annual Deductible |
|---|---|
| Conventional Single | $245 |
| Conventional Family | 605 |
| PPO (Inside Plan Network) | 190 |
| PPO (Out-of-Network) | 315 |
| POS (Inside Plan Network) | 41 |
| POS (Out-of-Network) | 359 |

A PPO is a preferred provider organization; POS signifies a point-of-service plan.

Source: Henry J. Kaiser Family Foundation/Health Reserach and Educational Trust: 1999 survey of employer-sponsored health benefits.

to meet a separate deductible, or will there be one blanket deductible for the entire family, after which insurance starts kicking in?

**Coinsurance.** After you've met the deductible, exactly what percentage of your costs will the plan pay? Some will cover the entire cost, but many others will require you to pick up a portion. (As a general rule, plans with a coinsurance feature will pick up 80 percent of the expenses after you meet the deductible; you pay the remaining 20 percent.)

**Out-of-pocket limits.** Even if a plan has a coinsurance feature, it may limit the overall amount you'll have to pay. Once you reach this out-of-pocket limit, the plan picks up 100 percent of your additional expenses. For example, after you meet a deductible, a plan may require you to pay 20 percent of the next $5,000 in expenses for the year; after that, the plan picks up 100 percent. (The average annual out-of-pocket maximum was $1,358 for individual-only coverage and $2,858 for family coverage, according to a 1998 report by the Employee Benefit Research Institute on group health plans at medium and large companies.) Find out if the plan's deductible or coinsurance features apply as a blanket, or if they vary according to the doctor or other health care provider you use, or the hospital or other facility you visit. If the limits vary, figure out your estimated costs based on the type of services you (or your family) used over the past year.

**Copayments.** Some plans do not require you to meet a deductible and do not have a coinsurance feature. They do, however, require you to pay a relatively small amount each time you visit a doctor or hospital or use another type of health service. How much will you have to pay? Here, too, the amount will vary by plan. Although the amount may seem small— anywhere from $5 to $25 or more per visit is typical—these "small" items can add up. Look back at the services you used over the past year to get an idea of how much you may have to pay in the coming year in copayments.

**Out-of-network care.** Some plans set different fees depending on exactly *where* you go for care. Using a plan's own network of doctors, hospitals, and other providers may result in the lowest out-of-pocket costs for you. If you use doctors, hospitals, or other providers outside the plan's network you may face an entirely different—and higher—set of charges. Figure out whether you can stick with a plan's network of health care providers and services, and estimate your costs from there. If you or a family member will have to go outside a plan's network, try to estimate how often this will happen, and how much you might wind up paying. (Remember that your calculations can never be exact; you're looking for estimates on which to base your decision about which plan is best.)

**Figure 2.8**   HMO Copayments

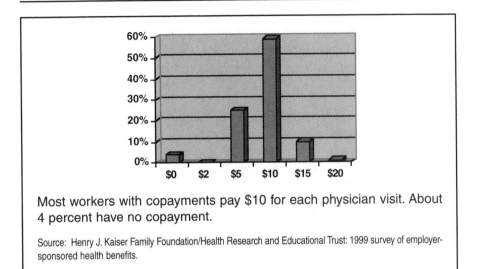

Most workers with copayments pay $10 for each physician visit. About 4 percent have no copayment.

Source: Henry J. Kaiser Family Foundation/Health Research and Educational Trust: 1999 survey of employer-sponsored health benefits.

**Emergency care.** For some plans, a visit to the emergency room is treated like any other health service. For other plans, however, there can be a big difference: you may wind up paying far more for a trip to a hospital's emergency room or emergency department than you would, say, for a visit to a doctor's office or a walk-in clinic. Check how often you (or your family members) visited the emergency room in recent years, and figure out how much you may wind up paying in the coming year in a certain plan. (This can be a good area in which to save money, too. If you use the emergency room for fairly routine health matters, you can probably save money through a certain plan by visiting the doctor's office or a walk-in clinic more often instead.)

**Prescriptions.** Some plans make no provision for prescription drugs. Other plans may treat them like any other health care expense, letting you apply the amount you pay out of pocket toward the deductible and the coinsurance limits. Still other plans (such as HMOs) include prescription medicines in their coverage, but require you to make a copayment ($5 or $10 for each prescription, for example). Check each plan so you'll know exactly how prescriptions are treated, then project your out-of-pocket costs based on how many prescriptions you had filled, on average, in past years.

**What isn't covered.** Keep in mind that from a cost standpoint what a plan *won't* cover can be just as important as—or even more important than—what it *will* cover. If a plan doesn't cover a service you or a family member requires, you may wind up paying for it out of your own pocket. Some things to look for are fairly obvious—regular physicals, mammograms, and Pap smears, for instance. However, there may be other services you or someone you love needs now or will need in the future, such as infertility treatment, medical equipment, or an organ transplant. It's crucial to consider such items when comparing plans, because the less a plan covers, the more you'll have to pay.

**Limited coverage for specific services.** Some plans place limits on what they'll pay for certain services, treatments, or illnesses. For example, some plans put a cap on how much they'll pay toward the cost of prescription medicines in a given year. Others agree to pay only a fixed amount for a hospital stay (per day, per month, or per illness, for example). Keep in mind, too, that some plans—especially traditional plans—agree to pay only a "usual, customary, and reasonable" (or "prevailing") charge for a particular service. This can wind up costing you. For instance, if your doctor normally charges $1,000 for a hernia operation, but most other doctors in the area charge $600, you could wind up paying the $400 difference out of pocket—in addition to your deductible and coinsurance. Consider such issues carefully. Based on your own health history or your family's health history, try to figure out whether you might bump up against these limits and clauses, and, if so, how much you may wind up paying. Will you have the resources to pay?

**Lifetime limits.** Many plans place an overall limit on how much they'll pay for your care—either over a year's time, or over your lifetime. These limits can be high—up to $1 million or more. Based on your health history or your family's health history, try to project whether you may wind up exceeding your policy's limit, and how much you may have to pay on your own for care beyond that limit. (The average lifetime maximum was $1.03 million, according to a 1998 report on group health insurance at medium and large companies by the Employee Benefit Research Institute.)

**Travel.** If you or your family members travel a lot, either in the U.S. or overseas, be sure to check how each plan you're reviewing will cover health care services, including routine care and urgent care, in other states and other countries. You may find that a plan with severe restrictions on out-of-town coverage could wind up costing you too much in out-of-pocket expenses.

**Changing circumstances.** When comparing plans, keep in mind that your personal circumstances may change. A plan that worked well for you last year may not be the best for you this year. For instance, are you planning to have a family? Are you expecting a child now? Did you have a baby or adopt a child recently? At one time in your life it may not have mattered whether your plan covered prenatal and well-baby care, but it may matter now. Starting a family may force you to either increase your budget for out-of-pocket health expenses or choose another plan entirely.

To do the comparisons, get to know the details about how each plan works. Ask your employer's human resources department or benefits administrator for a copy of the booklet or brochure that describes each plan. (Remember: Employers must, by law, offer you a copy of what is technically known as the "summary plan description." It explains your benefits and your legal rights under federal law and should also include such important details as how dependents are covered, which services require a copayment, and under what circumstances your employer can change—or end—the plan.)

As you make your comparison, use the handy worksheet on page 34. Use it only as a starting point, and feel free to personalize it, adding things that are important to you and your family.

Remember, too, that in the end you probably won't be able to figure out exactly what a particular plan will cost you over a year's time. But you can come up with a pretty good estimate based on the average of your health care claims in recent years under other plans.

## Understanding How Your Plan Works

Estimating how much various plans may cost you is an important step to take, even if you're already employed and you already take part in a company-sponsored health plan. From time to time, your employer may offer workers an open enrollment period during which you can switch from one health plan to another.

It's also important to evaluate the costs of various plans if you're taking a job for the first time or if you're moving from one job to another. Odds are pretty good that you'll have a choice of plans, and you'll need to know how much you may wind up paying for each.

Keep in mind that no plan will cover every expense. Still, some will do a better job than others covering the kinds of things that are most important to you.

Even if you don't want to switch plans, it's important to read your health benefits booklet from time to time so you'll be prepared to act if your circumstances change or if you need to resolve a problem with your coverage. For example:

- If you have a baby or adopt a child, you have 30 days to get the child covered under your plan. You must know the procedure for adding the child to your policy. (The child's enrollment will be retroactive to the date of the birth or adoption.)
- If you already have children, you'll need to know at exactly what age your plan will stop covering them. Many plans stop coverage on

**Worksheet**   Comparing Health Plans on Cost

When comparing health plans at your job, or at a job you're considering, check to see how much each will cost you, then figure out how each will fit in your budget. Study the booklets and other materials your employer gives you, talk with your company's benefits manager, or the plan's customer service office, then compare plans using this checklist.

| Find out about these costs: | Plan A | Plan B | Plan C |
|---|---|---|---|
| How much will the premium cost you per month? | | | |
| If there's a deductible, how much will you have to pay before the plan starts paying? | | | |
| Is there a separate deductible for prescription medicines? How much must you pay before the plan kicks in? | | | |
| How much is the copayment for a doctor's visit? | | | |
| How much is the copayment for a hospital visit? | | | |
| How much is the copayment for a prescription? | | | |
| How much must you pay to use doctors, hospitals, and other services outside the plan's usual network? | | | |
| Is there a coinsurance feature? What portion of expenses must you pay? Is there a limit? | | | |

Source: U.S. Department of Health and Human Services, Agency for Healthcare Research and Quality.

a child's nineteenth birthday but continue coverage to age 23 or 25 if the child is enrolled full-time in college. (Even afterward, the child may elect to continue coverage for up to 36 months thanks to a federal law known as COBRA, which will be explained in Chapter 4.)

* If your plan rejects your claim for benefits, you have the right to appeal, but you'll need to know exactly what your rights are and how they work. You'll also need to know your plan's time limit for filing an appeal. (Your rights in the appeal process are explained in Chapter 3.)

Another reason it's a good idea to keep current on your company-sponsored health benefits is that your employer generally has the right to change plans, or to change the rules for existing plans. Any change could affect how much you'll pay. If your company publishes a newsletter (in print or electronically), don't just file it; read it for notices and explanations about additions or changes to your health benefits.

Also, if you're in the job market—either for your first job or for a better job than you now have—bear in mind that companies in some industries generally contribute less toward health insurance premiums than companies in other industries, as Figure 2.9 shows. For example, about 42 percent of

**Figure 2.9**   Some Industries Pay Less in Premiums

Some industries are more likely to require workers to pay a big chunk of health insurance premiums.

| Industry | Percentage Paying Half or Less for Single Coverage | Percentage Paying Half or Less for Family Coverage |
|---|---|---|
| Construction | 41.5% | 60.5% |
| High-Tech | 34.1 | 29.0 |
| Transportation; Utilities; Communications | 17.4 | 21.9 |
| Service | 14.7 | 45.0 |
| Retail | 13.5 | 54.5 |
| Wholesale | 13.3 | 42.6 |
| Health Care | 12.9 | 42.6 |
| Manufacturing | 8.6 | 31.5 |
| Government | 8.4 | 37.0 |
| Finance | 7.4 | 34.6 |
| Mining | 6.0 | 29.6 |

Source: U.S. General Accounting Office (1999 report).

firms in the construction industry pay half or less of the cost for single coverage. In the mining industry, however, only 6 percent of firms pay that little.

It's also generally true that the more employees a company has, the more likely it is that the company will pay a bigger share of the premiums for workers' health insurance coverage, according to a study by the U.S. General Accounting Office.

## For More Information . . .

- The U.S. Department of Health and Human Services (HHS) publishes a consumer booklet, "Choosing and Using a Health Plan." It spells out costs, benefits, and other aspects of health plans, and offers tips for getting the most out of your plan. For a free copy of the guide, or for more information about the services available through HHS's Agency for Healthcare Research and Quality, call toll-free at 1-800-358-9295, or contact the agency's Web site: <www.ahrq.gov>.
- For more information about comparing plans based on quality, see Chapter 3. For information about paying for health insurance and medical expenses through cafeteria plans, flexible savings accounts (FSAs), or medical savings accounts (MSAs), see Chapter 5.

# 3

# Choosing a Plan
# Based on Quality

How much it'll cost you to get health insurance through your job is a big consideration. However, it's just as important—or even more important—to know whether the health plan you choose will deliver the benefits and services you need, when you need them.

In other words, you need to consider quality, too. No matter how much you wind up paying, you also need the security of knowing that the plan you've chosen will work—and work well—for you and your family.

Make no mistake: There can be big differences in the ways that health plans provide access to care, treat illnesses, deliver services, and generally keep customers satisfied.

For example, a 1997 study by the National Committee for Quality Assurance examined the use of so-called beta blocker drugs, which can save the lives of heart attack patients. Under some health plans, most heart attack patients got the drugs; under other plans, only one in three patients got the drugs, the study found.

It is true that cost is a big factor when choosing a health plan. How much you'll have to pay can go a long way toward helping you choose the health plan that is best for you and your family. However, there are lots of other factors to consider, and quality is critical.

## Another Language

The world of health insurance is confusing. No wonder! There's the conventional plan, the HMO, the PPO, and the POS plan. And it doesn't stop there. Among HMOs alone, there are the "staff model" HMO, the "group model" HMO, the "network model" HMO, the "Independent Practice Association" HMO, and the "open" HMO. There are also coinsurance, co-payments, deductibles, premiums, caps, and out-of-pocket limits.

Want more? Consider covered expenses, usual and customary fees, exclusions, preexisting conditions, primary-care physicians, and third-party payers. The list goes on and on.

Puzzled? You're not the only one. A survey by the Employee Benefit Research Institute found that 56 percent of the people enrolled in managed care plans *said they've never been in managed care.*

Don't worry, though. You needn't become a health care expert. You just need to find out how well a plan works and whether it can work for you. Fortunately, it's not that difficult. All it takes is some homework and a focus on the basics.

# Comparing the Quality of Various Plans

To start, you can use many of the same steps explained in Chapter 2 for figuring out costs. Then you can do a little extra research to find out such things as how a plan rates not only among the plan's members or participants, but also among professionals.

This is important stuff if you're considering moving from one plan to another at your current job. It's also important if you're thinking about moving to another job and weighing the benefits package the new employer has to offer.

Begin with the booklets and other materials from your employer (or prospective employer). For other basic information, you can talk with the company's human resources department or benefits administrator. You can also call each plan to get additional materials and details.

Once you've got the paperwork sorted into neat little piles before you at the kitchen table, you can begin to compare plans. Take some notes, or use the handy checklist on page 42. (Use the checklist as a starting point, adding or changing items as you go along.) Remember to stay focused, looking for the kinds of things that are—or can be—most important to you and your family.

## Key Points to Consider

Here are some key points to look for:

**Doctors.** Will you be able to keep seeing the same doctors, or will you need to switch to new ones? Different plans have different answers. Does the plan let you select a doctor? If you're considering a managed care plan, carefully check the list of doctors and specialists who are part of the plan's network. Are there enough doctors to choose from? Ask the doctors you now see for their opinions of the plan you're considering. Are they part of the plan? Are they thinking about joining? If not, why not? Some plans require you to use a primary-care doctor. This "gatekeeper" decides which other services

**Figure 3.1**   Checking a Plan for Quality

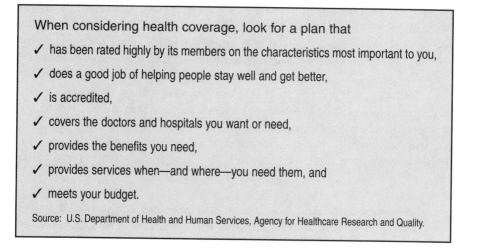

When considering health coverage, look for a plan that

✓ has been rated highly by its members on the characteristics most important to you,

✓ does a good job of helping people stay well and get better,

✓ is accredited,

✓ covers the doctors and hospitals you want or need,

✓ provides the benefits you need,

✓ provides services when—and where—you need them, and

✓ meets your budget.

Source: U.S. Department of Health and Human Services, Agency for Healthcare Research and Quality.

you'll need and whether you can see a specialist. (Remember: You should be able to see a specialist when you really need one.) What are the restrictions? Do you have the right to switch to a new primary-care doctor if you want to? Are there specialists in the plan who can treat a particular condition that afflicts you or a family member? Check how many of the doctors in the plan are board certified. (This generally means that a doctor has been trained in a specialty and meets certain standards set by the profession.) To determine whether a doctor is board certified, contact the American Board of Medical Specialties at 1-800-776-2378, or consult the group's Web site: <www.certifieddoctor. org>. The American Medical Association (AMA) also has information on the training, specialties, and board certification of many licensed doctors. Call 1-800-665-2882, or contact the AMA's Web site: <www.ama-assn.org>.

**The doctors' location.** Does the plan have any doctors in the area where you live or work, or will you have to travel a distance to see them? Some plans have groups of doctors located at one facility. Is that location convenient for you? And will you mind being restricted largely to those doctors and to that facility? Ask the insurance provider—or your benefits department—about the percentage of doctor turnover in the plan. A high rate of turnover (doctors leaving the plan) can be a symptom of underlying problems such as poor management.

**Hospitals.** Check which hospitals take part in the plan. Are they the ones you'd normally use? Are they in a convenient location? Do all the doctors in the plan (or the doctors you are likely to use) practice at all the plan's hospitals? Is a hospital limited in the types of services it provides? What's the reputation and rating of the hospital or hospitals in the plan? Do the hospitals meet the minimum standards set by the Joint Commission on the Accreditation of Healthcare Organizations? If they do, find out exactly how highly they rate. (The commission is an independent, nonprofit group that reviews and rates hospitals. You will read more about it later in this chapter.)

**Networks.** A plan may steer you toward certain doctors, hospitals, and other providers by offering financial incentives. You may be allowed to use services outside the network, but you'll have to pay. Consider the impact of such a plan carefully. If using certain doctors, hospitals, or other services is vitally important to you or your family, and they aren't included in a plan's network, the cost may warrant using another plan.

**Emergency care.** Find out how a plan provides for around-the-clock emergency care. Under what conditions will a plan cover emergency treatment? Will you need the plan's permission first? What are the consequences if you fail to get prior approval? Find out what provisions the plan has for urgent medical situations that require immediate care but aren't necessarily emergencies. In other words, find out what happens if you need medical care after the doctor's office is closed, or if a visit to the doctor can't be arranged. If you travel, find out how a plan provides for emergency or urgent care when you're outside the plan's normal service area—if you're on vacation in another part of the country, or if you're traveling in another country. Is the plan affiliated with any providers beyond the normal service area? If so, what steps must you take to use them? And what are the consequences if you don't take the proper steps or if you use a provider that isn't affiliated with the plan?

**Prescriptions.** Find out if the plan covers prescription medicines. If it does, be sure to check on restrictions. For instance, must you always use generic instead of brand-name drugs? Will the plan cover only certain drugs (and are the ones you need included)? If the plan steers you toward only certain pharmacies, are they conveniently located near your home or job, or will you have to go out of your way to get a prescription filled?

**Prevention.** Find out if the plan will cover preventive care. For instance, some plans emphasize early intervention and are eager to cover physicals, mammograms, Pap smears, and screening for high cholesterol, colorectal cancer, and prostate cancer. Some plans also embrace prenatal care and well-baby care. How important are these to you and your family? Preventive care for women is no small matter. A 1998 presidential report found that death rates associated with breast cancer, cervical cancer, ovarian cancer, and sexually transmitted diseases in women can be significantly reduced through preventive care and routine gynecological services. If preventive care is offered by the plan, find out if there are limits. Can you get a physical once a year? Once every two years?

**Utilization review.** Check carefully to find out what your responsibilities are under the plan. For instance, many plans carefully monitor the types of care you receive. The experts call this "utilization review." It's an ungraceful phrase, but if utilization review is part of a plan you're considering, you'll need to know what it is and how it works. For example, it may mean you'll need the plan's prior approval before you can qualify to get certain types of care. Does the plan require you to get a second opinion before it will agree to cover an operation? Is there a number you must call before you can be treated at a hospital? What are the consequences if you fail to contact the plan when you're supposed to? Consider, too, whether a plan has too many of these conditions.

**What isn't covered.** The materials you receive for each plan should include a list of benefits that aren't covered. Decide how important these are to you. For example, will a plan offer annual hearing and eye exams? Will it cover eyeglasses, contact lenses, and hearing aids? What about dental care, mental-health care, chiropractic care, foot care, or medical equipment? Keep in mind that what a plan *doesn't* cover may be just as important to you as what it *does* cover.

**Retiree coverage.** If you're planning to continue at your present job until you retire, or you're thinking of taking a job that'll be your last before retirement, find out whether the employer offers some sort of retiree health coverage. Most don't, because of the expense, but some do. Retiree health benefits are offered at about 8 percent of small firms (those with between 3 and 199 workers), and at about 41 percent of large firms (those with 200 or more workers), according to a study by the Henry J. Kaiser Family Foundation and the Health Research and Educational Trust. Overall, about 34 percent of people 65 and older have some form of employment-based health coverage, mainly as a supplement to Medicare, according to the Employee Benefit Research Institute. This can be a nice benefit to have, even if the plan serves only as a bare-bones supplement to other coverage you may have in retirement. Just remember that retiree coverage may not be there forever. Companies have the right to alter such plans, and some companies have tried to eliminate them because the costs can be exorbitant (but some of these efforts have been challenged in court). For instance, about 35 percent of large firms that offer retiree benefits have capped the maximum amount of employer contributions for this coverage. Many firms that offer retiree coverage have been increasing the amount that retirees must contribute.

**Worksheet**    Comparing Health Plans on Benefits

When comparing health plans at your job, or at a job you're considering, check to see which plan offers the kinds of health care services you— and your family—need most. Study the booklets and other materials your employer gives you, talk with the company benefits manager or the plan's customer-service office, and compare plans using this checklist.

| Does the Plan Cover These Services: | Plan A | Plan B | Plan C |
|---|---|---|---|
| Cancer Screening (colorectal cancer tests, mammograms, Pap smears) | | | |
| Cholesterol Screening | | | |
| Immunizations (shots) | | | |
| Prenatal Care | | | |
| Well-Baby Care | | | |
| Care for Preexisting Condition | | | |
| Diabetes Supplies | | | |
| Dental Exams and Treatments | | | |
| Eye Exams, Glasses, Contact Lenses | | | |
| Hearing Exams, Hearing Aids | | | |
| Outpatient Prescription Medicines | | | |
| Medical Equipment for Home Use | | | |
| Mental-Health Services | | | |
| Physical Therapy | | | |
| Hospice Care | | | |
| Stop-Smoking Programs; Drug, Alcohol Counseling | | | |
| Alternative Treatments (such as chiropractic services, acupuncture) | | | |
| Home Health Care, Adult Day Care, Nursing Home Care | | | |

Source: U.S. Department of Health and Human Services, Agency for Healthcare Research and Quality.

### Talk to Other Workers

All of this may seem to be a terribly involved process. It's isn't, though, because you have lots of resources available, most of them near at hand. Besides studying the written materials you've collected, you can talk to the people in your company's human resources department or a benefits administrator to get a better feel for how each plan works and which may be best for your particular circumstances.

Coworkers can also be a good source of information, especially those who've had health problems and can tell you in detail about how well their plan worked.

# How to Learn How Your Plan Rates

If you can't find any information about how a health plan rates, forget the plan and either stick with the one you've got or choose another. Your health is too important to get involved with a plan that either doesn't allow for ratings, or won't share the results with you and others.

This section looks at two key tools to help you figure out which plan is right for you. There are "consumer" ratings, which focus mainly on consumer likes and dislikes. There are also "seal of approval" ratings, known as accreditations, which are put together by independent professional groups and generally show how well a plan meets certain industry standards.

As you review this section, keep in mind that ratings aren't perfect. They won't tell you all you need to know. Nevertheless, they're a good start, and can be an important factor in helping you decide whether a plan is right for you and your family.

### Consumer Ratings

Whether you're looking to buy a car or make another major purchase (a refrigerator, stove, or washing machine, for example), it's always a good idea to find out what other people think about it. In other words, you want to know how the item you're buying rates for quality.

It's even more important to take this step when you're shopping for a health plan. After all, it's your health that's at stake, and the health of your family, too.

Fortunately, these ratings surveys aren't hard to come by. One such survey, the Consumer Assessment of Health Plans, is used by many states, businesses, health plans, and other organizations to find out what members think of the plans they're in.

The Consumer Assessment of Health Plans asks plan members the kind of questions that should be on your mind, too: Do members get the health services they need? How easy is it for members to get a doctor they're comfortable with? How easy is it to get to see a specialist? Do plan doctors listen carefully and explain things well? Are there too many forms to fill out? How do members rate the care they get from doctors and other providers in the plan? And how do members rate the plan overall?

## Surveying Treatment

Another type of survey, the Health Plan Employer Data and Information Set, compares how well plans prevent and treat illness. For example, one focus of the survey is on whether young children in a particular plan are current on recommended immunizations. Other parts of the survey look at breast cancer screening, at prenatal care, and at eye exams to prevent blindness in people who have diabetes.

Ask your employer (or prospective employer), your nearest Medicare or Medicaid office, or your state's insurance commissioner's office whether such surveys are available for the plan or plans you're considering. These surveys may be known by their technical name or may be called "performance reports," "consumer ratings," "membership satisfaction ratings," or simply "report cards." (For a state-by-state list of insurance regulators, see Appendix A.) The health plan itself may make a copy of the survey available, too.

No matter what they're called, these surveys are important because they can show you how other people view the plans you're considering. Match the results against the factors you find important in a health plan.

## Accreditation

Many health plans also choose to be formally reviewed and accredited by a nationally recognized organization. By displaying a seal of approval, a plan can get a leg up on competing plans. The accreditation process can also help a plan find ways to improve. The results of accreditation studies are used not only by consumers, but also by employers who try to get the best plans for their workers.

For information on whether a health plan (or provider) is accredited, rated, or reviewed, you may contact the plan itself, your state's insurance department (see the Appendix A for a list of your state's insurance regulator), or one of these organizations:

**National Committee for Quality Assurance (NCQA).** This is a private, nonprofit organization that assesses the quality of managed care plans—individually and as a group—and publishes the results. The NCQA began accrediting managed care organizations in 1991. The program is voluntary;

plans need not take part. Nevertheless, by 1999, almost half the HMOs in the country, covering three-fourths of all HMO enrollees, were involved in the group's accreditation process. Plans that publicly reported their data to the NCQA for two or three years outperformed the national average on every measure of clinical quality and member satisfaction, according to the group's 1999 report, "The State of Managed Care Quality." To see the list of 40 insurance plans that qualify for the group's rating of "Excellent," see Appendix B. To find out whether a plan is accredited by the group, call its toll-free "accreditation status" hotline at 1-888-275-7585. The group also publishes an "accreditation status list," which shows the status of all health plans the group has surveyed. It also shows plans that have a decision pending, and those for which a survey has been scheduled. For information on ordering the list by mail (it costs $10), call the group's publications center at 1-800-839-6487. You may also get a copy of the list, as well as free reports on the health care industry and on individual plans, by contacting NCQA's Web site: <www.ncqa.org>.

**Joint Commission on Accreditation of Healthcare Organizations.** This independent, nonprofit group evaluates and accredits more than 18,000 health care organizations nationwide, including hospitals, health care networks, managed care organizations, and others. At one time, it focused mainly on hospitals and other such facilities, but it has expanded its reach to include HMOs. To find out (at no charge) whether a managed care plan, hospital, or other organization has been accredited and how it rates, call the organization at 1-630-792-5000 or write to: Joint Commission on Accreditation of Healthcare Organizations, One Renaissance Boulevard, Oakbrook Terrace, IL 60181. You also can contact the organization's Web site: <www.jcaho.org>.

**American Accreditation HealthCare Commission/URAC.** This group also gives a seal of approval to managed care plans that meet its standards. For details on its accredited organizations, call 1-202-216-9010 or contact its Web site: <www.urac.org>.

## Problems with Managed Care

Late in July of 1999, when many workers were away on vacation or just enjoying part of a long, hot summer, a foundation published the results of a nationwide survey that rocked the health care industry.

The foundation didn't survey consumers, and it didn't poll specific health plans, either. Instead, it focused on the people on the front lines, people who work most closely with patients, people who provide direct care: doctors and nurses.

**Figure 3.2**   Patients Denied Care

---

In a national survey, doctors reported that their patients had been denied coverage by health plans for certain types of health services:

✓ 79 percent of doctors said patients had been denied coverage for a prescription drug that the doctors believed a patient needed.

✓ 69 percent of doctors said patients had been denied coverage for a diagnostic test or procedure.

✓ 60 percent of doctors said patients had been denied coverage for a hospital stay.

✓ 52 percent of doctors said patients had been denied referrals to specialists.

Denials had been issued by health plans during the two years before the survey was taken.

Source: Kaiser Family Foundation/Harvard University School of Public Health, "Survey of Physicians and Nurses," July 1999.

---

The survey's results were, in some ways, an indictment of managed care. For example, almost 9 out of 10 doctors said health plans had denied patients coverage for health services. Between one-third and two-thirds of the doctors surveyed said their patients had suffered adverse health consequences after being denied coverage by their health plans. In addition, about half of the nurses surveyed said that a health plan decision had resulted in a decline in health for patients.

The doctors and nurses in the survey gave some high marks to managed care plans for offering preventive care. In other words, with managed care, there was a greater likelihood that patients would receive preventive services.

Many of the doctors and nurses who responded to the survey also commended managed care for imposing certain types of guidelines and rules that resulted in improvements to the health care system. For example, some said that a health plan had given them guidelines or innovative tools to better manage a patient's illness.

### Troubling Questions

However, the report raised troubling questions about the impact of managed care on health care professionals and their patients. For example:

- 95 percent of doctors, and 92 percent of nurses, said that managed care had increased paperwork—for health care providers as well as for patients.

- 86 percent of doctors, and 82 percent of nurses, said that managed care had decreased patients' ability to see medical specialists.
- 83 percent of doctors, and 85 percent of nurses, said that managed care had decreased the amount of time they spent with patients.
- 72 percent of doctors, and 78 percent of nurses, said that managed care had decreased the quality of care for people who are sick.

## Focus on Doctors and Nurses

The survey was no broadside by a band of health care radicals; it was a national survey of more than 1,000 doctors and more than 750 nurses conducted by researchers at two respected organizations: the Kaiser Family Foundation, an independent national health care philanthropy, and the Harvard School of Public Health.

The report drew an immediate response from the health care industry. The American Association of Health Plans said that the report was inconsistent with other research that suggests that the overwhelming majority of patients in health plans are getting the care they need. Other industry groups criticized the survey, too.

The finer points of the Kaiser survey will likely be debated by experts for years to come. At the very least, however, it raises questions about how effective managed care plans have been from a provider standpoint, and affirms the suspicions of some consumers and others about the quality of care that managed care plans provide.

## Results of Other Studies on Managed Care

There's no question that managed care can work well, for patients as well as the health care industry. Indeed, a 1998 report by the President's Advisory Commission on Consumer Protection and Quality in the Health Care Industry found that managed care can result in improvements in care for patients. "When appropriately structured, a plan using a network of providers can improve the quality and coordination of care delivered to consumers through careful selection and credentialing of providers and through coordination of care by primary-care physicians and those with specialty training."

That same report, however, found that, in some cases, managed care can result in problems. For example, while nearly all workers covered by health plans can now choose a plan that covers non-network providers, "In some cases . . . the additional cost of these products, or of the option to go out of network, effectively puts such choice out of the reach of some consumers."

The President's commission also found that the "gatekeeper" provision in some plans can cause problems. One way health plans control costs is to limit your choices, or at least to carefully control your access to specialists and services. For some people, especially healthy people who seldom need care and rarely visit a doctor, this may not matter. For others, however, it can be a big deal.

If you have ongoing health needs, you may require regular access to doctors and other health care professionals who are specially trained to serve those needs. "This is especially true of those consumers who have disabling or terminal conditions. In such cases, the traditional 'gatekeeper' approach used by some health plans can be an impediment to access to quality care and result in unnecessary inconvenience to consumers," the President's commission said.

A national survey published in 1999 by Hewitt Associates, a management consulting firm, found that most people remain satisfied with their managed care health plans. However, the survey also showed that 22 percent of consumers weren't satisfied with their plans, and that consumer dissatisfaction had increased across the board, for all managed care plans—including HMOs, PPOs, and POS plans—and across all geographic regions.

The main reason for dissatisfaction was poor customer service. Indeed, more than one-third of employees said they weren't pleased with their plan's ability to resolve problems. In addition, 30 percent said they weren't satisfied with their plan's timeliness, professionalism, or accuracy.

Hewitt attributed the results in part to consolidation in the managed care industry, which has led to operational glitches, technical problems, and confusion for consumers. Hewitt also said plans face increasing pressure on keeping costs down. This has led to cutbacks in staff and service, frustrating consumers.

### The Importance of Research

What do all these studies, surveys, and reports mean to you? They underscore how important it is to research plans carefully so you can have a sound basis for deciding which plan is best for you—whether you're thinking about choosing another plan during "open enrollment" time at your existing job or you're evaluating one or more plans at a new job.

This is especially important because most health plans in the workplace nowadays are managed care plans. (Indeed, another Kaiser study showed that managed care covers more than 85 percent of health insurance enrollees among medium and large employers. Many small businesses offer only one health insurance plan, and it is likely to be a managed care plan.)

As the President's Commission put it, "Consumers' choice of a health plan has a significant impact on consumers' ability to make other choices about facilities, health professionals, and treatment options. Even in cases where consumers do not have a choice of plans, they require information on the plan in which they are enrolled to use the available services effectively."

The point, then, is clear: When you're faced with a decision about which health plan to choose, you have to do some homework. Cost alone isn't the only factor; quality is important, too.

## Your Right to Appeal

It's also important to know exactly how a plan will handle any complaints you may have, and what rights you have to appeal a plan's decision. For example, what procedures does a plan have for hearing your complaint and acting on it? How quickly will a plan respond—and act?

Keep in mind that if you have a complaint about a plan, or if a plan has denied you care, your company's benefits department or plan administrator may be able to resolve the problem for you. That's a good place to start.

Still, there are times when you may have to appeal a decision yourself, and it helps to know in advance how the complaint and appeal process works. The booklets, brochures, and other written materials your employer (or prospective employer) provides you can answer some of these questions, but not all of them.

### Federal Laws

First, keep in mind that employers who offer group health benefits to workers—either through managed care plans or conventional plans—have to follow some basic federal rules. These rules come from a landmark 1974 law, the Employee Retirement Income Security Act (ERISA).

Under the law, a health plan must set up procedures for handling complaints and appeals. The plan must also disclose these procedures to you.

A health plan generally has 90 days to approve or deny your claim for benefits. If a plan denies your claim, it must do so in writing and list specific reasons why the claim was denied. You also have a right to appeal this decision, and the plan has 60 days to approve or deny your appeal.

Another federal law deals specifically with HMOs. Under this law, if an HMO is federally qualified, it must have written procedures to deal with complaints and appeals. These procedures have to be written in plain language, and the HMO must give them to you if you ask for them.

### State Laws

Keep in mind that states often have lots of rules for health insurers, too, but these rules vary from state to state. Some states require that health insurers offer certain complaint procedures to enrollees. For example, under some state laws, you have the right to appeal a denial of coverage or denial of claim to an outside panel of medical experts if you're not satisfied with the outcome of the plan's internal appeals process.

About 30 states require HMOs to follow specific complaint procedures. Furthermore, at least seven states require HMOs to process your appeal quickly if the plan has denied you urgently needed care.

Within laws, however, there can be some wiggle room. It's worth talking with your company's benefits department and with people who are covered by a particular plan to find out exactly how the plan deals with complaints, denials, and appeals. Here are some good questions to ask:

- Does the plan issue timely notice of its decision to deny, reduce, or end treatment or to deny a claim? Are these actions written in plain language so that plan members or beneficiaries can understand them?
- Does the plan give you a plain-language description of its process for complaints and appeals?
- Does the plan provide for expedited procedures to handle complaints or appeals in certain types of cases, such as when claims for urgent care have been denied?
- Does the plan provide for an external appeals procedure? In other words, if the plan denies your claim, is the decision final and binding, or can you bring your appeal to an outside panel or organization that can review your appeal and reach its own independent decision?

### Additional Steps

There are some additional steps you can take to help ensure that a plan you're considering really works for consumers.

For example, you can contact your state insurance regulators (see the state-by-state list in Appendix A) to find out how many complaints have been filed against the health care plan, and what types of complaints have been filed. You can also make a sort of dry run by calling a plan's consumer complaint phone number to check how long it takes to reach a real person.

## Checking an Insurer's Financial Health

It's always a good idea to check on the financial health of an insurance company. A plan may offer a great deal, with low-cost premiums and lots of benefits, but if the insurer is on shaky financial ground, the deal—and the company—may disappear.

In 1999, a small HMO that mainly served Rhode Island and South-eastern Massachusetts ran into severe financial problems. State regulators finally stepped in to seize control. Thousands of subscribers—including individuals, families, and small businesses—were suddenly left scrambling to make other arrangements.

Had the consumers checked in advance on the HMO's financial ratings, however, they would have been forewarned: In the months before the collapse, most major ratings agencies had already downgraded the insurer. Indeed, one ratings agency, Weiss, had given the HMO a grade "D" as far back as 1994.

There are several established ratings agencies that review insurance companies' health from a financial standpoint. Many public libraries subscribe to publications from one or more of these agencies, so you may be able to get ratings at no charge simply by visiting—or calling—your local library. You may also contact the agencies directly. Just keep in mind that while some provide ratings at no charge, others levy fees.

**A.M. Best & Co. of Oldwick, New Jersey.** If you call 1-908-439-2200, you can order a full financial report on an insurer for $19.95. If you contact Best's Web site, you can get ratings and a brief financial report on an insurer at no charge: <www.ambest.com>.

**Standard & Poor's Corp. of New York.** If you call 1-212-438-2400, you can check the rating on an insurer at no charge (other than the price of the call). If you have access to the Internet, you can get ratings at no charge: <www. standardandpoor.com>.

**Weiss Ratings Inc. of Palm Beach Gardens, Florida.** By calling 1-800-289-9222, you can get a rating over the phone for $15. For $25, you can get a more detailed one-page ratings report sent to you by mail. For more information, contact the firm's Web site: <www.weissratings.com>.

## Where Federal and State Laws Come In

Whether you're comparing health plans or just trying to get the most out of the health plan you now have, keep in mind that federal law guarantees you certain types of protections and coverage.

For example, the Newborns' and Mothers' Health Protection Act, enacted in 1996, guarantees a minimum hospital stay for a mother or newborn in connection with childbirth. The law says that health plans cannot restrict a stay to less than 48 hours following a vaginal delivery, or less than 96 hours after a delivery by cesarean section. The attending doctor or midwife, in con-

**Figure 3.3**   Federal Laws on Health Care

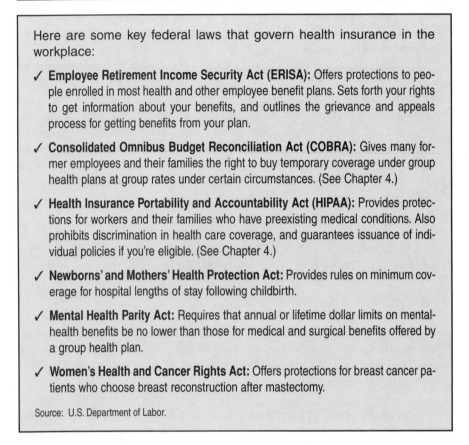

Here are some key federal laws that govern health insurance in the workplace:

✓ **Employee Retirement Income Security Act (ERISA):** Offers protections to people enrolled in most health and other employee benefit plans. Sets forth your rights to get information about your benefits, and outlines the grievance and appeals process for getting benefits from your plan.

✓ **Consolidated Omnibus Budget Reconciliation Act (COBRA):** Gives many former employees and their families the right to buy temporary coverage under group health plans at group rates under certain circumstances. (See Chapter 4.)

✓ **Health Insurance Portability and Accountability Act (HIPAA):** Provides protections for workers and their families who have preexisting medical conditions. Also prohibits discrimination in health care coverage, and guarantees issuance of individual policies if you're eligible. (See Chapter 4.)

✓ **Newborns' and Mothers' Health Protection Act:** Provides rules on minimum coverage for hospital lengths of stay following childbirth.

✓ **Mental Health Parity Act:** Requires that annual or lifetime dollar limits on mental-health benefits be no lower than those for medical and surgical benefits offered by a group health plan.

✓ **Women's Health and Cancer Rights Act:** Offers protections for breast cancer patients who choose breast reconstruction after mastectomy.

Source: U.S. Department of Labor.

sultation with the mother, has the right to call for an earlier discharge. (The law doesn't require plans to offer coverage in connection with childbirth. However, if a plan does offer such benefits, the plan must follow the rules outlined here.) Many states have adopted similar rules.

Another law enacted in 1996, the Mental Health Parity Act, says that annual or lifetime dollar limits that a group plan imposes on your mental-health benefits cannot be lower than the annual or lifetime dollar limits the plan imposes for medical and surgical benefits. (Small businesses—generally, those with fewer than 50 employees—are exempt from the law.)

The Women's Health and Cancer Rights Act, enacted in 1998, outlines protections for those who choose breast reconstruction in connection with a mastectomy. The general rule is that if your plan provides coverage for medical and surgical benefits in connection with a mastectomy, the plan must also provide coverage for reconstructive surgery.

Although federal law generally governs employer-sponsored health plans, state laws also play a role, especially in managed care. In some states, for instance, certain health plans must allow plan subscribers to go directly to a specialist without the requirement of a referral from the patient's primary-care doctor.

Some states require health plans to pay for certain types of care delivered in an emergency room. Certain states also require health plans to admit any provider to their networks who's willing to abide by the terms of the health plan's contract. (Although this rule typically applies to pharmacies, some states extend the rule to other providers, according to a report by the House Ways and Means Committee.)

## Other Considerations That May Influence Your Choice

As you do your research and make your choices, here are some other pointers to keep in mind:

### Carrying Two Plans

If you're married and your spouse works, you'll have to decide whether it's best to maintain two plans or to drop one. Keep in mind that even if you and your spouse are covered under separate group health insurance plans at work, you won't get more than the cost of a covered expense. That's because plans include a clause that's called "coordination of benefits." In effect, both plans get together to make sure that a plan beneficiary never receives more than 100 percent of the allowable cost of a covered medical expense.

Because of this, and for other reasons, it's seldom a good idea to pay for coverage under two plans, especially if you have children to include in your coverage. It's usually better to launch a detailed study to compare plans, then choose the one that is best for your situation.

### Lifetime Limits

Try to choose a plan that offers high lifetime limits on the amount of benefits you can receive. At first glance, a plan's lifetime limit may seem high, so high that you may figure you'll never reach it. But think more carefully about this important clause. Each year, about 1,500 to 2,500 people lose their private health insurance coverage because their medical expenses exceed the lifetime limit set by their health insurance policy, according to a 1998 report by the President's Advisory Commission on Consumer Protection and Quality in the Health Care Industry.

The result can be catastrophic. "Many of these consumers must exhaust their family savings before becoming eligible for Medicaid or other forms of public assistance," the report found. "This creates a tremendous hardship on these individuals and their families."

The commission urged employers, health plans, and others to consider taking steps to ease the burden: eliminate or increase lifetime limits, expand the use of high-risk pools so that people who reach a lifetime limit can get immediate coverage, or offer supplemental coverage for workers who want to increase their limits.

That's a wish list, however, and until these big-picture changes take place, you're on your own. Your best bet, then, is to choose a plan that has high limits. (You may also want to talk to an insurance agent about getting a catastrophic health insurance policy, one whose coverage kicks in once you reach the limit on your regular policy.)

## A Final Point

Is the quality of U.S. health care adequate? Is it getting better, worse, or staying the same? It's not easy to tell, according to RAND, a nonprofit research group. "More information is available on the quality of airlines, restaurants, cars, and VCRs than on the quality of health care," two of RAND's researchers said in a recent study.

Their study also suggested that quality varies substantially among physicians, hospitals, geographic locations, types of care, and age groups.

There are ways to measure quality in health plans, but they're not foolproof. Some plans simply do not report their data. Others report it in a confusing way. You can use this chapter as a starting point on which to base a decision about how to choose the best health plan for you and your family. Just keep in mind that you'll have to do some extra homework. Health care in America is complicated and rapidly changing. There still aren't any easy and accurate ways to fully evaluate a health care plan.

## For More Information . . .

- The U.S. Department of Health and Human Services (HHS) publishes a consumer booklet called *Your Guide to Choosing Quality Health Care,* and a shorter guide, *Quick Checks for Quality.* For a free copy, or for more information about the services available through HHS's

Agency for Healthcare Research and Quality, call toll free at 1-800-358-9295, or contact the agency's Web site: <www.ahrq.gov>.

- The U.S. Department of Labor publishes several booklets that explain changes in health care plans, your rights under federal law, and how to make health plans work for you. These include *Questions and Answers: Recent Changes in Health Care Law, Can the Retiree Health Benefits Provided By Your Employer Be Cut?* and *Health Benefits for Women.* For free copies of the brochures, call the agency's toll-free publications hotline at 1-800-998-7542. If you have access to the Internet, you may read or download copies of these and other health-benefits publications at the agency's Web site: <www.dol.gov>.

- If you have questions or problems with your health plan, the Department of Labor's Pension and Welfare Benefits Administration may be able to help. To find out how to contact the regional office nearest you, see the list in Appendix C. If you have access to the Internet, you may find out more by contacting the agency's Web site: <www.dol.gov/dol/pwba>.

- The AARP (formerly known as the American Association of Retired Persons) has several publications that can help you choose the health plan that best suits your and your family's needs. These include *9 Ways to Get the Most from Your Managed Care Plan,* and *Checkpoints for Managed Care: How to Choose a Health Plan.* Single copies are free. Write to AARP Fulfillment, 601 E Street NW, Washington, DC 20049, or contact the AARP's Web site: <www.aarp.org>.

- Consumer Reports, the national magazine published by the non-profit Consumers Union, regularly reports on health care issues and rates many of the nation's largest HMOs. The magazine is available on newsstands. For subscription information, call 1-800-765-1845. You may also obtain information and articles from past issues from the magazine's Web site: <www.ConsumerReports.org>.

- *Money* magazine regularly surveys large companies and publishes a "List of America's Best Company Benefits." The October 1999 issue carried the results of one such survey. The magazine is available on newsstands. For subscription information, or to order back issues, call 1-800-633-9970 or contact the magazine's Web site: <www.money.com>.

- If you have access to the Internet—at home, at work, or at your local library or community college—check the Healthfinder Web site offered by the Department of Health and Human Services. Launched in 1997, this is a free service that offers lots of information on consumer health issues. It also includes many links to other resources that you can access on the Internet, including online publications, clearinghouses, databases, support groups, and self-help groups, as well as government agencies and nonprofit organizations that produce reliable information: <www.healthfinder.gov>.

- The National Association of Insurance Commissioners (NAIC) has put together a Consumer Action Kit that you can use to evaluate health plans. Check with your state insurance department to see if it is available there (see the state-by-state list of insurance regulators in Appendix A). Some states also publish their own shopper's guide to health insurance.

# Continuing
# Your Coverage

When you leave your job, you can take your health insurance with you.

That's right. Whether you quit or you're fired, whether you're sick or healthy, whether you have another job to go to or none at all, you can continue your health insurance coverage for at least 18 months.

It's not a gift from your employer.

It's the law.

Your employer *must* extend your health insurance coverage if you want it—and not just for you, but for your family, too.

This is important stuff. Many Americans, particularly in the South and West, have no health insurance (see Figure 4.1). Altogether, about 44.3 million people in the United States are uninsured—about 16.3 percent of the population—according to a 1999 report by the U.S. Census Bureau. Financially and from a health standpoint, they are at risk. Your ability to maintain coverage under your former employer's health plan can be a great advantage—for your mental and physical health and for your pocketbook.

## Your Rights under Federal Law

Retaining your health benefits when you leave your job may not seem important to you now. After all, we've just lived through one of the best job markets in recent history. During the latter half of the 1990s, unemployment was low, job opportunities were plentiful, and job-hopping was commonplace.

This climate may still exist, depending on where you live, the industry in which you work, your level of skill, and other factors. Maybe you can get another job, whenever you like, and get a benefits package that's as good— or better—than the one you have now. That's great.

Nevertheless, there'll come a day when you or someone close to you leaves work and a satisfactory new health care plan isn't immediately available. That's the time you need to know about your right to extend health insurance coverage under the former employer's plan.

**Figure 4.1**    Uninsured by Region

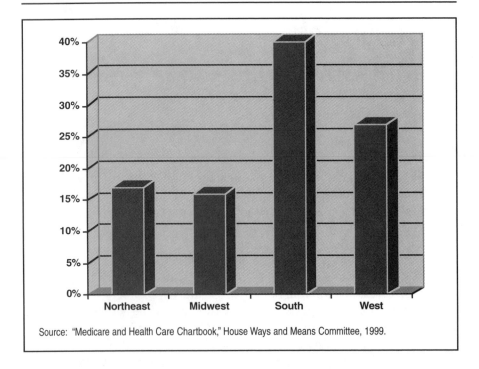

Source: "Medicare and Health Care Chartbook," House Ways and Means Committee, 1999.

That's the time you'll need to know about a law called COBRA and exactly how it applies to you and your loved ones. At any given time, about 4.7 million former employees rely on COBRA for their health insurance coverage, according to a study by the Henry J. Kaiser Family Foundation and the Health Research and Educational Trust. Here's another way to look at it: For every 100 active or former workers with job-based coverage, an average

**Figure 4.2**    What Is COBRA?

In 1985, Congress passed the Consolidated Omnibus Budget Reconciliation Act, or COBRA for short.

This landmark legislation was signed into law in April 1986 and took effect for plan years starting July 1986. Under the law, you have the right to continue group health insurance from your former employer—for you and your family—if you leave your job.

You may also exercise this option if you stay on the job but lose coverage because your hours have been cut back. In certain circumstances, coverage may continue for up to 36 months.

of 3 are former employees using COBRA to extend their coverage, the study found.

Under COBRA law, your former employer *must* give you the option to continue coverage under your old health insurance plan—at group rates—for you and your family members.

## How COBRA Applies to You

In effect, COBRA coverage can serve as a bridge for you and your loved ones until you get coverage under another plan. This could be helpful for any number of reasons:

- If you get laid off, it could be some time before you land another job.
- Even if you plan to step from your current job right into the job of your dreams, your new employer may require you to wait awhile before health coverage kicks in.
- If you take early retirement, you may not have a health plan to cover you between the time you leave and the time you enroll in the federal Medicare program (typically at age 65).

### Job Lock

Even if you're just thinking about taking another job, it's good to know that COBRA will be there to fill the gap. With COBRA, you won't be locked into a job you don't like simply because of uncertainty over health insurance coverage, and if you're thinking about leaving your job to start your own business, COBRA can tide you over until you've got your business up and running and you can get coverage on your own.

### Life Before COBRA

It wasn't always this way. Before the law was passed, if you lost your job, you could lose your health insurance coverage, too. Unless you quickly landed a new job—and new coverage—or managed to get an individual policy on your own, you were uninsured and potentially in deep financial trouble.

COBRA changed the landscape dramatically. Nowadays, your former employer must give you the option to continue coverage with the same provisions your old group plan had, whether it was a traditional health insurance plan, a managed care plan, a trust, a self-insured plan, or some combination of plan types.

**Figure 4.3**    What Does COBRA Cover?

---

COBRA says that you—and your beneficiaries—may continue to be covered under the terms of your old company-sponsored plan for items such as:

✓ Inpatient and outpatient hospital care

✓ Doctor's care

✓ Surgery and other major medical benefits

✓ Prescription drugs

✓ Dental, vision, and other care

✓ Drug or alcohol treatment

Source: IRS regulations.

---

You may also continue coverage if your hours have been cut back so much that you lose your eligibility for company-sponsored health insurance. (Many employer-sponsored health plans cover you only if you work a certain number of hours in a pay period.) For COBRA purposes, a cut in hours can also result from a strike or walkout.

Keep in mind, too, that neither you, your spouse, nor your children must provide evidence of insurability to continue coverage under COBRA. In other words, you don't have to undergo any tests or exams to try to qualify; COBRA requires that you continue to be covered under the same terms and conditions that applied under your old policy; coverage must be identical to what you had.

## Why Group Plans Cost Less

Continuing your coverage can be especially important if you, your spouse, or your children are in bad health: COBRA coverage can be a lot cheaper than buying an individual policy in the open market. Why? COBRA coverage is, after all, group coverage, through an employer-sponsored plan. These plans are typically less expensive—often a lot less expensive—than individual plans. A group plan covers people who are relatively healthy and will require few health care services as well as people with health problems who'll require more health care services. As a result, the risk—and the overall cost—is spread out over a large group, lowering the cost on a per-person basis. Administrative costs also are spread across the group. Further, some

**Figure 4.4**   Consumer Out-of-Pocket Costs Are 41% Lower in Employment-based Market

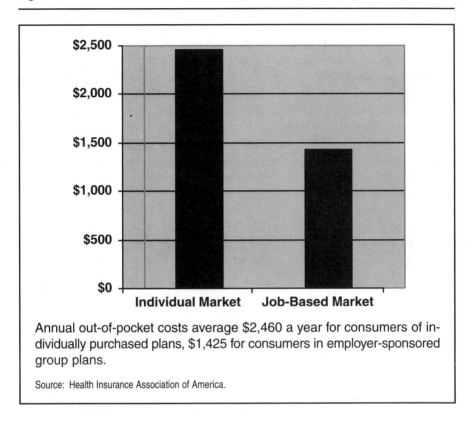

Annual out-of-pocket costs average $2,460 a year for consumers of individually purchased plans, $1,425 for consumers in employer-sponsored group plans.

Source: Health Insurance Association of America.

companies are in a better position than individuals are to negotiate for lower-cost health plans.

Even people who don't know about COBRA (perhaps because it's so seldom publicized) don't need to worry: employers *must* give workers a written notice about their right to choose COBRA.

Your employer must also spell out your right to COBRA coverage in a booklet, known as the "summary plan description," that explains your health benefits. If you haven't received a summary plan description, request one from your human resources department, benefits administrator, or whoever's responsible for running the plan; federal law requires that you be given a copy.

## Limits on COBRA

Is there a catch to COBRA? There are several. COBRA is, after all, a federal law, so it can be tricky. There are some drawbacks and loopholes.

First, the law applies only to the plans of organizations in the private sector, such as businesses, and to local and state government plans (although these government plans have a somewhat different set of rules).

Religious organizations and the federal government are typically exempt from COBRA although they may offer their own plans for continuation of coverage. The federal government is subject to separate rules under another law.

Second, although COBRA applies to most companies, some are exempt. In general, your employer must give you the COBRA option if the company has 20 or more workers (full-time and part-time workers are counted, and so is any other worker who may be covered by the company's plan).

In other words, only the very smallest of companies are exempt, and they may offer their own plans and may also be subject to state laws about extended coverage.

If you clear these hurdles, there are still some others in your path. For example, your company must give you the option to continue coverage if you leave work for any reason except for one: gross misconduct. Unfortunately, the law doesn't say what, exactly, "gross misconduct" means, but this much is clear: you must do something really bad in order to be disqualified. Your employer can't deny you coverage just because you'd been goofing off at the water cooler, for example. The stakes must be far higher (for instance, you hacked your way into the human resources computer, gave yourself a raise, then stole company secrets and sold them to the enemy).

In other words, you get to claim your rights under COBRA if you lose your job for just about any reason, voluntarily or not. This means that you may take advantage of COBRA if you quit, and you may take advantage of it if you are fired, laid off, downsized, rightsized, or just plain out-the-door sized.

## Costs of COBRA Coverage

Perhaps the most important catch, however, is this: COBRA may cost you. Employers are free to pay for the entire cost of your coverage, of course, but it's expensive. As a result, most employers require that people who receive continued coverage under COBRA pay some or all of the expense.

In fact, the law lets employers charge for the entire cost of the premium— including whatever portion the company formerly paid, *plus* whatever portion you used to pay. In addition, the law lets employers charge an additional 2 percent administration fee for clerical costs and the like. As a result, you may have to pay up to 102 percent of the overall cost of coverage.

For instance, suppose that the premium for covering you and your family under a group health insurance plan is $500 a month. You pay $100; the company pays $400. You leave your job and choose COBRA. Under the law, your employer can charge you up to $510 a month for the coverage—100 percent of the actual cost of the premium plus a 2 percent administrative fee ($10).

### You Still May Pay Less Than You Would without COBRA Coverage

Although you may have to pay some or all of the cost of your coverage under COBRA, it still may be a good deal for you. That's because group health insurance is usually less expensive than an individual policy. You may wind up paying less under COBRA—even if you must pay the entire cost—than you would for the same level of coverage under an individual policy purchased in the open market. (It's still a good idea to shop around, however; take your COBRA coverage first, then once you're covered, check around to see if you can get lower-cost coverage.)

### Deductibles, Caps, and Copayments

Picking up coverage under COBRA also means picking up all the terms and conditions that your old plan provided.

For example, if your company plan required you to meet deductibles, you'll also have to meet deductibles when you're covered by COBRA.

Plan limits are treated the same way as deductibles, too. This means that under COBRA you may face limits on plan benefits just as you did under regular coverage, such as a cap on the number of hospital days covered, a limit on the dollar amount of reimbursable expenses, a limit on out-of-pocket expenses, and a cap on copayments.

For example, suppose your company plan pays for a maximum of 150 days of hospitalization per person per year. While employed in early 2001, you spend 20 days in the hospital. In May of that year, you lose your job and choose to continue plan coverage under COBRA. In this example, the plan must pay for a maximum of 130 days of hospitalization for the rest of the year. In other words, the limit on hospitalization continues under COBRA.

This can work to your advantage, too. For example, if your old plan has annual deductibles, and you become covered under COBRA in the middle of the year, you'll get credit for expenses you paid toward your deductible earlier in the year when you were employed.

## Length of COBRA Coverage

How long can COBRA cover you? In general, if you (as an employee) lose coverage under your company plan—either because you lose your job or your hours are cut back—then you, your spouse, or your dependent children may choose COBRA coverage for up to 18 months (see Figure 4.5).

In some circumstances, however, coverage may extend even longer. For example, if you or a family member qualifies for Social Security disability benefits at any time during the first 60 days of COBRA coverage, the 18-month limit on COBRA coverage will be extended another 11 months, to a maximum of 29 months.

In addition, your spouse and dependent children may get COBRA coverage for 36 months for any of these reasons:

- You enroll in Medicare, the federal health insurance program that generally kicks in when you turn 65.
- You become divorced or legally separated.
- You die.

In addition, your children may choose to continue group coverage if they lose what the experts call "dependent child" status under your plan's rules.

**Figure 4.5**    How COBRA Rules Apply to You

| If This Happens to You, as an Employee . . . | These People Are Covered . . . | For This Amount of Time |
| --- | --- | --- |
| Job loss, cutback in hours* | You, your spouse, and dependents | 18 months |
| You enroll in Medicare, you become divorced or legally separated, or you die** | Your spouse and dependents | 36 months |

*Access to health coverage can be extended by another 11 months, for a maximum of 29 months, if beneficiary qualifies for Social Security disability benefits.

**If your child reaches a certain age that would normally trigger loss of coverage under your company plan (in other words, if he or she loses "dependent status" as defined by plan rules), he or she may choose to continue coverage under COBRA for up to 36 months.

Other rules apply for people whose companies enter bankruptcy proceedings. COBRA rules generally do not apply to plans offered by religious organizations and government agencies (separate continuation-of-coverage rules apply to most government agencies). Although some small businesses—generally those with fewer than 20 employees—are exempt from COBRA rules, they may be subject to state laws that require varying degrees of continuation of coverage.

Source: U.S. Department of Labor.

What does that mean? Suppose your company plan's rules require that coverage stop for a child once he or she reaches the age of 21. If this happens to your child, he or she may continue coverage under COBRA for up to 36 months—even if you keep working, and you continue to be covered under your company plan.

Keep in mind that these are the maximum time periods that federal law sets for COBRA coverage. Your employer may offer more generous terms, depending on the company and the plan. In other words, although the law says you must be covered for up to 18 months (or 36 months, depending on the circumstances), the law doesn't stop the company from covering you for longer periods. Your state's laws may also have rules that are more liberal for beneficiaries than the federal law.

Generally, however, coverage stops under any of these circumstances:

- You reach the last day of maximum coverage (18 months, 29 months, or 36 months, depending on the circumstances described in Figure 4.5).
- You stop paying COBRA premiums.
- The company ends its group health plan altogether.
- You become covered under another employer's group health plan (and the new plan doesn't have any exclusion or limitation on a pre-existing condition you have).
- You become covered under Medicare (although COBRA coverage for your spouse and dependent children may continue afterward).

The point to remember is that COBRA coverage is only temporary coverage.

## Your Responsibilities

Although your employer must give you notice about your right to choose COBRA coverage, there are some instances when the responsibility for COBRA falls on your shoulders.

For example, if your child will no longer be a dependent under your plan's rules, you must let your employer know. The same is true if you get divorced or legally separated. In all these cases, you must let your employer know within 60 days after the event occurs.

Once you notify your employer about the change, the company must automatically give a written notice, either in person or by mail, to you—and your spouse (or former spouse) and children—about your right to choose COBRA coverage.

Also, if you're eligible for COBRA coverage, you must let the employer know within 60 days whether you want to take advantage of it. The experts call this your "election period," and the clock generally starts ticking when you lose coverage. If you choose coverage within the 60-day limit, and you pay whatever cost your employer may require of you, COBRA coverage applies retroactively to the time when you lost normal coverage under your company plan.

## Put It in Writing

The government has established all sorts of detailed regulations about COBRA, and there will be more to come; regulators, employers, health insurance companies, and others will continue to debate and refine the rules.

You don't have to keep abreast of every development; focus instead on the main point: If you (or your spouse or children) want COBRA coverage, let your employer know about it as soon as possible after you (or they) lose regular coverage. Make your intentions clear in writing, and keep a copy for your files. COBRA coverage is valuable, and you don't want to lose it just because you didn't make a decision in time and document it properly.

## Rules for Spouse, Children

The same commonsense rule applies if you're a spouse or child of an employee. You have the right to choose COBRA coverage independently of the person on whose company plan you once relied. Know your rights and exercise them—putting your intentions in writing—as soon as possible.

Suppose you work at home raising your children, and you're all covered by your spouse's health insurance plan. Your spouse is laid off. You and your children have the right to choose COBRA coverage, even if your spouse does not. In this example, you and your children may get COBRA coverage for up to 18 months.

What if your spouse keeps working and continues to be covered under the company plan, but you get divorced or legally separated? Here, too, you and the children may get COBRA coverage, but in this example, you may be covered for up to 36 months.

In either case, be sure to let your spouse's employer know that you want to continue coverage. Do it as soon as you can, and put your request in writing; you want to ensure that you'll be covered.

Remember, too, that the same "identical coverage" rules that apply to a working spouse who loses coverage also apply to you and your children: under COBRA, you're entitled to the same coverage you had under the normal plan.

## Other Provisions of COBRA

COBRA offers some other benefits, too. For example, suppose your family expands while you're on COBRA coverage because you have a baby or adopt a child. The new family member is covered, too. What if the company offers an "open enrollment" period, allowing employees to pick from various plans, while you're on COBRA coverage? ("Open enrollment" generally gives workers the right to pick and choose among various health plans a company offers.) The company must offer you—and your spouse and dependent children—a chance to take part, too.

Keep in mind that while COBRA applies to health care and medical care plans in general, it doesn't include everything. In general, COBRA applies to core health benefits, not extras (see Figure 4.6).

Here are a few important points about core COBRA coverage:

- If the overall cost of your employer's health plan goes up, the law says your employer can charge you more, too (although the cost must be fixed in advance of each 12-month premium cycle).
- You can pay for the cost of COBRA coverage on a monthly basis if you want; you needn't pay in a lump sum quarterly, semiannually, or annually.
- You must make your first payment for COBRA coverage within 45 days after the date you originally choose COBRA. After that, you must make payments on the due date your plan requires (although you're entitled to a 30-day grace period).

**Figure 4.6**  What COBRA Does *Not* Cover

COBRA typically does not apply to certain types of coverage—for long-term care, for example. It also does not extend to programs, benefits, and services an employer may offer that simply further general good health, such as:

✓ Spa

✓ Swimming pool

✓ Gymnasium

✓ Exercise programs

✓ Fitness facility

Source: IRS regulations.

- As outlined earlier in this chapter, if you'd normally be entitled to COBRA coverage for 18 months, your coverage may be extended by an extra 11 months (for a total of 29 months) if you qualify for Social Security disability benefits. In that case, however, the law lets the employer charge you up to 150 percent of the total cost of health care coverage.
- If you file a claim for COBRA coverage and it's denied, you have 60 days to appeal.
- If you're retired and you're covered under your former employer's retiree health care plan, you have special protection if your employer files for creditor protection under Chapter 11 of the U.S. Bankruptcy Code. If your coverage is eliminated within 12 months before or 12 months after the bankruptcy proceeding begins, COBRA coverage must be continued until you die. Spouses and children also become eligible for special extended COBRA coverage in this case.

## The Family and Medical Leave Act

COBRA isn't the only federal law that helps to protect your right to health coverage. Another law covers you if you leave your job temporarily for family reasons.

A law passed in 1993—the Family and Medical Leave Act—generally requires your company to give you up to 12 weeks of unpaid leave because of the birth or adoption of a child, or because of a serious health problem of a family member.

When you return to work, the company must give you the same job back or an equivalent job. (The law generally applies only to companies with 50 or more workers.)

Where does your health plan fit in? The law says a company to which the Family and Medical Leave Act applies *must* continue to cover you under its group health plan, under the same terms and conditions for which you would have been eligible had you continued working. In other words, you can't be cut off just because you went on leave.

Where does COBRA fit in? If you decide while you're on leave that you won't be returning to work, and you notify your employer of your intention, COBRA coverage is triggered. You then have the right to continue coverage under COBRA according to the terms described earlier in this chapter. (The same holds true for your spouse and dependent children.) In this case, the maximum COBRA coverage period begins on the last day of your family leave period.

Suppose, for example, that you take a leave of absence under the Family and Medical Leave Act to care for your elderly parent, who's seriously ill.

You take the maximum period allowed under federal law: 12 weeks. You're scheduled to return to work on October 1.

While on leave, you decide you don't want to go back to work; you want to continue caring for your parent for as long as necessary. You also want to take advantage of COBRA. In other words, you want to continue coverage under your group health insurance plan for 18 more months. In this example, the 18-month COBRA coverage period begins on September 30, the last day of your family leave. Of course, you may have to pay for the cost of your COBRA coverage.

Keep in mind that these are the minimum requirements for continued coverage; your employer may have more generous terms (allowing a longer period for family leave, for example), and your state laws may require better terms, too.

## Preexisting Conditions

Another recent change in federal law limits—and in some cases eliminates—the length of time during which a health plan can refuse to pay for your health care costs associated with a preexisting condition.

A preexisting condition is a condition that you already have when your health coverage begins—and for which your health plan may not cover you initially. Under the Health Insurance Portability and Accountability Act, passed in 1996, if you have an illness or other health condition, your company plan may refuse to cover you for it, but only for a certain period of time. That length of time is called the "exclusion period." Because of the new law, the exclusion period can't last forever; it must end, and afterward you must be covered.

For some plans, this hasn't been a big deal: they simply don't apply restrictions for preexisting conditions. Indeed, a 1999 study of group health plans by the U.S. General Accounting Office found that of companies with more than 200 workers, fewer than half had plans that excluded employees from coverage for preexisting conditions. However, some companies—especially smaller and mid-sized firms—do have plans that exclude employees from coverage based on preexisting conditions.

That's where the Health Insurance Portability and Accountability Act kicks in. It's a fiendishly complicated law, and many employers, as well as employees, still aren't exactly aware of how it works, according to the government study. Still, it's important to have at least a general idea of how the law may apply to you, because it could come in handy, especially if you change jobs.

Keep in mind that the law doesn't prevent health plans from excluding you from coverage due to a preexisting condition, but it does limit the time during which you can be excluded.

In general, here's what the law says:

- The plan may "look back" only six months to see if you have a pre-existing condition that will trigger exclusion.
- Even if you wind up being excluded, the plan *must* start covering you for preexisting conditions after 12 months. (Technically, the exclusion period can last up to 18 months, but only if you enroll late in your plan. You're a "late enrollee" if you don't join the plan as soon as you're eligible. The message is clear: Join your health plan as soon as you're eligible.)
- Although a plan technically may exclude you from coverage for a preexisting condition for a time, you can get "credit" for health coverage you used to have. This is where the law can really help you, because the credit can reduce—or even eliminate—your exclusion period.

## The "Look-Back" Period

As you can see, the law can be confusing, but it's not that difficult if you take a moment to try to understand it.

Let's start with the look-back period. In effect, what the law says is this: A plan can't pore through your entire life's medical history to see if you've ever had a certain condition, then exclude you from coverage for it; the plan can only go back six months.

Even then, there are limits. The law says that a health plan may exclude you from coverage only for a condition for which you received medical

**Figure 4.7**   Limits on Exclusions

---

Federal law cannot stop a plan from refusing to cover you for preexisting conditions. However, there are some conditions for which you cannot be excluded from coverage:

✓ **Pregnancy:** A health plan cannot count pregnancy as a preexisting condition. In other words, a plan typically must pay your expenses associated with pregnancy (up to the usual limits outlined in the plan).

✓ **Conditions in newborn and newly adopted children:** A plan generally cannot exclude (and therefore refuse coverage for) conditions in a newborn, a newly adopted child under 18, or a child under 18 who's placed for adoption.

Source:  U.S. Department of Labor.

advice, diagnosis, care, or treatment during the six months before you enrolled in the plan.

For example, suppose you have asthma. You received treatment for it several times early last year, and were hospitalized for it at one point. Since early this year, however, you've been fine; you have received no medical advice, diagnosis, care, or treatment for asthma since that time.

Now you've landed a new job. The company-sponsored health plan has a clause about preexisting conditions, and asthma is on the list. Can you be excluded from coverage should you require treatment? No. Why? Because of the rule limiting the look-back period to six months.

## When a Plan Is Not Required to Pay

Here's another example:

Assume, once again, that the health plan at your new job has a clause about preexisting conditions, and asthma is on the list. Suppose you were treated for asthma two months ago. Now that you've started your new job, it flares up again. Can you be excluded from coverage for this latest battle with asthma? Yes. Why? Because the plan looked back at your medical treatment during the six months before you enrolled in the plan, and found that you were treated for asthma during that time. Therefore, the plan may exclude you under its provision regarding preexisting conditions.

How long can your plan refuse to cover you for treatment of asthma in this example? For 12 months from the date you enrolled in the plan, but no longer (unless you enrolled late in the plan, in which case the plan may exclude you for up to 18 months).

**Figure 4.8**  Waiting Periods

What if your new company's health plan has a waiting period before you're eligible to join the health plan? How does it apply when there's also a preexisting condition clause? There are two ways:

✓ **Look-back period:** The six-month look back starts on the day you enroll in your new company's plan. If your plan has a waiting period, it can look back to six months before the first day of your waiting period (typically your date of hire).

✓ **Credit for prior coverage:** The period during which a plan may refuse to cover your health expenses for a preexisting condition (technically known as the exclusion period for preexisting conditions) starts when your waiting period starts.

Source: U.S. Department of Labor.

Is there any way around this dilemma? Yes. It depends on whether you were previously covered by a different plan. If so, you're generally entitled to get credit for this prior coverage. You can apply this credit against the exclusion period under your new plan.

## How Credits Work

Suppose you had a job for three years and were covered by your company's group health plan all the while. Now you've taken a new job, and you immediately switched over to your new employer's health plan.

If the new plan has an exclusion period for preexisting conditions, and you have one of those conditions, can you be excluded? No. Why? A plan can exclude you from coverage for a preexisting condition for 12 months, but if you've had coverage under a previous plan, you get credit for it, and you can apply that credit against the exclusion period in your new plan. In this example, you get credit for three years of group health coverage at your old job. That's more than enough to wipe out the maximum 12-month exclusion period that is part of your new plan.

Here's how it applies to the asthma example. You were treated for asthma 2 months ago. Now you start a new job, and your asthma flares up again. Because of the look-back rule, it appears as though your company's health plan can refuse to cover costs associated with this latest bout, and can keep on refusing to pay asthma-related expenses for 12 months.

But what if you came to your new job immediately after working at another job? And what if you were covered under a health plan at your old job for the past year? You get full credit for that coverage—one year's worth—and you apply that credit against the 12-month exclusion period in your new plan. You have so much credit that you wipe out the 12-month exclusion period. As a result, in this example, your new company's health plan *must* cover your expenses for asthma treatment.

What if you were covered under your old company's plan for only 8 months before you took your new job? You get credit for the 8 months, which you can apply against your new plan's 12-month exclusion period. As a result, your new plan may refuse to pay for your asthma treatments for only 4 months (the 12 months in the exclusion period, minus your 8 months of credit).

## Breaks in Coverage

There's a catch, however, and it's an important one. If you had a break in coverage, the new plan doesn't have to give you credit for the coverage you had before the break occurred.

In other words, if there was a time that you weren't covered under a health plan, your new plan may not give you credit for the time you were covered before the break in service occurred. It all depends on how long the break was.

Here's the rule-of-thumb: If the break in service was 63 days or longer, your new plan doesn't have to give you credit for the months of coverage that preceded the break; if the break was shorter than 63 days, the plan must give you credit.

Tricky? Here's an example: Suppose you receive regular monthly treatment for carpal tunnel syndrome. The health plan at your new company considers this to be a preexisting condition. As a result, the health plan is busy trying to figure out exactly how long it may exclude you from coverage for your carpal tunnel treatments.

Here are the facts: In your first-ever job, you worked for two years, and were covered by a health plan all the while. You left that job for three months (90 days) and did not continue your coverage. Then you started another job, where you worked—and were covered by a health plan—for nine months. Immediately after that you joined your present company.

How long can your new plan refuse to pay for your carpal tunnel treatments? Three months. Why? It's because of the break-in-service rule. In this example, you went without health coverage for 90 days. That's longer than the 63 days allowed under the break-in-service rule. As a result, you get no credit for the time you were covered in your first job. However, you do get credit for the nine months you were covered at your second job. Why? Although your new company's plan need not give you credit for the coverage you had before your lengthy break in service, it must recognize the coverage you had after your break in service.

## Applying the Credit

How can you make sure you get the proper credit? You can get credit for the time you were covered by almost any type of health plan, including a traditional group plan, a managed care plan, an individual health insurance policy, the federal health program for people with low incomes (Medicaid), and the federal health plan for retirees (Medicare). You can get credit for general health coverage, but not for specific, "noncore" benefits, such as dental or vision coverage.

Your old plan must, by law, give you a certificate that shows you were covered and for how long. You may then present this certificate to the new plan, which must take it into account when figuring how much time—if any—it may refuse to cover you for a preexisting condition.

**Figure 4.9**    Paying for COBRA

---

What if you can't afford to pay for COBRA coverage? Look to your IRA.

Under the old rules, if you withdrew money from your IRA before you turned 59½, you generally would have to pay a 10 percent "early withdrawal" penalty—in addition to paying income tax on the amount you withdrew.

Under a law passed in 1997, however, you may avoid the 10 percent penalty altogether if you use the money to pay for health insurance premiums—including COBRA coverage—for you, your spouse, and/or your children.

You'll still have to pay federal income tax on the amount you withdraw, but at least you won't have to pay the 10 percent penalty, too.

Source: Taxpayer Relief Act of 1997.

---

## COBRA's Role

This is where COBRA coverage can come in handy in the case of pre-existing conditions. It's a good idea to try to keep your COBRA coverage going as long as possible because *COBRA counts as prior coverage.*

For example, suppose you lose your job and you continue health insurance coverage under your former employer's plan for 18 months, as allowed by law. A month after your COBRA coverage lapses, you get another job, and your new employer's health insurance plan starts covering you right away.

You file a claim under the new plan for treatment of a serious, long-term illness. Ordinarily, the new plan might deny your claim, citing its clause for excluding preexisting conditions.

In this example, however, your claim cannot be denied, because you had only a 1-month break in coverage—between the time your COBRA coverage lapsed and the time your new employer's plan took over. COBRA coverage counts as credit that you can apply against the 12-month exclusion period.

## COBRA Isn't Forever

This raises an important planning point to keep in mind: COBRA coverage is only temporary coverage. What happens if it runs out?

The Health Insurance Portability and Accountability Act also guarantees you access to health care coverage if you lose coverage under a group plan (including group coverage under COBRA).

To comply with this law, some states offer coverage under a so-called high-risk insurance pool. This is generally a state-run plan that provides comprehensive health insurance if you have preexisting health conditions and can't otherwise get coverage, or if the coverage you can get is too expensive.

For the state-run plan you may have to pay more—perhaps much more—than the standard rate. That's because the law doesn't limit the price that insurers may charge you for coverage. Still, the law requires that coverage be made available. Before this law took hold, you could have been rejected outright and left without coverage altogether.

## The Health Expenses Tax Deduction

You may claim a federal income tax deduction for the premiums you pay for health insurance—for you, your spouse, and your children. Ordinarily, the only way you can get such a break is by clearing a couple of big tax hurdles.

First, you must have enough deductions to list them separately on Schedule A of your federal income tax return instead of taking the one-size-fits-all standard deduction. Second, after you lump together your health insurance premiums with all your out-of-pocket medical expenses, you can claim a deduction only for the amount that exceeds 7.5 percent of your adjusted gross income.

For most people, that's a pretty tall order. If you're self-employed, however, you can get two bites at the apple. You may claim the deduction (within the limits shown in the nearby table) directly against your business income.

**Figure 4.10**　Health Deduction for the Self-Employed

---

If you're self-employed, you may get a tax break for the premiums you pay for health insurance. The premiums can be for a plan that covers not only you, but also your spouse and children. You may deduct a portion of your premiums from your business income according to this schedule:

| Year | Percent of Expenses |
|------|---------------------|
| 2000 | 60% |
| 2001 | 60 |
| 2002 | 70 |
| 2003 | 100 |

Source: Internal Revenue Service.

What about the portion of your health insurance premiums that you cannot deduct against your business income because of the limits shown in the table? You may lump them in with the rest of your out-of-pocket medical expenses, for you, your spouse, and your children, and claim them as itemized deductions on Schedule A (assuming that you itemize, and that you've enough of these expenses to clear the hurdle of 7.5 percent of your adjusted gross income).

Why this break for the self-employed? If your business was set up as a regular corporation, you would generally get to claim a full federal income tax deduction for the money you spend on employee health insurance. Congress decided to level the playing field between corporations and small businesses run as sole proprietorships (the self-employed).

## Other Sources of Coverage

If you do not receive health care coverage from an employer, check with your state insurance regulators to see what plans might be available for you.

For example, each state has its own program that makes health insurance available to children. The Children's Health Insurance Program (CHIP) is paid for by the federal government and run by the states. Its goal is simple: to expand health insurance to children whose families earn too much to qualify for the federal Medicaid program, but not enough to afford private health insurance.

You may qualify for this low-cost or free health insurance for your children if they are 18 or younger and you meet program guidelines. For details, call the information clearinghouse for children's health insurance toll-free at 1-877-543-7669. If you have access to the Internet, you may get more information by contacting the clearinghouse's Web site: <www.insurekidsnow.gov>.

In addition, many group health plans offer a so-called conversion right. (Your state may require group plans to offer this right.) This generally means you have the right to convert to an individual policy if your coverage under a group policy runs out, and you won't have to go through a medical exam or a lengthy application process. If you convert, you'll have to pay the premiums at individual rates, not group rates, and they can be expensive. (You typically have 31 days after your group coverage ends to exercise your right to convert. If you choose to continue your group coverage under COBRA, your right to convert to an individual policy ends 31 days after your COBRA coverage runs out.)

In addition, be sure to check with any professional, union, or other membership groups to see if they offer group health insurance. College graduates, for example, may find that various types of insurance—including health insurance—are available through their alumni associations. A building trades union may offer group insurance, too, either through a local chapter or through an affiliation with a national union. You can also check with your local Blue Cross and Blue Shield insurance organization or with local HMOs to see when their open enrollment periods occur and whether you're eligible to buy in.

## For More Information . . .

- The U.S. Department of Labor publishes a booklet on COBRA, "Health Benefits Under the Consolidated Omnibus Budget Reconciliation Act (COBRA)." For a free copy, call the agency's toll-free publications hotline at 1-800-998-7542. If you have access to the Internet, you may read or download a copy by contacting the agency's Web site: <www.dol.gov>.
- The IRS publishes a booklet about IRAs that explains how to avoid the 10 percent penalty on withdrawals that are used for health insurance costs. For a copy of Publication 590, "Individual Retirement Arrangements," visit your local IRS office, call the agency at 1-800-829-3676, or contact the IRS's Web site: <www.irs.gov>.
- Insure.com, an online news organization that focuses exclusively on insurance, provides lots of information and resources for getting individual health coverage. For information, contact the site at this address: <www.insure.com>.

# 5

# Cafeteria Plans and
# Other Flexible Benefits

There was a time when the employee benefits you received at work were fixed by your employer. You typically were covered by a certain type of health plan, a certain type of pension plan, and perhaps a few extras, too.

You may have had a comprehensive benefits package, giving you most or all of the coverage you needed. You didn't have to give much thought to it. You didn't have a choice in the matter; you got whatever the boss ordered.

Nowadays, you may have a lot more say, and a lot more flexibility. You may be able to choose from a menu of benefits through a "cafeteria" plan. You may be able to contribute to a plan that gives you tax benefits for what you spend on childcare (a dependent-care assistance plan). You may be able to pay for medical expenses that aren't otherwise covered by your health insurance (if you have a flexible spending account or medical reimbursement account), and get immediate tax benefits, too.

## How Cafeteria Plans Work

Imagine being able to pick the type of benefits you want, the kind that most suit your personal circumstances, instead of the ones mandated for all workers by your employer. You can do this through a cafeteria plan, also called a Section 125 plan.

Under this arrangement, you typically receive a varied menu of benefits from which to choose. In effect, you go through the line in the "cafeteria" of benefits, picking the ones that you and your family most desire.

This can be a pretty good deal because of its flexibility. For example, a young worker with children may need to bulk up on some relatively low-cost group term life insurance. An older worker who has no young children for whom to provide may choose to skip the life insurance altogether and focus more on health insurance or vision care, for example.

**Figure 5.1** What's on the Menu?

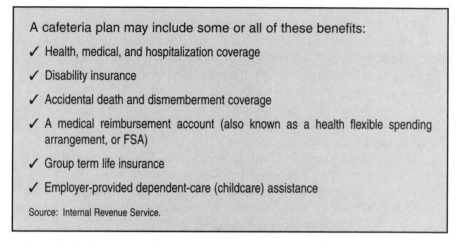

A cafeteria plan may include some or all of these benefits:

✓ Health, medical, and hospitalization coverage

✓ Disability insurance

✓ Accidental death and dismemberment coverage

✓ A medical reimbursement account (also known as a health flexible spending arrangement, or FSA)

✓ Group term life insurance

✓ Employer-provided dependent-care (childcare) assistance

Source: Internal Revenue Service.

## Tax Benefits of Cafeteria Plans

Freedom to choose can be a big benefit in itself, but there's something else these plans offer that can be an even greater advantage: tax benefits.

Under federal law, money your employer gives you is generally taxable. In other words, you must pay tax on it. That's true whether you actually receive the money or it's simply made available to you—you're given the right to receive it.

There's a big exception to this rule, however. If a company makes money available to you through a cafeteria plan, and you have the right to

**Figure 5.2** What's *off* the Menu?

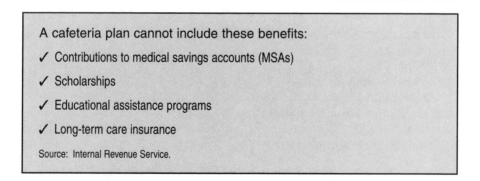

A cafeteria plan cannot include these benefits:

✓ Contributions to medical savings accounts (MSAs)

✓ Scholarships

✓ Educational assistance programs

✓ Long-term care insurance

Source: Internal Revenue Service.

receive this money either in cash or in the form of employee benefits under the plan, you do not get taxed on the money that goes to benefits (as long as the plan meets government rules).

To put it another way, if you apply a dollar of your pay to a cafeteria plan, you can use the full dollar; if you instead take that dollar as cash, you wind up receiving only 85 cents—and probably less—after federal income taxes and Social Security taxes are taken out. In other words, the dollar you apply to a cafeteria plan can go a lot further.

As you peruse the menu of benefits in a company-sponsored cafeteria plan, you won't find everything. That's because cafeteria plans are limited in the types of benefits they can provide.

Nevertheless, you'll be likely to see most of the key types of benefits that you'd normally be interested in, such as accident or health coverage, group term life insurance, and programs to help pay for childcare. (Cafeteria plans may not, however, offer educational assistance and certain other types of fringe benefits such as those listed in Figure 5.2).

How large is the tax advantage to you? Suppose your childcare expenses total $3,400 a year. Then $4,000 of your earnings from your job will be needed to meet those expenses. Why? If you're in the 15 percent federal income tax bracket, that $4,000 in wages from your job will be taxed at 15 percent: you'll pay $600 in tax ($4,000 times 0.15). That'll leave you with $3,400 after taxes to pay the childcare expenses.

**Figure 5.3**   Cafeteria Plans by Industry

Some industries are more likely than others to offer cafeteria plans to workers.

| Industry | Percentage of Workers in Firms Offering Cafeteria Plans |
|---|---|
| Finance | 45% |
| Transportation/Communications/Utilities | 40 |
| Health Care | 32 |
| Service | 31 |
| High Technology | 29 |
| Manufacturing | 29 |
| Mining/Construction/Wholesale | 26 |
| Retail | 12 |
| State, Local Government | 10 |

Source: Henry J. Kaiser Family Foundation and the Health Research and Educational Trust: 1999 survey of employer-sponsored health benefits.

However, if you pay the childcare expenses through a special benefit plan at work—a cafeteria plan or a flexible spending account—when you earn $4,000, you'll get the childcare, plus some extra cash in your pocket. The $600 you save in taxes in this example is yours to keep.

The tax benefits don't stop there. For each dollar you contribute to a cafeteria plan or flexible spending account at work, you lower your income for tax purposes; in other words, you get to report less income on your tax return. This, in turn, could make you eligible for other tax breaks.

Some tax breaks are tied to your income. If you make too much money, you won't be eligible for the tax break (or you'll be eligible for only a partial break). For example, your ability to claim the Hope Scholarship Credit or Lifetime Learning Credit depends on the level of income you report on your federal income tax return.

Keep in mind, too, that the money you set aside in a cafeteria plan or flexible spending account escapes Social Security tax and may also escape state income tax (depending on the rules of the state where you live.)

Small wonder, then, that cafeteria plans have grown in popularity. In 1986, only about 5 percent of employees at large and medium-sized firms were eligible for some type of cafeteria plan. By 1995, 55 percent of employees at these firms were eligible, according to a report by the U.S. House Ways and Means Committee.

# Flexible Spending Accounts (FSAs) and Similar Accounts

Even if your employer doesn't offer a full-blown cafeteria plan, you may have access to a similar plan that can stand on its own—a kind of "a la carte" benefit.

It may be called a flexible benefit plan, a flexible spending account (FSA), a medical spending account, a medical reimbursement account, or something similar.

These plans are about twice as common in the workplace as cafeteria plans (perhaps because cafeteria plans can be more complicated and expensive for an employer to set up, pay for, and maintain). Whatever the name they go by, these plans all work in essentially the same way.

Shortly before the year begins and before taxes are applied, you decide to set aside money in the account. Each dollar you contribute to the account out of your wages or salary is a full dollar; it's not reduced by income taxes or Social Security taxes.

The money sits in the account during the year as you incur ordinary expenses—out-of-pocket medical expenses and other costs that aren't covered under your employer's group health insurance and other benefit plans.

For instance, during the year, you may have to reach into your wallet to buy new contact lenses or eyeglasses, or to pay for prescription drugs, eye exams, or the cost of childcare.

You get a receipt for these expenses and bring the receipt to your employer or to an agent or intermediary who works for your employer. You are then reimbursed for the full amount.

Where does the reimbursement come from? It's drawn from your flexible spending account, reimbursement account, medical spending account, or other such arrangement.

The advantage of all this is probably obvious. You get to pay pre-tax dollars for things that your health insurance and other employee benefits don't cover. As a result, you save yourself some money.

### Claiming Tax Breaks Up Front

You may also be able to cash in on another tax benefit involving medical expenses. Suppose you ring up thousands of dollars one year in medical expenses that aren't covered by your employer's health plan. You want to claim a federal income tax deduction for these expenses, but you can't because the government sets some high hurdles.

In general, you get to claim a federal income tax deduction for such things as mortgage interest, property taxes, union dues, medical expenses, and the like only if you itemize your deductions. You have to have enough of these expenses to list them separately on Schedule A of your federal income tax return instead of claiming the lump-sum deduction known as the standard deduction (which is what most people wind up claiming).

That's not all, however. Even if you have enough expenses to itemize, you still can't claim a tax break for your unreimbursed medical expenses—those out-of-pocket health-related expenses that aren't covered by your health insurance plan—unless the total of these expenses is greater than 7.5 percent of your adjusted gross income.

With FSAs, medical reimbursement accounts, and similar arrangements, however, you typically can pay for these expenses with pre-tax dollars. In other words, you get a tax break up front, even if you wouldn't qualify under the rules that apply to your income tax return.

### Uniform Coverage

Another advantage is that with some of these plans the money is available to you even if it isn't already in your account. For instance, suppose you agree to set aside $50 a week from your paycheck into a health FSA. Over the course of a year, you'll have set aside $2,600.

During the first few weeks of the year, however, you need an eye exam and new contact lenses, which cost you $200. These expenses aren't covered by your health insurance, so you look to your health FSA. There's only $100 in the account because it's so early in the plan year, and you haven't had time to contribute more. Still, the account must reimburse you in full. Why? "A health FSA must provide 'uniform coverage' throughout the coverage period," the Internal Revenue Service says. "This means that the maximum amount of reimbursement . . . must be available to the participant at all times."

What happens if a worker leaves the job before contributing enough to "catch up" with the amount withdrawn from the account earlier in the year? Originally, the IRS said that the employer must make up the difference. There's been debate over this point, and the rule could change.

## Complex Rules

The rules for FSAs, dependent-care assistance accounts, and similar arrangements are mostly the same, but there are key differences. For instance, with a dependent-care account (which you can use for childcare, for example), coverage doesn't have to be uniform throughout the coverage period. In other words, you're entitled to reimbursement only for the amount you've already contributed. Also, the most you can contribute to a dependent-care plan is generally $5,000 a year. (Keep in mind, too, that you generally can't simultaneously take advantage of the tax break for an employer-sponsored dependent-care assistance plan and the federal income tax credit for dependent-care expenses; it's one or the other.)

## Advantages for Employers

What's in it for employers? Companies aren't stupid. Setting up and running FSAs and similar plans can be expensive. There are, however, some advantages. These plans are not just exempt from income tax; Social Security taxes don't get applied to these dollars, either, and you're not the only one who pays Social Security tax. Your employer must pay it, too. In general, for every dollar of Social Security, or FICA, tax that you pay, your employer must fork over a matching amount. The reverse is also true. For every dollar of Social Security tax you do not pay because of your participation in an FSA or similar arrangement, your employer doesn't have to pay the tax, either. In other words, your employer gets a tax break. (For some workers, especially lower-paid workers, this can result in lower Social Security benefits in retirement. That's because, as a general rule, the less you put into the Social Security system, the less in benefits you might be eligible to receive later on. The overall reduction in Social Security benefits may be modest, but it's a factor to consider, especially for lower-paid workers.)

And that's not the only advantage. Your employer knows you will get all sorts of tax breaks for setting aside money in an FSA or similar plan, so the employer may simultaneously increase the amount you pay toward health insurance premiums and other benefits.

It's also true, however, that an FSA can give an employer the opportunity to offer you more benefits than you had before. This can make for a happier and more productive workforce and can help an employer attract and retain good workers. FSAs can also make essential benefits such as health insurance more affordable to workers, and they can cause workers to be more aware of the value of the benefits they receive.

## Planning and Paperwork

FSAs and similar plans offer a lot of advantages to employees, but these arrangements also have potential drawbacks.

With flexible spending accounts or other reimbursement arrangements, you must tell your employer, in advance—sometimes *way* in advance—approximately how much you expect to spend during the year on eye care, childcare, and other expenses. That may not sound like such a big deal. Remember, however, that you may have to estimate in November how much you and your family will spend for the entire following year.

If you don't salt away enough in one of these accounts, there's no real damage done. If it turns out that the total of your out-of-pocket expenses is greater than the amount that's in your flexible spending or other such reimbursement account, you simply must decide whether to pay the expenses out of your after-tax dollars. That's something you'd have to do anyway, even if you had no flexible spending or other such reimbursement account.

What if the reverse happens? In other words, what if the total that's in your flexible spending or reimbursement account is greater than the amount of your out-of-pocket expenses? That's where the trouble comes in. The general rule is: Use it or lose it. In effect, you've got to spend the entire amount by the end of the year or you forfeit what's left in the account.

This is why some people call it a "use it or lose it" benefit. Suppose you decided a year ago to set aside $1,000 in one of these accounts to pay for things that may not be covered by your insurance plan. Now it's November, and you've used up only $700 of the $1,000 that was in your account. If you don't use up the remaining $300 by year-end, you forfeit that money, and it reverts to the plan.

# Deciding Whether Flexible Benefits Are for You

Cafeteria plans, FSAs, and similar arrangements aren't available in every workplace. Whether flexible benefits are offered can depend on the size of the company you work for (or are thinking of working for), the part of the country in which you live, or the industry in which you work.

For example, workers at large firms are far more likely than those at small firms to be offered a flexible benefit plan, according to a 1999 survey by the Henry J. Kaiser Family Foundation and the Health Research and Educational Trust. Only 19 percent of workers at small firms were offered flex plans, but 65 percent of workers at giant firms were offered them.

If you're involved in such a plan, or you're considering taking a job that offers one, take some time to understand clearly how it works. Talk with your human resources department, the plan administrator, and fellow workers. These plans can be confusing. For example, an FSA, medical reimbursement account, or similar plan can be offered as part of a cafeteria plan, not just as a stand-alone benefit.

**Figure 5.4**   Flexible Benefits

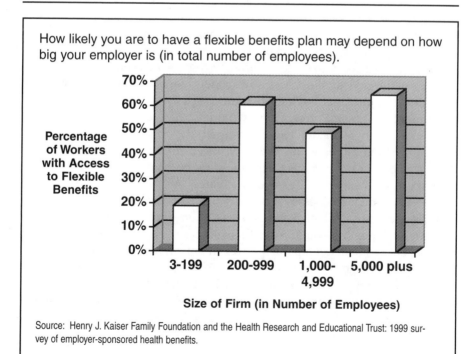

How likely you are to have a flexible benefits plan may depend on how big your employer is (in total number of employees).

Percentage of Workers with Access to Flexible Benefits

Size of Firm (in Number of Employees)

Source: Henry J. Kaiser Family Foundation and the Health Research and Educational Trust: 1999 survey of employer-sponsored health benefits.

Bear in mind, too, that there's some paperwork involved, and you must estimate your expenses carefully. With some reimbursement accounts, such as those for childcare or other dependent-care expenses, this may not be a big problem: the costs are predictable and usually annual dependent-care expenses exceed the amount that an employee can set aside in a pre-tax account. But medical expenses, for example, can vary widely, so they're much more difficult to estimate. If there's money left in your reimbursement account by year-end, you may lose it.

Despite the complexities involved, most flexible benefits arrangements can be a good way to help pay for the ever-increasing cost of health insurance—especially for small businesses. An employer can use the tax savings available from a cafeteria plan, for example, to offset the cost of offering group health insurance. An employee can use the tax savings from a cafeteria plan or an FSA or similar arrangement to help offset the premiums, deductibles, copayments, and other costs of group health insurance. Still another way to pay for health insurance is the medical savings account, which we turn to now.

## Medical Savings Accounts

In 1996, Congress cobbled together a plan to try to extend health insurance to more people while also trying to gain some control over health care costs. Thus was born the medical savings account (MSA)—a way to save for, and pay for, medical expenses.

MSAs aren't easy to understand; they come with a complex set of rules and regulations. And they're relatively new, so few people know about them. In addition, Congress launched medical savings accounts as a kind of experiment; in general, new MSAs would be allowed after December 31, 2000, only if Congress extended (or changed) the program.

Still, MSAs can be your ticket to health insurance coverage, especially if your employer doesn't offer a health plan, or if you're self-employed or own your own business. The law that created MSAs targeted them specifically toward small businesses (generally those with no more than 50 workers). This was no accident. Workers at medium-sized and large companies are far more likely to be offered health insurance as an employee benefit than are workers at smaller companies, government surveys have found.

To understand how MSAs work, you've got to concentrate, because they can be incredibly complicated (which may account for why they haven't exactly caught on in the marketplace). MSAs are really two plans in one: a savings account, and a high-deductible health insurance plan. In addition, they combine elements of the FSAs and the individual retirement account (IRA).

In other words, they are confusing.

**Figure 5.5** Limits on Medical Savings Accounts for 2000

| Type of Coverage | Minimum Annual Deductible | Maximum Annual Deductible | Maximum Annual Out-of-Pocket Expenses |
|---|---|---|---|
| Individual | $1,550 | $2,350 | $3,100 |
| Family | 3,100 | 4,650 | 5,700 |

Figures are for 2000, and are subject to adjustment annually.

Source: Internal Revenue Bulletin 99-46.

## The Insurance Part

Workers can take part in a medical savings account only if their employer offers a health plan that comes with a high deductible. In other words, you've got to be covered by a plan that requires you to pay, out of pocket, all your medical expenses up to a certain limit in a given year before the health plan's coverage takes over. (The expenses can include doctors' fees, prescription drugs, hospital charges, and the like.)

- For individual coverage through a health plan, the deductible must be at least $1,550 and no more than $2,350.
- For family coverage through a health plan, the high deductible must be at least $3,100 and no more than $4,650.

There are also limits on how much you can be expected to spend out of your own pocket, overall, on health expenses in any given year before the health plan takes over. If you're covered as an individual, the limit is $3,100. If you have a family plan, your annual out-of-pocket expenses can't be more than $5,700.

## The Savings Account Part

Is this a good deal? No, not in itself. That's where the savings account comes in. It's an interest-bearing account that is set up with an insurance company or bank, which acts as the account's trustee or custodian (just as a bank does for an IRA).

You contribute money to your account, or your employer makes the contribution. (It has to be one or the other; you and your employer can't both contribute to your account in the same year.) The contributions are tax-deductible. An employer that contributes gets to claim an income tax deduction and doesn't have to pay employment taxes on the amount of the contribution. If you are the one who contributes, you claim a deduction on your federal income tax return (even if you claim the lump-sum standard deduction on your return instead of itemizing your deductions). In addition, the money your account earns isn't taxed.

## Comparing MSAs and IRAs

Medical savings accounts, then, work like traditional IRAs: you get a tax break for the money you set aside, and the money your account earns doesn't get taxed, at least not immediately. But there's also a big difference between MSAs and IRAs. IRA rules generally require you to keep the money in your account until retirement. Indeed, you may have to pay taxes—and a penalty—on money you withdraw prematurely.

Medical savings accounts work differently. Even though you get a tax break for putting money into the account, you can take the money out tax-free if you use it to pay for medical expenses, including those that aren't covered by your insurance.

It is true that the deductible on the insurance plan is high, but you can withdraw money from your medical savings account to pay for the medical expenses you have to cover before the insurance kicks in.

Any money that's left in your medical savings account can stay there and grow on a tax-deferred basis until retirement, when you can withdraw it and use it however you like. It'll be taxed at that point, but you'll pay no penalty. (You may even avoid tax on the withdrawals in retirement if you use the money to pay medical expenses.)

## Paying for the Small Stuff

You withdraw money that's in a medical savings account to cover the relatively small stuff; your health plan kicks in only to cover the big bills. This is one of the things that appealed to Congress when it enacted the law about medical savings accounts. Because you pay for the "small stuff" yourself out of the money that's in your medical savings account, you're likely to be a lot more careful about the kinds of expenses you incur—more careful than you would be if you had to pay only a small deductible and your insurance company paid the rest. In other words, because the money is coming directly out of your own account, there's a big financial incentive for you to use only those health care services that you and your family members really need. This, in turn, is supposed to help make our nation's health care system more efficient overall.

It's a little like homeowners insurance: If you carry a low deductible, you're more likely to file lots of claims for relatively small expenses, raising the cost of insurance for everyone; if you carry a high deductible, you're forced to pay for the small stuff out of your own pocket and you'll file fewer claims, so there's less upward pressure on premiums for all homeowners.

## Limits and Penalties

Do MSAs have limits? Yes. If you're single, you (or your employer) may contribute no more than 65 percent of the insurance plan's annual deductible to your MSA. For example, if the plan's deductible is $2,000, the most that you or your employer can contribute to your medical savings account is $1,300.

With a family plan, the contribution limit is 75 percent of the deductible. If the deductible is $4,000, the most that you or your employer can contribute to your medical savings account is $3,000.

There's also a penalty to consider. The money you withdraw from your medical savings account comes out tax-free and penalty-free if it's used for medical expenses, but withdrawals used for other purposes are taxed and are also subject to a 15 percent penalty. (Withdrawals made for other than medical purposes after you turn 65, after your death, or if you have become disabled are not penalized.)

## More Points to Consider about MSAs

Here are some other points to consider about MSAs:

- To be eligible for a medical savings account, neither you nor your spouse (if you're married and file a joint federal income tax return) can have any other health insurance plan. (Certain types of plans aren't counted toward this rule, such as accident, disability, dental, vision, and long-term care insurance.)
- You can't contribute to your account more than what you earned for the year from your employer. (If you're self-employed, you can't contribute more than the amount of your net self-employment income.)
- As with an IRA, you have until April 15 to contribute to your MSA and claim the contribution as a deduction for the preceding year.
- You don't have to contribute to your medical savings account—nor do you have to withdraw money from it—in any given year.
- Medical savings accounts are portable. In other words, if you change companies, and you still meet the rules for having an MSA, you can keep using your MSA.

- If you lose health coverage because you lose your job or your hours are cut back, you can make tax-free withdrawals from your MSA to pay for health insurance premiums—including coverage you get under COBRA.
- You should pick a beneficiary for your MSA. If your spouse is your beneficiary, your spouse can treat the account as his or her own after you die. If the beneficiary is someone else, your MSA ends at your death, and the amount that's in the account will be treated as taxable income for the beneficiary.
- If you have a medical savings account, you'll have to file Form 8853, "Medical Savings Accounts and Long-Term Care Insurance Contracts," with your federal income tax return each year you have an MSA. You'll have to file it with a Form 1040 (the "long form"); you won't be able to file the shorter Form 1040A or Form 1040EZ.

## The Advantages of MSAs

There is an incentive for a company to install the type of health plan that will make you eligible to open an MSA: high-deductible plans typically cost an employer less than low-deductible plans.

What's in it for you? If all your employer can afford is a high-deductible health insurance plan, that's better than no plan at all, and if you have a medical savings account, you can better afford to pay your out-of-pocket medical expenses.

## Lots of Complications

If you're thinking about opening a medical savings account or trying to persuade your employer to offer them, keep in mind two points: (1) they're complicated, and (2) they're not popular, partly because of their complexity.

In late 1998, almost two full years after medical savings accounts first became available, the U.S. General Accounting Office (GAO) reported to Congress about the status of medical savings accounts. The study found that insurance companies were quick to offer MSAs. By the summer of 1997, just a few months after the law allowed MSAs to take effect, more than 50 insurers offered them.

The insurers offered all sorts of bells and whistles to make MSAs appealing. Some MSAs were linked to traditional indemnity (fee-for-service) plans; others were linked to managed care plans (mainly Preferred Provider Organizations—PPOs). As for the savings element, most insurers offered various investment options and banking features.

**Figure 5.6**  Number of MSAs Is Far Below Limit

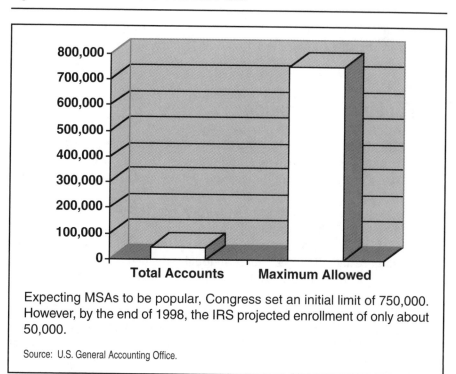

**Total Accounts**     **Maximum Allowed**

Expecting MSAs to be popular, Congress set an initial limit of 750,000. However, by the end of 1998, the IRS projected enrollment of only about 50,000.

Source: U.S. General Accounting Office.

MSAs were widely available, too. By the summer of 1998, MSAs that qualified under government rules were available in almost all states, and there were several competing plans available in most states. The price for plans had come down, and insurers were offering even more options and features.

And yet the GAO study found that "consumer demand has been lower than many in the industry anticipated." Why? "Lower demand reflects, in part, the complexity of [MSAs] for both agents and consumers."

The numbers tell the story: By the end of 1998—two full years after MSAs first became available—the government projected enrollment at only about 50,000, well below the legal limit of 750,000 accounts. Indeed, the IRS later reported that by April 15, 1999, only about 36,600 tax filers had claimed either an exclusion or deduction for contributions to MSAs for 1998.

A study on MSAs by the National Center for Policy Analysis, a public policy research institute, noted that there are all sorts of legal, regulatory, and other obstacles. "Considering the circumstances, it is remarkable that the MSA program has been as successful as it is."

In spite of the obstacles, MSAs "are an important alternative to other forms of health care financing," the study said. "They may not be for everybody, but they offer people more control over their own health care needs and financing."

If you're planning to offer MSAs to employees, or if you're considering opening an MSA, be sure to check first with the IRS, at 1-800-829-1040, to see if the program has been extended.

## For More Information . . .

- The IRS publishes a booklet that explains what medical savings accounts are, how they work, and whether you may be eligible to open one. For a free copy of Publication 969, *Medical Savings Accounts*, and a copy of Form 8853, "Medical Savings Accounts and Long-Term Care Insurance Contracts," visit your local IRS office, call the IRS at 1-800-829-3676, or contact the agency's Web site: <www.irs.gov>.
- Golden Rule is an insurance company that specializes in health insurance and offers plans for individuals and medical savings accounts. For information, call 1-800-444-8990 or contact the firm's Web site: <www.goldenrule.com>.
- For more about childcare and dependent-care accounts, see IRS Publication 503, *Child and Dependent Care Expenses.* For a copy, visit your local IRS office, call the IRS at 1-800-829-3676, or contact the IRS at their Web site: <www.irs.gov>.

# 2

# *RETIREMENT PLANS*

If you had to pick the two most important benefits out of all those offered in your employee benefits package, odds are that you'd choose these two: health insurance and your pension.

For most working Americans, saving for retirement is a top goal, and being able to achieve that through the workplace is a great opportunity.

It's also important from a public policy standpoint. By allowing special tax breaks for employer-sponsored retirement plans (contributions are generally deductible, and plan earnings grow tax-free), the federal government passes up the chance to rake in more than $76 billion a year in income tax revenue, according to estimates by the Congress Joint Committee on Taxation. Why? These tax breaks encourage employers to provide retirement benefits for their workers. "This reduces the need for public assistance and reduces pressure on the Social Security system," the committee found.

You may be eligible to take part in a traditional pension plan, a "defined benefit" plan to which only your employer is required to contribute. A defined benefit plan can generate a guaranteed source of steady income for you in retirement.

You may also be eligible for a "defined contribution" plan to which you make your own contributions through payroll deduction. With a defined contribution plan, you choose how the money is to be invested.

No matter what type of coverage is available at your job, you need to know how it works and how to make the most of it. We will discuss one of the most popular types of retirement plans available today: the 401(k) plan. You'll find out how the rules work, how you can best take advantage of them, and when other savings options may be a better choice.

You'll also find out about traditional pension plans, and why there's such controversy when companies convert traditional plans.

You'll also learn why a relatively new type of retirement savings plan, the SIMPLE plan, has become wildly popular among small businesses. And you'll read about the many other types of retirement plans available in the private and public sectors, including SEP, 403(b), Section 457, and other plans.

As you read about retirement plans, keep this point in mind: If your employer offers a pension or retirement savings plan at work, you can count yourself lucky. About 47 million workers in the private sector are earning pension benefits in their current jobs, and about two of three families will reach retirement with at least some private pension benefits, according to U.S. Treasury statistics. Still, less than half of the private-sector workforce is covered by an employer-sponsored retirement plan, according to the Pension Benefit Guaranty Corporation, a federal agency. Among small businesses, only 20 percent of employers offer retirement plans. And among low-wage workers, the picture is even bleaker: only 8 percent have any sort of retirement plan.

If you're not covered, use this section as a blueprint—either in your search for a job that does offer this important employee benefit, or as a tool to try to persuade your employer to add a pension or retirement savings plan to the employee benefits package.

# 6

# Traditional
# Pensions

$I$t provides a steady stream of income to countless retirees and their families. It is the rock upon which millions of retirements have been built. It is, in short, the granddaddy of pension plans.

Why, then, is the traditional pension plan—the "defined benefit" plan—so seldom publicized? One reason is that it's dull. Face it: The defined benefit pension plan is like a refrigerator—it does its job, all right, but you don't think too much about it unless it breaks.

Indeed, the only time workers generally give these plans any attention is when they're nearing retirement. And the only time they're likely to talk about them is after they've retired. Small wonder, then, that there's probably not a lot of buzz in your workplace about your company's defined benefit plan.

In addition, employers have generally failed to let workers know how important these plans are to a worker's retirement security. (Part of the problem is that defined benefit plans have complex rules that can be hard to explain.) The plans don't get much attention in the news media, either, partly because so few reporters understand what a defined benefit plan is, how it works, and why it's so important.

That's too bad. If more employees were aware of the significance of defined benefit plans, they might work for improvements, and employers might be more reluctant to send traditional pensions to the scrap heap in favor of plans that can pose more risk to workers, such as the 401(k) plan, and plans that can spark controversy, such as the cash balance plan.

## Why Defined Benefit Plans Are Vital

What makes defined benefit plans so vital? Mainly, it's because they promise to pay you a specific monthly benefit when you retire. That's why they're called defined benefit plans: the benefit you'll receive is "defined" by the plan in advance. Your employer must make sure there's enough money stored in the plan to pay out all the benefits as required.

**Figure 6.1**  Defined Benefit Plans Cover Millions

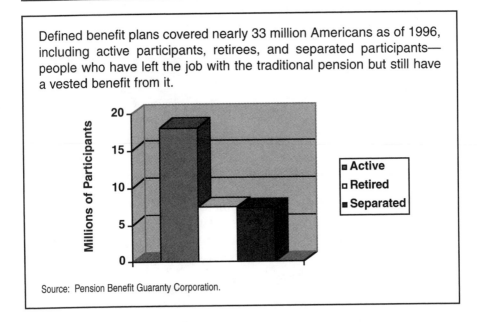

Defined benefit plans covered nearly 33 million Americans as of 1996, including active participants, retirees, and separated participants— people who have left the job with the traditional pension but still have a vested benefit from it.

Source: Pension Benefit Guaranty Corporation.

In other words, your employer shoulders all the risk. No matter how the stock market fares, no matter the vagaries of the business cycle, your employer is required to pump enough money into a defined benefit plan to make sure that current retirees get paid and that future retirees will receive the benefits they've been promised.

The other main type of employer-sponsored retirement plan, defined contribution plans, which include the 401(k) plan, cannot make this claim. A defined contribution plan spells out how contributions are made (it "defines" the contribution in plan documents in advance), but it does not make any promises as to how much you'll receive in benefits when you retire. Your employer generally isn't required to maintain a certain level of funding. With a defined contribution plan, in other words, *you* shoulder the risk.

## Insurance for Pension Plans

Still not convinced? Bear this in mind: The defined benefit plan is the *only* employer-sponsored retirement plan that's backed by the federal government. You won't hear much about this advantage of traditional pensions when coworkers talk about their 401(k) balances or their profit-sharing plans, but it's true nonetheless.

The Washington-based Pension Benefit Guaranty Corporation (PBGC) insures and protects your benefits in a defined benefit plan. This agency *guarantees* your pension benefits (up to certain legal limits).

If your employer gets into financial problems and can't maintain the required level of funding in your defined benefit plan, the PBGC will take it over (after some intervening steps) and keep the plan running, ensuring that you'll get what's coming to you. (About 472,000 workers and retirees in about 2,660 pension plans rely on the agency for their retirement income. For the year 2000, the agency's maximum benefit was generally set at $3,220 a month, a little over $38,600 a year.)

To make sure the PBGC has enough money to do the job, it levies premiums on employers who offer traditional pensions. In other words, employers who operate defined benefit plans must regularly pay a fee.

Overall, a defined benefit plan can be attractive to employees because it promises a specific benefit at retirement. There's no guesswork; employees know in advance the amount of benefits they're supposed to receive. The amount won't fluctuate with the ups and downs of the stock market. In addition, the employer—not the employee—is responsible for making sure the benefits are there.

## Peace of Mind: One Family's Story

A traditional pension—a defined benefit pension plan—can make a big difference in a worker's retirement years. David M. Strauss, executive director of the PBGC, suggests his own father as an example of how defined benefit plans can help.

Strauss's father worked as a meat cutter in a grocery store in Valley City, North Dakota. When he retired in the early 1970s at age 62, he had no pension. He then took a part-time job as a janitor at the local high school. He earned just $1.75 an hour, but he was covered by a defined benefit pension plan—for the first time in his life.

Strauss's father worked at the high school for 16 years, until he retired again. This time, however, he retired with a pension benefit. Although the benefit totaled only $169 a month, it made a difference, Strauss said. "While it may not seem to be a large amount, $169 a month has real purchasing power in Valley City, North Dakota."

That's not the only advantage, according to Strauss. "My father doesn't have to worry about running out of money. He doesn't have to worry about how much he can afford to take out of his savings each month or what the market will do. His pension is not dependent on his investing skill or his investing luck. For as long as he lives, he's going to get a monthly check; he can spend it all every month and not worry.

**Figure 6.2**    Important Moments in Pension History

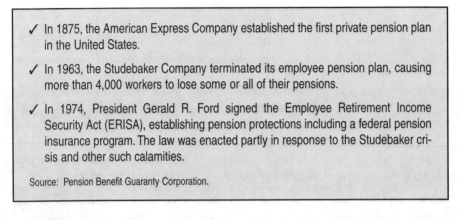

✓ In 1875, the American Express Company established the first private pension plan in the United States.

✓ In 1963, the Studebaker Company terminated its employee pension plan, causing more than 4,000 workers to lose some or all of their pensions.

✓ In 1974, President Gerald R. Ford signed the Employee Retirement Income Security Act (ERISA), establishing pension protections including a federal pension insurance program. The law was enacted partly in response to the Studebaker crisis and other such calamities.

Source: Pension Benefit Guaranty Corporation.

"Plus, if my father dies before my mother, the pension plan will provide *her* with a survivor benefit for the remainder of her life. You can't put a value on the peace of mind this guaranteed income for life gives people like my mother and father, or, for that matter, their children."

Strauss says his family's story illustrates several key points about defined benefit pension plans. For example, a worker is never too old to enter a traditional pension plan. A defined benefit plan can make a big difference even for workers making very modest salaries. Finally, you can never overestimate the value of even a small amount of guaranteed income for life, an amount that can never be taken away.

## How Defined Benefit Plans Work

Defined benefit plans have been around since 1875, when the first corporate pension plan was set up by the American Express Company. Traditional pension plans work pretty much the same way now as they did back then, pledging to provide workers with a stream of income during their retirement years.

To meet that promise, defined benefit plans must build up assets and generate income. The point is to ensure that the plan will have the wherewithal to cover its obligations to current and future retirees.

In most cases, only the employer contributes to the defined benefit plan; employees typically don't pitch in. The employer gets to claim a federal income tax deduction for the amount of the contribution, and earnings inside the plan grow on a tax-deferred basis. In general, the only time plan benefits are taxed is when they're withdrawn; then the employee pays the tax, and because retirees may be in a lower tax bracket, the tax consequence may not be great.

In some years, a plan earns enough money through investments to cover expenses, and the amount of the employer's contribution is small. In other years, however, a plan's investments may not earn enough, or may actually lose money. That's when the employer may have to contribute a significant amount to make sure the plan can cover its costs.

## "Joining" a Traditional Pension Plan

How can you wind up getting benefits from a defined benefit plan? The rules are a bit complicated, but with a little effort, you can quickly see how it all works.

First, you have to actually take part in a plan. In other words, you must become a "plan participant," as pension experts say. To do that, you typically have to clear two hurdles, one having to do with your age, the other involving how much time you have put in on the job.

In general, you're allowed to take part in a plan if you're at least 21 and you've completed at least one year of service with your employer. (A year of service generally means a 12-month period during which you've logged at least 1,000 hours of work. That rounds off to a minimum of about 20 hours a week.)

When you become a plan participant, you start earning benefits under the plan's rules—you're on your way to eventually receiving a pension from the plan.

## Vesting

To actually receive a benefit, however, you must overcome one more obstacle. It has to do with how long you work for your employer.

That's right. Just because you become a plan participant and start earning credit toward a benefit, you are not automatically entitled to receive the benefit. You have to put some more time in on the job.

This is where "vesting" comes in. Essentially, for every year you work, you earn the unforfeitable right to at least some level of benefit under the plan, no matter what. If you don't put in the required number of years, you'll get no benefit, or you'll get only a partial benefit—even though you technically were a participant in the plan. Exactly how many years you must put in depends on how the plan is set up.

At one time, plans routinely required participants to work at least ten years—or even longer in some cases—before they could qualify to receive a benefit out of the plan.

Nowadays, however, you don't have to put in as many years. There are two vesting formulas, or schedules. Your plan can use one or the other.

One of these formulas, known as "cliff" vesting, essentially works like this: If you work a certain number of years (plans may require no more than five years and often require less time), you'll eventually be paid the entire benefit that you've earned. If your plan uses the five-year rule, you must work at least five years for that employer to eventually get the entire benefit that you've earned. If you leave before the five years is up, you'll get nothing.

The other formula is known as "graded" vesting. Under this method, you qualify for a certain portion of your benefit every year. If you log enough years, you'll become entitled to the full benefit. Seven years is the legal limit. (Keep in mind that here, too, your employer is free to set a limit that's more favorable to workers.)

If your plan has a graded vesting formula that stretches to seven years, it probably works this way: after three years, you earn the unforfeitable right to 20 percent of your benefit; after four years, to 40 percent; after five years, to 60 percent; after six years, to 80 percent; and after seven years, to 100 percent.

What if you switch jobs after four years and go to work at another company? When you reach retirement age, the employer that offered the plan will have to pay you 40 percent of the benefit to which you were entitled under plan rules at the time you left.

## Figuring Your Benefits

Exactly how much money your defined benefit plan will pay you when you retire depends on the plan's rules. In general, the amount of your retirement benefit will be linked to your pay, to your years of service, or to both.

One plan may promise to pay you a flat amount per month, based on your years of service. (This is technically known as the "flat benefit" formula.)

Another plan may figure your monthly benefit based on both how many years you worked and an average of the amount you earned in salary or wages each year. (This is technically known as the "career average" formula.) A plan may calculate your pension benefit as a percentage of the salary or wages you earned over your entire career. Another plan, using a slightly different version of the career average formula, may calculate your benefit in essentially the same way, but add another feature to the formula to boost benefits based on how many years you worked overall.

Still another method (one that's potentially more favorable to workers) is the "final pay" formula. Under this method, the plan uses an average of how much you earned, in salary or wages, during a certain number of years toward the end of your career—perhaps three out of your last five working years. The plan may use a percentage of the amount you were paid in your highest-earning years and multiply that figure by the total number of years you worked. Because this formula focuses on how much you earned only in your final working years, the benefit you get in retirement may be higher because you typically earn the most in wages or salary in your final working years.

A typical defined benefit plan might provide an annual retirement benefit of 2 percent of your final average compensation, multiplied by your total years of service, according to the Congress Joint Committee on Taxation.

As of 1999, 72 percent of large employers with defined benefit plans used a "highest average pay" formula in calculating pension benefits, according to a report by the Employee Benefit Research Institute. Only about 9 percent used a "career average pay" formula.

Although the exact formula can vary from plan to plan, there are a few rules of thumb. In general, the longer you've worked under the same plan, the more money you've earned, and the older you are at retirement, the higher your pension benefit will be under a defined benefit plan.

## Getting Your Money

You typically receive your benefits when you reach normal retirement age (usually age 65, although this can vary from plan to plan). You may receive your payment in a lump sum or in a series of payments—an "annuity"—for the rest of your life. (Annuity payments are made at regular intervals, usually monthly.)

If you're married, you'll be paid what's known as a "joint and survivor annuity": you'll get a certain amount while you're alive, and your spouse will receive a reduced amount after you die. By law, the surviving spouse must get an amount that's at least half of the amount of the worker's full benefit. If a lump-sum option is available, and you want to choose it, you must get your spouse's written consent. By law, these plans are set up to provide retirement security not only to a worker, but also to the worker's spouse.

(If the value of your benefit under the plan is $5,000 or less, the plan has the legal right to cash you out in a lump sum, even if you—and your spouse—would prefer to have the benefit paid in the form of an annuity.)

Defined benefit plans also typically allow for other payments under certain circumstances. For example:

- If you've reached a certain age and have put in a certain number of years on the job, you may be eligible to receive an early-retirement benefit. If you decide to retire early, the amount you receive will probably be less than if you continued working until you reached normal retirement age. (You may also become eligible for early-retirement benefits as part of an early-retirement package, when an employer wants to cut the workforce and encourages older workers to leave earlier than scheduled, or when a company closes a division, subsidiary, or plant.)

- Many defined benefit plans also provide for disability benefits. Here, too, your ability to qualify may depend on such factors as the number of years of service you've logged.
- Your plan may pay a benefit to your spouse if you die before you reach retirement.
- If you keep working beyond normal retirement age, the plan must give you credit for this when it finally comes time to calculate the amount of your benefit. It must take into account your additional years of service and higher annual pay during these years. Although the general rule requires you to start pulling benefits out of the plan at about the time you turn 70½, you typically can postpone receipt of plan benefits until April 1 of the year following the year in which you finally retire. (If you're an owner of the company, however, you must start taking plan benefits under the age 70½ rule.)

## The Decline in Popularity of Traditional Pensions

Given the advantages of defined benefit pension plans—to employees and employers alike—you might think that they're the most popular type of employer-sponsored retirement savings plan in the marketplace today.

The truth is, however, that defined benefit plans have fallen from grace in recent years. In 1985, there were more than 112,000 such plans. By 1998, however, the number had fallen to only about 42,000.

Why the decline? One big reason is money. The fact is that defined benefit plans can be expensive to operate. For example, employers must hire specialists, known as actuaries, to make careful projections about the number of workers who are likely to take part in the plan in the future, how long they're likely to live, how much they're likely to earn, and other factors.

Employers must also hire other specialists to check the plans on a regular basis to make sure they're running properly and will be funded sufficiently to ensure that they'll meet their future obligations. There are lots of forms to file and other regulatory burdens, all of which add up to a heavy administrative expense.

In addition, employers can sometimes be on the hook to make large contributions. In good times, defined benefit plans can pretty much run by themselves. Plan assets, prudently invested, can earn enough on their own to cover much of the cost of payouts to current and future retirees. Employers don't have to contribute much, sometimes for years at a stretch.

In bad times, however, a defined benefit plan's investments may not earn enough to meet requirements. Indeed, they may even lose money and

**Figure 6.3**   A Fall from Grace

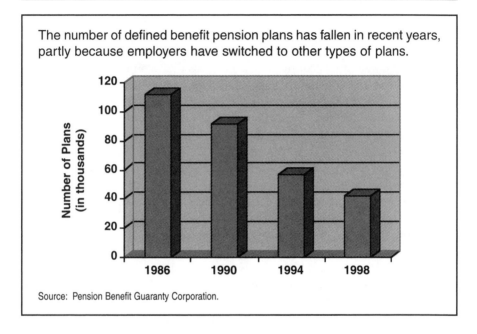

The number of defined benefit pension plans has fallen in recent years, partly because employers have switched to other types of plans.

Number of Plans (in thousands)

120 — 100 — 80 — 60 — 40 — 20 — 0

1986   1990   1994   1998

Source: Pension Benefit Guaranty Corporation.

become "underfunded." It is at that point that an employer will have to step up to the plate, kicking in enough money to make up for the shortfall. And this may occur at precisely the wrong the time in the business cycle—amid an economic downturn when corporate profits are squeezed the most.

That's not the only problem. Keep in mind that workers typically don't earn the most benefits from these plans until late in their working years. Because of the baby boom, unusually large numbers of workers are just now entering the late stage of their working careers, or will be soon. This could require employers to sharply step up the amount they contribute to traditional pension plans.

Don't forget, too, that employers must regularly fork over premiums to the Pension Benefit Guaranty Corporation to maintain the special fund that covers plans that fail.

In addition, defined benefit plans have potential drawbacks in the way they're designed and in the way they operate. For example:

- Although defined benefit plans can provide a steady stream of income, that stream can be pretty small. In some cases, retired workers and their spouses wind up getting only a nominal monthly benefit— perhaps $100 a month or so. (This can be especially true if the plan's benefits are somehow "integrated" with Social Security, and the

worker wasn't highly paid. For example, a plan can promise to provide you with a monthly benefit that amounts to a certain percentage of your income. However, the percentage may take into account
what you'll receive in Social Security benefits. As a result, the actual
percentage you receive from the plan—after Social Security benefits
are taken into account—can be far less than you had hoped.)

- Few defined benefit plans, especially in the private sector, are indexed to increase with inflation. This means that the amount of the
monthly benefit you receive can be fixed for your life—no matter
how long you live. The employer can change the terms of the plan
and give you a "raise" in retirement. That's rare, however. As a result,
as time goes on, the real value of your monthly pension check can be
eroded by inflation.

- Unlike 401(k) plans and many other types of retirement savings
plans in the workplace, defined benefit plans aren't "portable." In
other words, you can't take the benefits with you. You don't have
the option, therefore, of rolling over the benefits from a plan at your
old job into a plan at your new job. If you leave and you were vested,
your vested benefit typically stays with the plan at your old job until
you reach normal retirement age.

- Defined benefit plans may require longer vesting than other plans.
As a result, you may have to work a relatively long time at one employer to be eligible to earn a pension benefit from that employer.
Many defined contribution plans, such as 401(k) plans, have faster
vesting schedules, allowing you to qualify for the benefits under the
plan far sooner.

- With a defined benefit plan, there are no individual accounts, as
there are with 401(k) and some other types of employer-sponsored
retirement plans. You also typically don't get to have a say in how
the plan assets are invested. With 401(k) plans and the like, you get
to direct the investments yourself. Furthermore, 401(k) and similar
plans generally give you a range of investment choices. It's possible,
therefore, that if you invest prudently and general market conditions are right, you could profit handsomely, developing a huge nest
egg over time. With defined benefit plans, you don't have that option. (Indeed, the maximum benefit from a defined benefit plan is
capped by law. In recent years, the maximum annual benefit payable
under a traditional pension plan was generally either $135,000 or
100 percent of your average compensation over your three highest-
earning consecutive years.)

- Because of the way that most defined benefit plans are set up, they
favor long-term workers, people who stick with the same company
over a long period of time—perhaps their entire career. Critics argue

that these plans are outdated in today's workplace because fewer workers nowadays stick with one employer for a long period of time. Because of the way they are structured, defined benefit plans don't generally favor younger workers and those who change jobs a lot. They aren't set up to meet the need of a mobile workforce.

## Employers Are Switching to Other Plans

For these and other reasons, lots of companies have been scuttling their defined benefit plans in favor of other retirement savings programs that are less costly to run and pose less risk to an employer's financial position.

Lots of companies have started defined contribution plans, including the popular 401(k) plan. In 1979, defined benefit plans were the primary source of pension coverage for private-sector workers who had pension coverage. By 1998, however, the figure had dropped to less than 50 percent. During the same period, defined contribution plans have grown to become the primary source of pension coverage, to more than 50 percent of workers with pension coverage as of 1998.

**Figure 6.4**  Other Plans Gain Favor

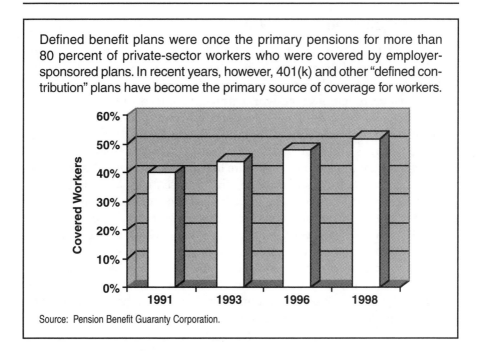

Source: Pension Benefit Guaranty Corporation.

You need only look at your local newsstand to confirm this transformation. Month after month, the covers of personal finance magazines trumpet the advantages of defined contribution plans such as the 401(k). The bold headlines scream from magazine racks: "Ten Ways to Improve Your 401(k) Plan—Now!" or "Take Charge of Your 401(k) and Retire at 40." You rarely, if ever, will see a headline like "Get the Most from Your Defined Benefit Plan!"

## Traditional Pension Plans Under Attack

Defined benefit plans were also under siege for a time by corporate raiders, who regularly looted them with abandon, especially in the 1980s. They would shut down a traditional pension plan and pirate the assets, then use the money to help pay for acquisitions, which were often made at wildly inflated prices. Eventually, the government caught on and established tax and other rules that made this practice difficult to carry out.

The plundering of traditional pension plans has now all but ended. More recently, however, the traditional pension plan has again been a lightning rod for controversy, as some companies have converted them to "hybrid" plans, primarily cash balance plans. They're called hybrid plans because they resemble defined benefit plans in some ways and defined contribution plans in others.

## How Cash Balance Plans Work

Cash balance plans are governed by the same rules that govern traditional defined benefit plans. They also offer some of the same features. For instance, only the employer contributes to the plan, only the employer assumes the investment risk, and workers are guaranteed a retirement benefit. In addition, cash balance plans—like defined benefit plans—are insured by the Pension Benefit Guaranty Corporation.

However, as an Employee Benefit Research Institute report said, cash balance plans are designed to look more like defined contribution plans. For example, cash balance plans provide what is essentially an individual account for each worker, and these hypothetical accounts grow each year for every participant in the plan. A cash balance plan may pledge to credit a worker's "account" each year, in an amount that equals a certain percent of his or her pay. A plan may also pledge to have a worker's "account" grow by a certain amount each year, based on some investment benchmark.

Because of the way cash balance plans operate, the individual "accounts" exist for recordkeeping purposes only. Amounts that employers contribute are really based on actuarial assumptions, not on actual fixed contributions to individual accounts, according to the Employee Benefit Research Institute report.

In addition, cash balance plans calculate a worker's retirement benefit by using the formulas in the plan's official document; benefits aren't based on the assets in a worker's "account."

Because there is at least a theoretical individual account involved, an employer may find it easier to explain a cash balance plan to workers than to explain a far more complex traditional plan. In addition, it may be easier for workers to understand how they may benefit from a cash balance plan.

A report by the Employee Benefit Research Institute summarized some key differences between defined benefit plans and cash balance plans. Under a typical defined benefit plan that uses a "final average pay" formula, the value of your benefit generally depends on your age, your years of service, and your pay. Under a cash balance plan, the value of your benefit generally depends on your pay and years of service, not your age.

As a result, younger workers generally accrue a greater benefit under a cash balance plan than they would under a typical defined benefit plan. For older workers the opposite is generally true.

## The Growth in Popularity of Cash Balance Plans

Although cash balance plans started to appear in the mid-1980s, it wasn't until about a decade later that they really began to grow in popularity among employers. By 1999, more than 300 large companies, including about one-fourth of the nation's 100 largest corporations, had adopted cash balance plans.

Why have the new plans become so popular? The ERISA Industry Committee, a nonprofit group that speaks for the employee benefit plans run by America's largest employers, says the plans offer lots of advantages when compared with traditional pension plans and defined contribution plans such as the 401(k). In testimony before a U.S. Senate hearing on cash balance and other hybrid pension plans, the group listed some of the advantages:

- Unlike traditional plans, cash balance plans provide an account balance for each participant, something that workers easily understand.
- Employers contribute money automatically to the accounts of all workers who are eligible to participate. Workers don't have to decide whether to take part, and they don't have to make decisions about contributing from their own paychecks.
- The employer bears the investment risk; a drop in the stock or bond markets doesn't affect the benefit promised to the plan participant.
- Benefits from the plan are protected by PBGC insurance.

**Figure 6.5**    Converting to Cash Balance Plans

Some of the nation's largest companies have converted their traditional defined benefit plans to cash balance plans, or have begun the process.

| Company | Year of Conversion | Number of Employees (as of 1998) |
| --- | --- | --- |
| IBM Corp. | 1999 | 291,067 |
| CitiGroup Inc. | 2000 | 173,700 |
| AT&T Co. | 1998 | 107,800 |
| Bell Atlantic Corp. | 1996 | 140,000 |
| SBC Communications | 1998 | 129,850 |
| CIGNA Corp. | 1998 | 49,900 |
| Aetna Inc. | 1999 | 33,500 |
| Eastman Kodak | 1999 | 86,200 |
| CBS Corp. | 1999 | 46,189 |

Source: U.S. Senate Committee on Health, Education, Labor, and Pensions.

- The plans deliver benefits more evenly over a worker's entire career, unlike defined benefit plans, in which a worker earns most of his or her benefit in the last few years before retirement.
- Cash balance and other such hybrid plans are portable. In other words, a worker who changes jobs before retirement can bring the benefits along with him or her, either transferring the money to an Individual Retirement Account, or moving it to another employer's plan. This helps to cut down on "job lock," which occurs when a worker decides to stick with a job—even though he or she would prefer to move elsewhere—just to qualify for the pension credits available to older, long-serving workers through traditional defined benefit plans.
- Cash balance plans can be especially attractive to new industries that are trying to attract highly talented and mobile workers. They can also appeal to people with family commitments and others who may be unwilling or unable to spend long years of service with a single employer.

## Controversy over Cash Balance Plans

Cash balance plans have prompted controversy primarily because of concerns about the rights of older workers. Keep in mind that workers typically earn the most from a defined benefit plan in their final working years.

That's when their annual pay is usually highest, and defined benefit plans typically calculate a worker's retirement benefits based, at least in part, on how much a worker earned during those years.

In some cases, when a defined benefit plan is converted to a cash balance plan, older workers eventually receive a lower retirement benefit than they would have received from a defined benefit plan.

Senator Tom Harkin, D-Iowa, puts it this way: "Many companies are changing to so-called cash balance plans, which often saves [companies] millions of dollars in pension costs each year by taking a substantial cut out of employee pensions. This practice allows employers to unfairly profit at the expense of retirees."

How does this happen? At a 1999 Senate hearing on cash balance plans, Harkin offered this explanation: When a worker shifts from a defined benefit plan to a cash balance plan, the employer calculates the benefits that the worker has earned under the old plan. An older worker typically has accrued a significant benefit under the traditional plan, higher than it would have been under the new cash balance plan. As a result, an employer can stop contributing to the cash balance plan on that worker's behalf, at least for a time. That's because under the rules of the cash balance plan, the older worker has, in effect, accumulated too great a benefit—more than what's called for under the new plan's rules. Therefore, the employer doesn't have to contribute to that worker's account until it is required to do so under the rules of the cash balance plan—sometimes years later.

When an East Chicago steel company, Ispat Inland Inc., converted to a cash balance plan in 1999, one of its workers, a 44-year-old engineer who had worked for the company for 19 years, calculated that it could take him up to 13 years to acquire additional benefits, Harkin said.

In some cases, employers have also used the switch to cash balance plans to reduce or eliminate early retirement and other benefits that workers formerly had under their traditional defined benefit plans. In other cases, employers have switched to cash balance plans at least in part to avoid the huge tax they would have had to pay if they had converted the defined benefit plan to a defined contribution plan.

Another common complaint is disclosure. In some cases, workers say that their employers haven't explained clearly enough how workers will be affected by a conversion to a cash balance plan.

## National Attention

Except for some isolated outcries by workers who had been caught up in the changeover, the trend toward cash balance plans went all but unnoticed until Ellen E. Schultz, a reporter at *The Wall Street Journal,* brought the matter to national attention.

**Figure 6.6**    Eastman Kodak: A Choice of Retirement Plans

When Eastman Kodak switched from a defined benefit plan to a cash balance plan for new hires, it allowed workers already on the payroll to stick with the old retirement program or go with the new one.

| Old Retirement Benefits | New Retirement Benefits |
| --- | --- |
| Defined benefit plan | Cash balance plan |
| 401(k) with no company match | 401(k) with company match |
| Company contribution to retiree health care and dental | No company contribution to retiree health care and dental, but access to plans at company rates |
| Company-paid life insurance in retirement (at 1 or 2 times pay) | $10,000 company-paid life insurance in retirement |
| Access to financial planning | Access to financial planning |

Source: U.S. Senate Committee on Health, Education, Labor, and Pensions.

She highlighted campaigns at IBM, AT&T, and other companies by workers who asserted that changeovers to cash balance plans were hurting older employees. In some cases, the employers were using the switch to cash balance plans to also reduce or eliminate early-retirement and other benefits that workers formerly had under their traditional defined benefit plans.

In time, Congress and the White House reacted, and in late 1999 the government began moving to protect the rights of those workers who might suffer losses from the shutdown of their defined benefit plans, and to require improved disclosure.

## Protections for Older Workers

Keep in mind that a switch to a cash balance plan doesn't necessarily mean that older workers will suffer. Some employers who've made the change have created built-in protections for older workers. In some cases, employers have kept their old plan in place and have given workers a choice of whether to stay in the traditional plan or join the cash balance plan.

For example, when Eastman Kodak began changing its retirement program for all its new hires from a traditional defined benefit plan to a cash balance plan (plus a 401(k) plan with a company matching contribution), the company gave existing employees the option to remain in the old retirement program or choose the new one.

When IBM announced its switch to a cash balance plan, the conversion was denounced by many workers, members of Congress, and others—in part because not enough workers were allowed the opportunity to stick with the old defined benefit plan. (IBM later announced it would sharply increase the number of older workers who could decide to stick with the company's traditional plan.)

In other instances, employers have established supplemental retirement savings plans or have redesigned cash balance plans to help make up for losses in future benefits older workers might otherwise suffer.

It's clear that the controversy over the switch to cash balance plans won't go away. If your company decides to make the switch, take a careful look not only at the advantages of the cash balance plan, but also at the potential benefits you might earn by sticking with your traditional plan—if you have the choice.

## For More Information . . .

- The Pension Benefit Guaranty Corporation has several publications that explain how defined benefit plans work, how your plan is protected by insurance, and what benefits you can expect to receive if your plan is taken over by the PBGC. For a free copy of the booklet *Defined Benefit Pensions: A Predictable, Secure Pension for Life,* write to: Consumer Information Center, Dept. 639E, Pueblo, Colorado 81009. For a free copy of the booklet *Your Guaranteed Pension,* write to: Pension Benefit Guaranty Corporation, Communications and Public Affairs Department, 1200 K Street NW, Washington, DC 20005-4026. You may also read these and other materials at the agency's Web site: <www.pbgc.gov>.
- The U.S. Department of Labor's Pension and Welfare Benefits Administration publishes several booklets about pensions, including *What You Should Know about Your Pension Rights; Protect Your Pension; Women and Pensions: What Women Need to Know and Do;* and *QDROs—The Division of Pensions through Qualified Domestic Relations Orders.* For free copies, write to: Pension and Welfare Benefits Administration, U.S. Department of Labor, 200 Constitution Avenue NW, Room N-5619, Washington, DC 20210. You may also call the agency's toll-free publications hotline at 1-800-998-7542, or contact the its Web site: <www.dol.gov/dol/pwba>.
- The AARP publishes lots of booklets about pension plans, including *A Guide to Understanding Your Pension Plan* and *A Woman's Guide to Pension Rights.* For free copies of these and other publications, write to: AARP Fulfillment, 601 E Street NW, Washington, DC 20049.

- The Pension Rights Center is a nonprofit group whose mission includes helping to inform workers about their pension rights. For information about their publications and other services, send a self-addressed, stamped envelope to: Pension Rights Center, 918 16th Street NW, Washington, DC 20006.
- A group of IBM employees formed a coalition in 1999, the IBM Employee Benefits Action Coalition, to help protect workers' pension rights when a defined benefit plan is converted to a cash balance plan. To reach the group or read its materials, contact its Web site: <www.cashpensions.com>.
- The Coalition for Retirement Security works to correct what it views as inequities in the areas of pensions and health care, and also tries to teach people about how important pensions and health care are to retirees. For more information, contact the group's Web site: <www.pensions-r-us.org>.
- BenefitsLink is a clearinghouse for information on employee benefits. Through its Web site, it offers background on benefits, updates throughout the day on news affecting benefits, and message boards for hot topics, including one on cash balance plans. If you're serious about benefits, this is an essential resource: <www.benefitslink.com>.

# 7

# 401(k) Plans

If you're eligible to take part in a retirement savings plan at work known as a 401(k) plan, do it. If your employer is thinking about offering a 401(k) plan as a benefit, lobby for it. If you're already in such a plan and you can afford to save some more, get going.

The truth is that the 401(k) retirement savings plan is one great way to save. Why? You get your own account. You can put money into it directly out of your paycheck, through the convenience of payroll deduction. For every dollar you save in your 401(k), you get a tax break. Your employer may contribute to your account, too. You generally get a choice of investment options. The money your account earns doesn't get taxed each year, as it would in an ordinary savings account at the bank; it's taxed only when you withdraw it. If an emergency arises, you probably can tap into your account if you need to—by borrowing from the account or making hardship withdrawals. Perhaps the biggest benefit, however, comes at the end: If you save faithfully and make some prudent investment choices, you can find yourself sitting on a big fat nest egg at retirement.

That's why there's been so much publicity about these savings programs, and why there'll be more to come. The 401(k) plan has become extraordinarily popular, so much so that American workers are projected to have more than $1.45 trillion tucked away in 401(k) plans in 2000, with more than 31 million people actively taking part, according to estimates by Spectrem Group, a national provider of consulting, research, and merger and acquisition advisory services.

To understand how 401(k) plans can help you, and to make sure you get the most out of this remarkable employee benefit, it helps to know exactly what they are and how they work.

## What 401(k) Plans Are

The 401(k) plan was named after a section in federal tax law—Section 401(k) of the Internal Revenue Code. The 401(k) plan (sometimes called a

**Figure 7.1** 401(k) Plan Assets Are Growing . . .

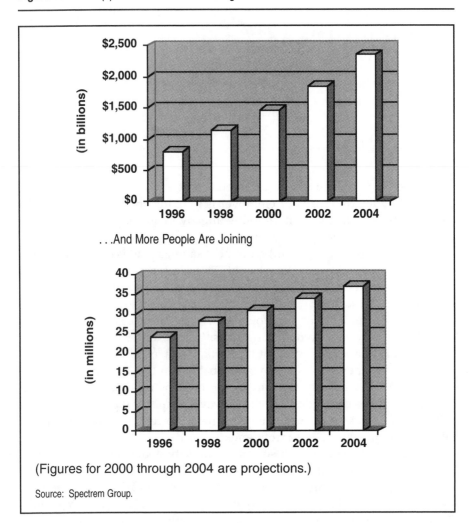

. . .And More People Are Joining

(Figures for 2000 through 2004 are projections.)

Source: Spectrem Group.

"cash or deferred arrangement," or CODA), was created as a result of a 1978 change in tax law. Because of this change, which took effect in 1980, employers were able to offer a special kind of retirement savings plan at work, and employees were able to use it to make their own contributions toward their retirement—and take advantage of tax incentives along the way.

The plans were slow to catch on at first because they were so new and because companies weren't certain about how the plans' benefits worked and how to put the plans in place. R. Theodore "Ted" Benna, who now runs the 401(k) Association, a nonprofit group in Pennsylvania that encourages

**Figure 7.2**   401(k) Plans by the Numbers

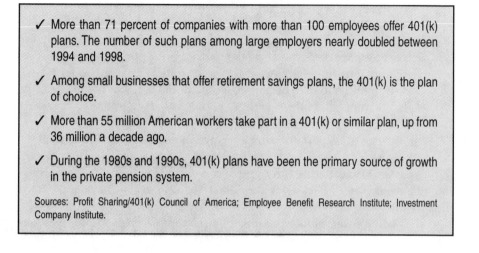

✓ More than 71 percent of companies with more than 100 employees offer 401(k) plans. The number of such plans among large employers nearly doubled between 1994 and 1998.

✓ Among small businesses that offer retirement savings plans, the 401(k) is the plan of choice.

✓ More than 55 million American workers take part in a 401(k) or similar plan, up from 36 million a decade ago.

✓ During the 1980s and 1990s, 401(k) plans have been the primary source of growth in the private pension system.

Sources: Profit Sharing/401(k) Council of America; Employee Benefit Research Institute; Investment Company Institute.

the development of 401(k) plans, is widely credited with putting the first such plan in place.

## Getting a Piece of the Action

If your employer offers a 401(k) plan—or if you're considering a job that has a 401(k) plan in the benefits package—can you get a piece of the action? You probably can. Unlike some other plans that can make you jump through some hoops before you join, most 401(k) plans let you join shortly after you become employed. The rules for 401(k)s are typically far less rigid than those for other retirement plans.

For instance, under federal law, you generally become eligible to take part in a 401(k) plan once you turn 21 and you've logged at least one year of service with your employer, according to the Congress Joint Committee on Taxation. These are the limits of how long a company can delay your participation. In practice, some employers allow you to join sooner than that.

Consider these points from a survey by Buck Consultants, a worldwide human resources consulting firm:

- With some 401(k) plans, you don't have to wait before you become eligible to take part in the plan. For plans that do make you wait, the typical wait is a year, but in some cases it is far less.

- Some plans impose an age requirement. In other words, you have to reach a certain age before you can join. Seventy-eight percent of such plans set the required age at 21. In other cases, however, the required age is lower.
- 401(k) plans are widely available to full-time workers, and many part-time workers can also take part. About 71 percent of employers require part-time employees to work a minimum of 20 hours a week to be eligible to take part in the plan. (Some employers require more hours, others less.)

If you can take part in your employer's plan, should you? In most cases, the answer is yes—a resounding yes. One big reason is convenience. In most cases, you can save through payroll deduction: you save money before you even "see" it because it gets taken out of your paycheck and placed directly into your account.

You tell your employer how much you want to save—typically a percentage of your pay—and that's how much gets taken out of your check. (For most employers, your "pay" includes not only your base pay, but also any commissions, bonuses, overtime pay, and shift differentials you may earn.) These plans are flexible, too; you typically get lots of chances to change your mind, to either increase or lower the amount you want taken out of your check, as Figure 7.3 shows.

**Figure 7.3**   Changing Your Mind

Most 401(k) plans give you the flexibility to periodically change how much you want to contribute.

| How Frequently You May Change Your Contribution | Percentage of Plans |
| --- | --- |
| Every pay period | 27% |
| Quarterly | 27 |
| Monthly | 21 |
| Daily, or on request | 15 |
| Certain number of times per year | 5 |
| Other | 5 |
| Annually | 2 |
| Never | 0 |

Note: Plans surveyed were allowed to select more than one option.

Source: Buck Consultants Inc.

There is a limit to the amount you can save (before tax) in a 401(k). For 2000, the limit was set at $10,500 a year. Because the limit is tied to inflation, it can increase each year.

## Employer Matching Contributions

Another attractive feature of 401(k) plans comes from employers. To encourage you to save, many employers contribute something to your account, too. In some cases, the employer contributes money to your account no matter how much you contribute. In many other cases, however, an employer will contribute a certain amount depending on how much you put into the account. This is called the "employer match." If you don't contribute, the employer doesn't contribute, either. If you *do* contribute, however, the employer kicks in something, too.

Almost 90 percent of employers with 401(k) plans make matching contributions, according to a survey by Buck Consultants. Frequently the amount the employer contributes is very attractive, a sweetener you almost cannot refuse.

Exactly how much an employer will invest in your account is spelled out in your employee benefits booklet or brochure (called the summary plan description) that companies are required, by law, to give to workers.

**Figure 7.4**   When Employers Sweeten the Deal

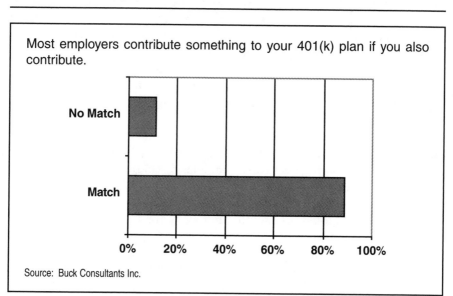

Source: Buck Consultants Inc.

## Limits to the Employer Match

Although formulas vary depending on the company, most employers kick in a fixed amount for every dollar a worker contributes, up to a certain limit. The most common such formula calls for an employer to kick in 50 cents for every dollar a worker contributes up to a maximum of 6 percent of the worker's pay.

Suppose you earn $40,000 in gross pay in a year. You contribute 10 percent of that to your 401(k) account, a total of $4,000. Your employer will not match the whole $4,000, but will match the amount that is equal to 6 percent of your pay—$2,400. The employer kicks in 50 cents for every dollar you contribute up to the $2,400 limit, and the result is an extra $1,200 in your account. In other words, your employer is handing you $1,200, no strings attached.

Now assume, for convenience, that your annual pay stays the same each year and that your employer continues putting up the $1,200 a year. If your 401(k) earns a 7 percent return each year, the annual employer matching contribution alone will be worth about $16,580 in 10 years, and nearly $50,000 in 20 years—and that doesn't include all the money that you contribute yourself, or the amount that your contributions earn.

## Why Employers Are Motivated to Contribute

Why are companies so generous? Some companies contribute to workers' accounts simply to help them save money toward their retirement. It's the kind of thing that helps attract and keep good workers. The plans also can be somewhat less expensive than some other types of retirement plans. For example, other plans may require more administration, more reports to file with the government, and steady annual contributions. In addition, the business gets to claim a tax deduction for the amount it contributes, and helping employees save for retirement is good public policy to boot.

Keep in mind, however, that some employers offer matching contributions to make sure you kick in at least something—especially if you are a rank-and-file worker with low or moderate pay.

Why? In general, 401(k) plans have to meet strict government rules to ensure that a plan doesn't overly favor the highest paid workers. The government requires employers to apply antibias tests known as "nondiscrimination" tests to their 401(k) plans.

These tests, which can be complicated and costly to run, generally boil down to this: If the plan is benefiting too many high-paid workers and too few low-paid workers, the high-paid workers (including the boss!) may have to lower—or even eliminate—their contributions for the year.

To make sure that the high-paid workers can take full advantage of the 401(k) plan, employers have to make sure that enough lower-paid workers are using the plan, too. A matching contribution from an employer, if the match is sweet enough, may be just the ticket to coax lower-paid workers to get involved.

Whatever the reason a company contributes, there's no doubt that its investments can quickly increase the amount of money in your account. And the more money there is in your account, the more money your account can earn.

## Tax Benefits

The real beauty of the 401(k) plan is the tax benefits. For every dollar you contribute, you save money in federal income tax (and possibly in state income tax, too, depending on where you live and your state's tax rules).

In a sense, then, a 401(k) plan is kind of like a traditional IRA, except that you can save more money each year (IRAs have a $2,000 annual contri-

**Figure 7.5**   What Tax Bracket Are You In?

To see how much in federal income tax you can save by contributing to a 401(k) plan, you need to know your federal tax bracket.

### For a Single Taxpayer

| Your Taxable Income ... | ... Is Taxed at This Federal Rate |
|---|---|
| $      0 to $  26,250 | 15  % |
| $  26,251 to $  63,550 | 28 |
| $  63,551 to $132,600 | 31 |
| $132,601 to $288,350 | 36 |
| $288,351 and above | 39.6 |

### For Married Taxpayers Filing a Joint Return

| Your Taxable Income ... | ... Is Taxed at This Federal Rate |
|---|---|
| $      0 to $  43,850 | 15  % |
| $  43,851 to $105,950 | 28 |
| $105,951 to $161,450 | 31 |
| $161,451 to $288,350 | 36 |
| $288,351 and above | 39.6 |

NOTE: Figures apply to the 2000 tax year and are subject to change annually. (For updated figures, call the IRS at 1-800-829-1040, or contact the agency's Web site: <www.irs.gov>). Figures for married taxpayers filing jointly also apply to qualifying widow(er)s. Contact the IRS for figures if your filing status is head of household or married filing separately.

Source: Internal Revenue Service.

bution limit), and you typically get the tax break no matter how much you earn (with an IRA, your ability to claim a tax deduction is affected by how much you earn overall).

Exactly how much you save in taxes with a 401(k) depends on your tax bracket, how much you invest, and other factors. Suppose, for example, that you earn $40,000 in gross pay a year. You decide to put 10 percent of your pay into your 401(k) account—for a total of $4,000.

That $4,000 investment reduces your taxable income to $36,000. In other words, even though you really earn $40,000, for tax purposes you earn only $36,000. Therefore, the IRS taxes you only on $36,000, not the $40,000 that you really earned.

As a result, if you're in the 15 percent federal income tax bracket, you save $600 in federal income tax simply by investing $4,000 in your 401(k). If you're in a higher tax bracket, you save even more.

In this example, then, it costs you only $3,400 to invest $4,000 in your 401(k), once you consider the tax break.

Here's another way to look at it: For every dollar you invest in your 401(k) in this example, you save 15 cents in taxes. The higher your tax bracket, the more you'll save in taxes. If you're in the 28 percent federal income tax bracket, you'll save 28 cents in tax for every dollar you contribute to your 401(k) plan. The more you invest, the more in taxes you'll save.

And yet another way to look at it: If you're in the 15 percent federal income tax bracket and you take the tax break into account, you give yourself an automatic 15 percent "return" on every dollar you invest. In other words, you're already 15 percent ahead of the game—and you haven't even considered what your 401(k) investments might generate in earnings.

Perhaps the biggest advantage that 401(k) plans offer is the tax deferment on earnings. Tax-deferred compounding is one of the main reasons that workers who've contributed faithfully to their 401(k) plans each year, and who've invested their money prudently, have wound up big winners in retirement.

Suppose you've got $20,000 in your 401(k) plan and $20,000 in a certificate of deposit (CD) at the bank. For convenience, suppose that each earns 5 percent a year, and neither you nor your employer contributes another cent. Both accounts, in other words, are frozen for the purpose of this example.

After 20 years, your 401(k) will be worth about $53,000. Your CD, however, will be worth only about $46,000. Why the difference? It's taxes. Each year, your 401(k) account earns the full 5 percent. The interest earned by your CD, however, gets taxed each year, so you don't earn the full 5 percent: after you account for federal income taxes (and assuming that you're in the 15 percent tax bracket), your CD really earns only 4.25 percent a year.

When you combine all of these factors—the tax break you get for contributing, your employer's matching contributions, and tax-deferred compounding—you get quite a stew. Keep it bubbling on the back burner throughout your working career and you could wind up with a big pot of money on retirement.

## Portability

One other attractive feature of 401(k) plans is something the experts call "portability." You generally can take your plan assets with you when you change jobs or retire. With some other types of employer-sponsored retirement plans or pension plans, the money stays with the company even if you leave, and you typically get the money only when you retire.

With 401(k) plans, however, not only do you typically get control of how your money is invested, but you also get to take the money along with you when you leave. In general, you can move the money either to a traditional IRA or to another employer's plan. (We'll discuss transfers and rollovers later in this section.)

## Other Key Points about 401(k)s

Here are some other points key points to bear in mind about 401(k) plans:

- Just as there is a variety of employer-sponsored retirement plans, there is also a variety of 401(k) plans. For example, some plans are funded entirely by worker contributions; others are funded through contributions by employers and workers. An employer may contribute a fixed amount or a variable amount. When a company contributes a portion of its profits to a 401(k) plan, the plan is said to have a "profit-sharing" element.
- Although there is a limit to the amount of your pre-tax contributions ($10,500 in the year 2000), your plan may let you contribute after-tax dollars to your account. (About one-third of plans permit employee after-tax contributions.)
- The limit on pre-tax contributions (again $10,500 in the year 2000) applies to all of your employer-sponsored plans that allow tax-free contributions put together. So if it's the year 2000 and you're covered by more than one 401(k) plan, or if you have both a 401(k) plan and a SIMPLE plan or SEP plan (these are covered in Chapter 10), you cannot save more than $10,500 altogether in pre-tax dollars.
- The most money that can flow into your account in a year from all sources is either 25 percent of your pay or $30,000, whichever is less. This is technically called the "annual additions" limit. It applies to all the contributions that can flow into your accounts *combined,* includ-

ing your contributions, your employer's contributions, and any "for-feitures" (money that another worker forfeited on leaving, which gets carved up and distributed to the remaining people in the plan).

- Here's another confusing rule. It applies to employers, not to workers, but it's something you should understand. If a 401(k) plan is set up as a profit-sharing plan, as most are, the maximum total contribution for which an employer may claim a federal income tax deduction is generally 15 percent of all workers' pay. This is the employer's deductible limit. The limit generally is applied to the combined pay of all people who take part in the plan. It's possible, therefore, that you will personally see going into your account an amount—including your contributions, your company match, and forfeitures—that equals more than 15 percent of your pay in a particular year.

# How to Invest Your 401(k) Dollars

Every working day, people spend a lot of time worrying about 401(k) investment choices. Around the water cooler or on the loading dock, during coffee breaks or lunch breaks, in person or by e-mail, workers like to discuss their investment choices, looking for the best places to put their 401(k) dollars. Most employers offer you a choice of where to invest your 401(k) dollars. A survey by the Profit Sharing/401(k) Council of America found that almost 40 percent of plans offer 10 or more mutual funds to choose from. Some employers offer far more. You really needn't be an expert, however, to come out ahead with your 401(k) investments. All you really need is to do a little bit of homework and to use some common sense.

## Choosing an Investment Strategy

Where to start? First, step back and choose a basic investment strategy. Here are some general guidelines to bear in mind:

- If you're young and you have plenty of time to go before retirement, consider taking a mostly aggressive approach, investing mainly in stock mutual funds.
- If you're middle-aged, consider a more balanced approach: Invest about half of your money in stock funds and about half in more conservative things, such as short-term bond funds.
- If you're older, nearing retirement, and you think you'll need your 401(k) assets to help supplement your income after you retire, invest more conservatively, mainly in such things as money market mutual funds, short-term bond funds, and stable-value funds (also called

d that a fund has consistently done poorly, you may want to stay away. tual funds may be the darling of the news media, but stinkers do exist.

It's also true that some funds have consistently performed well when asured both against other funds in the same category and against a standard market benchmark. These are the funds to keep in mind.

One approach to selecting a fund is to simply go with the benchmark elf. Many 401(k) plans now offer at least one "index" fund. This is simply und whose fate is tied directly to a well-known stock market barometer, ch as the Standard & Poor's 500 index, which follows the stock prices of 0 big companies. When you check the index, you can tell at a glance how 500 companies, as a group, are doing. (Some people use the S&P 500 as a ay to tell how the entire stock market is doing. Even though it tracks just 0 stocks—and there are thousands of stocks—the index is a pretty good indicator of the performance of the stock market as a whole.)

A mutual fund that's tied to the S&P 500 simply buys and holds stock all 500 companies that make up the index. As a result, if the index goes up, e value of a share in the mutual fund goes up; if the index falls, the value f a share in the mutual fund falls, too.

An index fund is said to be "passively" managed. In other words, it oesn't have a portfolio manager who decides which stocks to buy and sell; simply buys the stocks in the index, usually relying on a computer to do ost of the work.

Investing in an index fund such as one that tracks the S&P 500 can be n effective way to invest in the stock market. In fact, when you invest in an ndex fund, you can give your money broad domestic and international exposure because many of the companies that make up the index have substantial business interests overseas as well as at home.

**Expenses.** Once you've culled several well-performing funds from the list your employer gives you to choose from, it's a good idea to check on their level of expenses because high expense levels can eat into returns.

Picture a mutual fund as a giant pile of money. At regular intervals, the mutual fund company calculates the value of that pile so it can tell you how much each piece is worth.

Before shareholders get their pieces, however, the mutual fund company takes its piece to cover its costs. In other words, the mutual fund company takes a chunk off of the top of the pile. What's left is divided up by shareholders. The bigger the chunk the mutual fund company takes, the smaller the pieces that are left for you and other shareholders.

Running a mutual fund is expensive, of course, but some funds and fund companies charge more than others. A fund's expenses are typically expressed as a percentage of assets, called the "expense ratio." Here are some industry averages as of late 1999:

**Figure 7.6**   A Variety of Investment Options

At one time, 401(k) plans offered few investment options to participants. Things have changed:

✓ Nearly 40 percent of plans offer ten or more funds into which participants may funnel their contributions.

✓ The average number of funds available is 9.6.

✓ The three most frequently offered types of investment funds are actively managed domestic stock funds, actively managed international stock funds, and balanced stock/bond funds.

Source: Profit Sharing/401(k) Council of America.

guaranteed investment contracts). Keep in mind, however, that your retirement may last a long time, so if you won't need a huge chunk of your 401(k) money right away, consider the balanced approach I recommended for middle-aged investors.

## Staying the Course

No matter which investment strategy you choose or which funds you pick, determine to stay the course. Even if your plan gives you the chance to change investment options frequently—and more than 70 percent of plans allow for daily fund transfers, according to the Profit Sharing/401(k) Council of America—don't be tempted. There's no point in trying to time the market. Even most investment professionals can't do this successfully with any consistency.

The 1990s produced a strong bull market, generating sometimes incredible year-to-year gains. Even while the Dow Jones Industrial Average, the Standard & Poor's 500 Index, and other broad market barometers moved up, however, some mutual funds didn't perform well. Some individual stock sectors, and many individual stocks, either fell behind or lost money. It's impossible for average investors (or professional investors for that matter) to know exactly when the market as a whole, or individual funds or stocks, have hit their peak or hit bottom; for most people, such wisdom comes only in hindsight.

Your best bet, then, is to choose an investment strategy and stick with it. In your early years, you can afford to take more risk by investing more aggressively, in stock mutual funds, for example. As you age and the time for retirement and for withdrawing your money draws near, gradually change

**Figure 7.7    401(k) Assets in Equities**

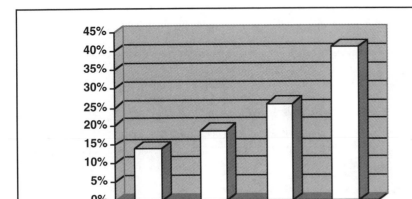

Source: Spectrem Group.

your investment mix to reflect a more conservative strategy. Otherwise, take a hands-off approach. Ignore the market timers, the day-to-day changes in investment values, and all the chatter you hear at work, on the TV and radio, and in newspapers and magazines. Tune out all the noise and stay the course.

## Choosing Specific Options

Once you know *how* to invest your money, you must decide *where* to invest it. This isn't a very difficult step either. Although your employer may offer you a lot of choices, your basic investment strategy can help narrow down the list.

For example, if you've decided to invest mainly in stock funds, you don't have to worry about the more conservative investment options available in your plan. If you've decided to stick mainly with the more conservative choices, such as short-term bond funds and stable-value funds, you don't have to pay as much attention to all the stock funds on the list.

Once you've narrowed your search, you can compare various funds based on such factors as past performance and expenses. Start with the fund prospectuses and other summary information that your employer gives you. If you don't have the information you need, ask for it. If your employer's human resources department or plan administrator doesn't have it, you can ask the funds themselves. (Most funds have toll-free phone numbers; a quick call should get you all the information you need. Many funds also offer the material on their Web sites.)

**Performance.** Next, check your local public library for the [ ] fin [ ] manuals compiled regularly by the Value Line Mutual Fund Su [ ] M [ ] York, and the Morningstar mutual fund information group, b [ ] cago. Value Line or Morningstar will tell you not only how each f [ ] me [ ] formed but also how funds have done when compared with sim [ ] da [ ] the same category.

You'll be looking for something called "total return." Thi [ ] its [ ] pressed as a percentage, generally shows how a fund has perfor [ ] a [ ] certain period. It takes into account such factors as the increase i [ ] su [ ] price per share and any dividends the fund has generated for sh [ ] 50 [ ]

When you consider performance, focus on the long term. [ ] al [ ] fund tables commonly found in newspapers and magazines focu [ ] w [ ] short-term performance. How a fund has done in the last month [ ] 50 [ ] week, however, is of little practical value, because individual [ ] di [ ] bonds—as well as stock and bond funds—usually change in value [ ] It's far more important to see how funds have performed over the l [ ] in [ ] five or ten years, for example. [ ] tl [ ]

Past performance is no guarantee of future results; neverthe [ ] o [ ] funds have consistently performed worse than a standard market [ ] (called a "benchmark") against which funds are typically measur [ ] d [ ] i [ ] n [ ]

**Figure 7.8    Mutual Funds Have Become Dominant Managers of 401(k)s**

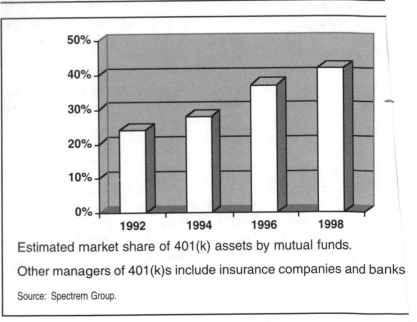

Estimated market share of 401(k) assets by mutual funds.

Other managers of 401(k)s include insurance companies and banks

Source: Spectrem Group.

- The average expense ratio for all the stock funds tracked by Value Line was 1.55 percent.
- The average expense ratio for all the bond funds tracked by Value Line was 1.10 percent.
- Overall, the average expense ratio for all of the mutual funds tracked in the Morningstar database was 1.37 percent.

If an individual fund has an expense ratio that's well above the average, be wary, especially if the fund's performance isn't particularly outstanding. On the other hand, if a fund's expense ratio is at or below average and the fund has a good performance record, you may have a winner.

### Diversifying

Be careful about concentrating your investments in just one area. A survey published in 1999 by the Profit Sharing/401(k) Council of America showed that, on average, workers invest more than 45 percent of plan assets in their own company's stock.

This is dangerous. Sure, you may know a lot about your own company. After all, you work there. Still, you don't know all there is to know. Moreover, your company's stock price may rise or fall independently of the company's true value. When it comes to investing, sticking to something you know well is generally a good idea. However, you should never put all your eggs in one basket. In investing, diversification is critical; spread your money around among different types of funds to reduce risk.

# Drawbacks of 401(k) Plans

It may be hard to think of any drawbacks to 401(k) plans, but they do exist. 401(k) plans have lots of advocates. Indeed, the more money a plan participant has in a 401(k) account, it seems, the more likely he or she is to promote these plans. If your company offers a 401(k) plan, you probably have some of these people in your workplace. They are almost obsessed with their accounts. They calculate their plan values daily, they boast about their returns, and they try get you to invest as much as you possibly can and to put your money in the funds they favor.

Remember, however, that 401(k) plans have some problems. For instance, as a general rule, the money you're saving is your own. 401(k) plans aren't like traditional pension plans, such as the defined benefit plan, which require *employer* contributions (and often prohibit *employee* contributions). At least some of the money that gets contributed to your 401(k) account—in

some cases, *all* the money—comes from your paycheck. As a result, 401(k) plans can't really be called pension plans at all; they're really retirement savings plans. As such, they're best suited for those who can afford to save. For people who can afford to save a lot, the 401(k) plan can be a terrific deal.

The trouble is that some people simply can't afford to sock away money—in a 401(k) plan or in any other type of savings vehicle. They may face huge medical bills or childcare expenses, for example, or they simply don't earn enough money and can barely afford to make ends meet.

For these people, the 401(k) plan is little more than a curiosity. If their employer has no other plan available—such as a traditional pension plan—these people are out of luck: they may wind up with little or nothing to help supplement their Social Security income in retirement.

There are other potential problems with 401(k) plans, too. For instance, some plans fail to adequately disclose information to plan participants. You may be offered a number of different mutual funds as investment choices in your plan, but there's no requirement for your employer to provide you with detailed information, such as a prospectus, about each of the funds. You may get some glossy brochures, but you really need more detail to make a prudent selection.

Keep in mind, too, that the popularity of 401(k) plans hasn't been a secret; investment companies and others know about it, and some of them see 401(k) plans as a great way to generate fee income. When the stock market is generating huge gains, you may not care much about the level of the fees that are charged to your plan. The truth is, however, that fees can cut into the return your account may earn. Fat fees take money right out of your pocket, and you may have little to say about it, especially if your employer isn't

**Figure 7.9**   A Snapshot of 401(k) Accounts

---

✓ Most workers don't contribute the maximum.

✓ Lower-earning participants are more likely to contribute just enough to get the employer matching contribution; higher-earning participants are more likely to contribute the maximum.

✓ Nearly half of participants have account balances with their current employer of less than $10,000; less than 10 percent have balances of more than $100,000.

✓ Those with balances of less than $10,000 tend to be younger workers or those who've worked only a short time with their current employer; those with balances of more than $100,000 tend to be older workers with long tenures.

Source: Employee Benefit Research Institute.

keeping careful track (and you don't have a union or other advocate to fight back).

In addition, although many 401(k) plans offer lots of investment choices, some offer only a few. In some cases, you may be better off saving your money in another type of account, such as a Roth IRA, that can give you more flexibility, as well as greater access to your money should you need it.

## For More Information . . .

- The U.S. Department of Labor has been keeping a close watch on 401(k) fees and publishes several booklets about retirement plans. For more information, call the agency's toll-free publications hotline at 1-800-998-7542, or contact the agency's Web site: <www.dol.gov>.
- The National Association of Investors Corporation (NAIC) is an umbrella organization for more than 36,000 investment clubs nationwide. Membership benefits include a monthly magazine, *Better Investing,* a low-cost investment program, and research services, as well as discounts on educational publications, products, and services. Joining the NAIC through an investment club or as an individual can be a great way to learn more about the world of investing. An individual membership costs about $40 a year. For more details, call 1-877-275-6242, or write to: NAIC, 711 West Thirteen Mile Road, Madison Heights, MI 48071. You also can contact the NAIC Web site: <www.better-investing.org>.
- *Everyone's Money Book,* by Jordan E. Goodman (Chicago: Dearborn Financial Publishing, 1998), is a clearly written, comprehensive book about all issues relating to your money matters. It's a handy how-to guide on issues such as household budgeting; planning and paying for retirement and other long-range goals; and money strategies for each stage of your life. It's also an excellent resource for information on investing. This essential guide deserves a spot on everybody's home bookshelf.
- The T. Rowe Price group publishes the *T. Rowe Price Retirement Planning Kit,* designed for people who have more than five years to go before retirement. It includes a workbook to help you figure out how much money you'll need for retirement and how much you must save to reach your goal. It also offers tips on putting together a retirement investment strategy. Another publication, the *T. Rowe Price Retirees Financial Guide,* is for those who are already retired or who are close to retirement. It includes a workbook to help retirees estimate how much money they can afford to spend in retirement so that they can maintain their standard of living. It takes into account

taxes, inflation, and various sources of retirement income, including Social Security. Both kits are available free by calling 1-800-541-8460, or by writing: T. Rowe Price, P.O. Box 17302, Baltimore, MD 21297-1302.

- The Investment Company Institute in Washington, a trade group for the mutual fund industry, publishes a comprehensive listing of thousands of mutual funds. Its annual directory includes the name, address, and phone number for each fund. The directory is available for about $10. The institute also publishes free brochures and booklets about the basics of mutual fund investing and on other investment topics. One of these, *A Guide to Mutual Funds,* is available in both English and Spanish. For order information, write to: Investment Company Institute, 1401 H Street NW, Washington, DC 20005, or visit the institute's Web site: <www.ici.org>.

- The Mutual Fund Education Alliance, a nonprofit group for mutual funds that are sold directly to the public, also publishes guides and booklets about funds and fund investing. Its Web site has tools to help you learn about, choose, and monitor mutual funds. It also features links to the Web sites of specific mutual funds and has a section you can use to set up and keep track of your own portfolio of funds. Here's the address: <www.mfea.com>.

- The American Association of Individual Investors (AAII) is a nonprofit group that has local chapters throughout the country to help people learn more about investing. You can join one of the chapters or just belong to the national organization. The annual membership fee of about $40 includes a subscription to the *AAII Journal,* a magazine that accepts no advertising and includes articles, charts, and tables for the individual investor. For information, write to: AAII, 625 N. Michigan Avenue, Chicago, IL 60611. You can also get information at the group's Web site: <www.aaii.com>.

- The Vanguard group of mutual funds, of Valley Forge, Pennsylvania, publishes a wide range of clearly written booklets on investing, retirement planning, and other topics. For information, call Van - guard at 1-800-523-8552 or write to: Vanguard, P.O. Box 2600, Valley Forge, PA 19482. If you have access to a computer, visit Vanguard's Web site: <www.vanguard.com>.

# 8

# 401(k) Loans and
# Hardship Withdrawals

If you take part in a 401(k) plan at work, the rules about taking money out of your account are just as important as the rules for putting money into your account. This chapter looks at the rules and strategies for getting access to your account while you're still at work, mainly through 401(k) loans and hardship withdrawals.

## Vesting

It's your money. When can you get it? To find out, first you must know whether you'll have access to all the money in your account or only part of it. In other words, it's important to know something about what the experts call "vesting." You need to know about vesting not only when you're looking to tap into your account, but also when you're deciding if—or when—to leave your job.

When you put money in your 401(k) account, your own contributions are immediately vested. This means you have the legal right to get that money when the time comes, a right you cannot forfeit. This money is yours; you own it.

But what about the money your employer contributes on your behalf? That's another story altogether. Exactly when you can have access to the money that your employer contributes to your account depends on your plan's rules and how long you've been at your job. That's what vesting is all about.

### How Vesting Works

There are three main vesting schedules that employers use:

1. Immediate vesting
2. Graded vesting
3. Cliff vesting

**Figure 8.1**    Graded Vesting

In some 401(k) plans, you gradually become entitled to your employer's contributions to your account—the "graded vesting" method. Seven years is the longest you can be required to wait before you're fully vested, as shown:

| Years of Service | Percent Vested |
|---|---|
| 1 year | 0% |
| 2 years | 0 |
| 3 years | 20 |
| 4 years | 40 |
| 5 years | 60 |
| 6 years | 80 |
| 7 years | 100 |

Source: Internal Revenue Code.

Some plans say that you immediately get the right to the dollars that your employer contributes to your account. This is what's known as "immediate" vesting. About 30 percent of companies say that this money is yours immediately, according to a study by Buck Consultants, a worldwide human resources consulting firm.

With other plans, you must wait awhile. Exactly how long you must wait depends on the plan and the vesting schedule it uses.

In some plans, for example, you become entitled to an increasing percentage of these dollars each year over a certain period of years until you're fully vested. This is what's known as graded vesting: you become vested in stages, over a certain number of years.

From time to time, Congress proposes changes in the rules governing vesting to allow workers to vest more rapidly in their employer's contributions. As of 1999, however, there was one overriding rule: If a plan uses the graded vesting method, seven years is the longest you can be required to wait before you're fully vested.

About 33 percent of plans use some kind of graded vesting schedule, according to the Buck survey. The most common is a five-year graded schedule. Under this schedule, you become vested in stages until you're fully vested after five years.

Other plans use an entirely different method, called "cliff" vesting, to decide when you will be vested in your employer's contributions. Under this method, you become vested all at once, but only after you've worked for the company for a certain number of years. If you stay for the specified num-

**Figure 7.6**   A Variety of Investment Options

At one time, 401(k) plans offered few investment options to participants. Things have changed:

✓ Nearly 40 percent of plans offer ten or more funds into which participants may funnel their contributions.

✓ The average number of funds available is 9.6.

✓ The three most frequently offered types of investment funds are actively managed domestic stock funds, actively managed international stock funds, and balanced stock/bond funds.

Source: Profit Sharing/401(k) Council of America.

guaranteed investment contracts). Keep in mind, however, that your retirement may last a long time, so if you won't need a huge chunk of your 401(k) money right away, consider the balanced approach I recommended for middle-aged investors.

## Staying the Course

No matter which investment strategy you choose or which funds you pick, determine to stay the course. Even if your plan gives you the chance to change investment options frequently—and more than 70 percent of plans allow for daily fund transfers, according to the Profit Sharing/401(k) Council of America—don't be tempted. There's no point in trying to time the market. Even most investment professionals can't do this successfully with any consistency.

The 1990s produced a strong bull market, generating sometimes incredible year-to-year gains. Even while the Dow Jones Industrial Average, the Standard & Poor's 500 Index, and other broad market barometers moved up, however, some mutual funds didn't perform well. Some individual stock sectors, and many individual stocks, either fell behind or lost money. It's impossible for average investors (or professional investors for that matter) to know exactly when the market as a whole, or individual funds or stocks, have hit their peak or hit bottom; for most people, such wisdom comes only in hindsight.

Your best bet, then, is to choose an investment strategy and stick with it. In your early years, you can afford to take more risk by investing more aggressively, in stock mutual funds, for example. As you age and the time for retirement and for withdrawing your money draws near, gradually change

**Figure 7.7**    401(k) Assets in Equities

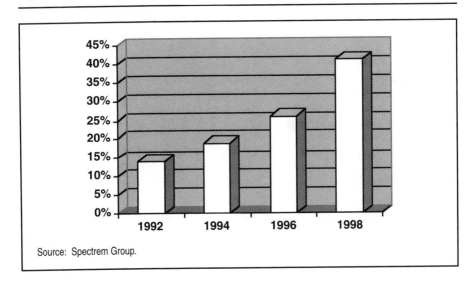

Source: Spectrem Group.

your investment mix to reflect a more conservative strategy. Otherwise, take a hands-off approach. Ignore the market timers, the day-to-day changes in investment values, and all the chatter you hear at work, on the TV and radio, and in newspapers and magazines. Tune out all the noise and stay the course.

## Choosing Specific Options

Once you know *how* to invest your money, you must decide *where* to invest it. This isn't a very difficult step either. Although your employer may offer you a lot of choices, your basic investment strategy can help narrow down the list.

For example, if you've decided to invest mainly in stock funds, you don't have to worry about the more conservative investment options available in your plan. If you've decided to stick mainly with the more conservative choices, such as short-term bond funds and stable-value funds, you don't have to pay as much attention to all the stock funds on the list.

Once you've narrowed your search, you can compare various funds based on such factors as past performance and expenses. Start with the fund prospectuses and other summary information that your employer gives you. If you don't have the information you need, ask for it. If your employer's human resources department or plan administrator doesn't have it, you can ask the funds themselves. (Most funds have toll-free phone numbers; a quick call should get you all the information you need. Many funds also offer the material on their Web sites.)

**Performance.** Next, check your local public library for the information manuals compiled regularly by the Value Line Mutual Fund Survey, of New York, and the Morningstar mutual fund information group, based in Chicago. Value Line or Morningstar will tell you not only how each fund has performed but also how funds have done when compared with similar funds in the same category.

You'll be looking for something called "total return." This figure, expressed as a percentage, generally shows how a fund has performed over a certain period. It takes into account such factors as the increase in the fund's price per share and any dividends the fund has generated for shareholders.

When you consider performance, focus on the long term. The mutual fund tables commonly found in newspapers and magazines focus mainly on short-term performance. How a fund has done in the last month or the last week, however, is of little practical value, because individual stocks and bonds—as well as stock and bond funds—usually change in value frequently. It's far more important to see how funds have performed over the long term— five or ten years, for example.

Past performance is no guarantee of future results; nevertheless, some funds have consistently performed worse than a standard market barometer (called a "benchmark") against which funds are typically measured. If you

**Figure 7.8**  Mutual Funds Have Become Dominant Managers of 401(k)s

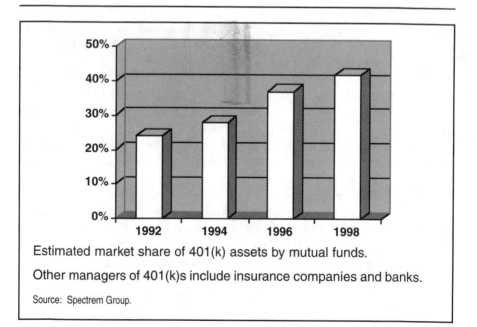

Estimated market share of 401(k) assets by mutual funds.

Other managers of 401(k)s include insurance companies and banks.

Source: Spectrem Group.

find that a fund has consistently done poorly, you may want to stay away. Mutual funds may be the darling of the news media, but stinkers do exist.

It's also true that some funds have consistently performed well when measured both against other funds in the same category and against a standard market benchmark. These are the funds to keep in mind.

One approach to selecting a fund is to simply go with the benchmark itself. Many 401(k) plans now offer at least one "index" fund. This is simply a fund whose fate is tied directly to a well-known stock market barometer, such as the Standard & Poor's 500 index, which follows the stock prices of 500 big companies. When you check the index, you can tell at a glance how all 500 companies, as a group, are doing. (Some people use the S&P 500 as a way to tell how the entire stock market is doing. Even though it tracks just 500 stocks—and there are thousands of stocks—the index is a pretty good indicator of the performance of the stock market as a whole.)

A mutual fund that's tied to the S&P 500 simply buys and holds stock in all 500 companies that make up the index. As a result, if the index goes up, the value of a share in the mutual fund goes up; if the index falls, the value of a share in the mutual fund falls, too.

An index fund is said to be "passively" managed. In other words, it doesn't have a portfolio manager who decides which stocks to buy and sell; it simply buys the stocks in the index, usually relying on a computer to do most of the work.

Investing in an index fund such as one that tracks the S&P 500 can be an effective way to invest in the stock market. In fact, when you invest in an index fund, you can give your money broad domestic and international exposure because many of the companies that make up the index have substantial business interests overseas as well as at home.

**Expenses.** Once you've culled several well-performing funds from the list your employer gives you to choose from, it's a good idea to check on their level of expenses because high expense levels can eat into returns.

Picture a mutual fund as a giant pile of money. At regular intervals, the mutual fund company calculates the value of that pile so it can tell you how much each piece is worth.

Before shareholders get their pieces, however, the mutual fund company takes its piece to cover its costs. In other words, the mutual fund company takes a chunk off of the top of the pile. What's left is divided up by shareholders. The bigger the chunk the mutual fund company takes, the smaller the pieces that are left for you and other shareholders.

Running a mutual fund is expensive, of course, but some funds and fund companies charge more than others. A fund's expenses are typically expressed as a percentage of assets, called the "expense ratio." Here are some industry averages as of late 1999:

some cases, *all* the money—comes from your paycheck. As a result, 401(k) plans can't really be called pension plans at all; they're really retirement savings plans. As such, they're best suited for those who can afford to save. For people who can afford to save a lot, the 401(k) plan can be a terrific deal.

The trouble is that some people simply can't afford to sock away money—in a 401(k) plan or in any other type of savings vehicle. They may face huge medical bills or childcare expenses, for example, or they simply don't earn enough money and can barely afford to make ends meet.

For these people, the 401(k) plan is little more than a curiosity. If their employer has no other plan available—such as a traditional pension plan— these people are out of luck: they may wind up with little or nothing to help supplement their Social Security income in retirement.

There are other potential problems with 401(k) plans, too. For instance, some plans fail to adequately disclose information to plan participants. You may be offered a number of different mutual funds as investment choices in your plan, but there's no requirement for your employer to provide you with detailed information, such as a prospectus, about each of the funds. You may get some glossy brochures, but you really need more detail to make a prudent selection.

Keep in mind, too, that the popularity of 401(k) plans hasn't been a secret; investment companies and others know about it, and some of them see 401(k) plans as a great way to generate fee income. When the stock market is generating huge gains, you may not care much about the level of the fees that are charged to your plan. The truth is, however, that fees can cut into the return your account may earn. Fat fees take money right out of your pocket, and you may have little to say about it, especially if your employer isn't

**Figure 7.9**   A Snapshot of 401(k) Accounts

✓ Most workers don't contribute the maximum.

✓ Lower-earning participants are more likely to contribute just enough to get the employer matching contribution; higher-earning participants are more likely to contribute the maximum.

✓ Nearly half of participants have account balances with their current employer of less than $10,000; less than 10 percent have balances of more than $100,000.

✓ Those with balances of less than $10,000 tend to be younger workers or those who've worked only a short time with their current employer; those with balances of more than $100,000 tend to be older workers with long tenures.

Source: Employee Benefit Research Institute.

ber of years, you get access to 100 percent of the dollars. If you don't, you get access to none of them.

About 31 percent of 401(k) plans use some kind of cliff vesting schedule. The most common is the five-year cliff. This means you must wait five years before you become vested in your employer's contributions. Leave your job before then and you can kiss these dollars goodbye.

## Why Employers Use Vesting

Why have vesting at all? High levels of staff turnover can cost a company money, not just in training and related expenses, but also in administrative costs for employee benefits, including pensions and 401(k) plans. Having a vesting schedule encourages workers to stay on the job longer. This can help cut staff turnover and reduce expenses.

**Figure 8.2** Vesting

---

When it comes time to leave your job, you may lay claim to the money your employer contributed to your 401(k) account only if you've been on the job long enough. How long depends on the vesting schedule your employer requires.

Some companies say the money belongs to you as soon as they contribute it; others make you wait.

| Vesting Schedule | Percent of Employers with 401(k) Plans Offering This Schedule |
|---|---|
| • Immediate | 29% |
| • 1-year cliff | 1 |
| • 2-year cliff | 1 |
| • 3-year cliff | 6 |
| • 4-year cliff | 0 |
| • 5-year cliff | 23 |
| • 3-year graded | 2 |
| • 4-year graded | 4 |
| • 5-year graded | 17 |
| • 6-year graded | 3 |
| • 7-year graded | 7 |
| • Other | 6 |

NOTE: "Cliff" means you become vested all at once at the end of the period; "graded" means you vest in stages.

Source: Buck Consultants Inc.

What does this mean to you? Where possible, you should try to stay on the job at least until you're fully vested. That way, you'll get access to all the money to which you're entitled. (Of course, if you have a better deal elsewhere, go for it; don't let the vesting issue alone hold you back.)

You can find out exactly how long you'll have to wait to be fully vested by reading your employee benefits handbook. Even if you don't have one, the law requires your company to give you an official document known as the "summary plan description," which shows how your 401(k) or other pension plan works.

## How 401(k) Loans Work

"It's my money! Why shouldn't I borrow it? And I'll be paying myself back. That's better than paying a bank!"

These words, or something similar, are heard all the time from workers who take part in 401(k) retirement savings plans. A worker puts money into his or her 401(k) account, saving faithfully year in and year out. Perhaps the

**Figure 8.3**   Most 401(k) Plans Allow for Loans

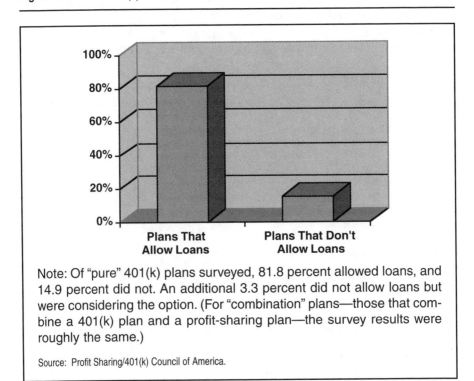

Note: Of "pure" 401(k) plans surveyed, 81.8 percent allowed loans, and 14.9 percent did not. An additional 3.3 percent did not allow loans but were considering the option. (For "combination" plans—those that combine a 401(k) plan and a profit-sharing plan—the survey results were roughly the same.)

Source: Profit Sharing/401(k) Council of America.

employer also throws in some money as a matching contribution, to encourage the worker to save. The account is prudently invested, and its value increases over time.

Then something happens on the home front. There's a roof that needs repairing, a car that needs replacing, a house that needs reshingling. Or maybe a college tuition bill demands payment. Suddenly, you're looking for a ready source of cash. The pile of money stashed away in your 401(k) looks mighty tempting, and when the account statement arrives, it seems to scream out, ever more loudly each time, "Here I am! Take me!"

Can you tap into your 401(k)? Yes.

If you're thinking about borrowing from your 401(k) plan, you'll have to find out whether your plan allows for loans. About 82 percent of plans do, but about 18 percent don't, according to a survey by the Profit Sharing/401(k) Council of America, an industry group. (Just because the law allows 401(k) plans to offer loans doesn't mean that all plans are required to offer them.)

If your plan offers a loan feature, you'll have to get acquainted with its terms and conditions. This information may be available in the employee benefits booklet your employer gives you. If not, you can get the details from your plan administrator or trustee.

Here are some key points about 401(k) loans:

- The most you can borrow is either half of the amount in your account or $50,000, whichever is less. (Technically, that's half of the *vested* amount in your 401(k) account. In other words, you do count

**Figure 8.4**    Most Plans That Let You Borrow Also Require a Minimum Amount

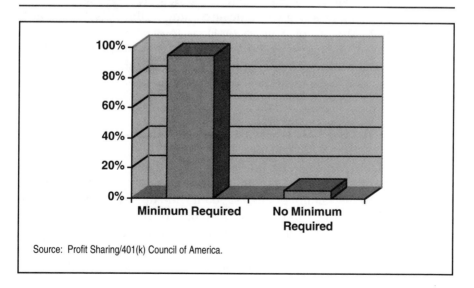

Source: Profit Sharing/401(k) Council of America.

all the contributions you've made plus the amount your contributions have earned. But whether you can also count your employer's contributions—and related earnings—depends on whether you're "vested" in them. This generally depends on how long you've taken part in the plan, and what kind of vesting schedule your employer has in place.)

- You may have to borrow a minimum amount in order to get a loan. That's because processing and keeping track of loans is expensive; a lot of tiny loans drive up a plan's overall administrative cost. (Almost all plans require a minimum dollar amount, according to the Profit Sharing/401(k) Council survey. The most common minimum is $1,000.)

- You'll probably have to fill out some paperwork to get the loan processed. Your company's human resources department will handle the loan, or it will be processed by the outfit your employer has hired to oversee your plan (a mutual fund company, for example). In general, the paperwork is completed fairly easily, and you get your loan promptly. In this respect, 401(k) loans can be easier to get than loans from outside sources, such as banks.

- Federal rules require you to make loan payments at least quarterly, and in equal installments. Most plans require you to pay by payroll deduction, with loan payments deducted from your paycheck each pay period. You also must pay back your loan within five years. If you're using the loan to buy a house, your plan will probably give you a longer time to repay the loan—perhaps as long as 25 years.

- Although the law lets you take more than one loan out on your 401(k) account, about 57 percent of plans permit only one loan to be outstanding at any given time, according to the Buck Consultants survey. (Also, if a plan allows for loans, most employees are eligible. However, you may not be eligible if your company is organized as a so-called Subchapter S corporation or partnership and you're an owner as well as a worker.)

## What 401(k) Loans Can Cost You

Some plans charge fees for processing the loan and keeping track of it. These fees are often added to the amount you borrow, increasing the amount of your loan and the amount of interest you'll wind up paying over the term of the loan. (Not all plans add fees to the amount of your loan, some let you pay the fee yourself, with a check; others deduct the amount from the assets in your 401(k) account.) Altogether, about 70 percent of plans charge a fee for borrowing, according to the Buck Consultants survey. Of these, about half

**Figure 8.5**   Most Plans That Let You Borrow Also Charge a Transaction Fee

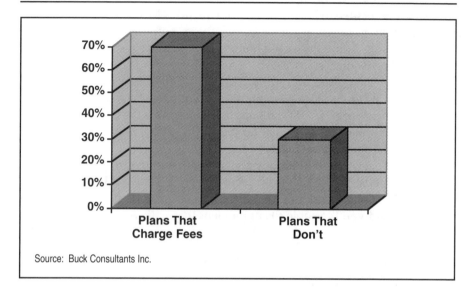

Source: Buck Consultants Inc.

charge a one-time fee, typically $50, but sometimes less. The terms depend on the plan. In some cases, the one-time fee per loan amounts to $100 or more. Some plans not only charge a one-time transaction fee, but also charge ongoing fees annually or quarterly.

Although you may view a 401(k) loan as simply a matter of borrowing from yourself, keep in mind that almost all plans require you to pay interest on your loan. This obviously adds to the cost of repayment and reduces your financial ability to continue contributing to your plan while the loan is outstanding.

Federal rules require plans to charge a "reasonable" rate of interest on plan loans; you can't get a 401(k) loan at a discounted rate. Nearly 90 percent of plans use the so-called prime rate. This is the rate that banks charge their "prime" customers (usually big companies with good credit records). You can check your daily newspaper or contact your bank—or the plan itself—to find out the current prime rate. (The rate changes from time to time, and usually increases—sometimes sharply—in times of inflation.)

About 21 percent of 401(k) plans with loan provisions use the prime rate itself; more than two-thirds of plans use the prime rate as a starting point and add on something extra (usually up to 3 percentage points). In other words, if the current prime rate is 7.5 percent, your plan may wind up charging you as much as 10.5 percent on your loan. This is one reason it's a good idea to check around first before applying for a 401(k) loan; you may be able to get a better deal from a local credit union or community bank, especially one with which you already have a financial relationship.

## Look Elsewhere First

Is it a good idea to borrow from your 401(k)? No. Look to other sources first. Consider borrowing from a credit union, tapping the equity you've built up on your home through a home equity loan, or just tightening your belt by cutting expenses.

Why? As tempting as your 401(k) balance may appear, you must remember that it is there for one main reason: your retirement. That old story about the "three-legged stool" still applies. You can't have just one source of income in retirement. You need at least three to get by: Social Security, your pension, and your own savings.

Social Security will likely supply you with enough to cover only your very basic needs. You'll also need income from a pension. If you're lucky, you'll get regular checks from a traditional pension—a defined benefit pension plan—and you'll be able to supplement that with your 401(k) plan. It's also possible that your 401(k) will be your *only* pension. In either case, why tinker with it now?

True, the ability to borrow from your 401(k) now may seem appealing. The law allows 401(k) plans to offer a loan provision, and most plans do. In fact, far more plans today offer a loan feature than did 15 years ago. Why not take advantage of it?

## Missed Opportunities

There are two main reasons to avoid borrowing from your 401(k). The first has to do with missing an opportunity. True, you'll be paying the loan back to your own account, and whatever rate of interest you pay will be credited to your account, along with the principal. In a sense, then, you will indeed be paying yourself back. Still, the actual cost to you can be enormous, especially when viewed over a long period of time.

For example, what if the rate of interest you'll be paying isn't as high as the amount your money could earn if it stayed in the plan? There's no guarantee, of course, that your account will earn a high rate of return year after year. That depends on how the money is invested and how the investments perform. It is possible, however, that your account will perform well in the long term, and generate a higher rate of return than whatever interest rate you might pay on a loan.

## You May Stop Contributing

An even more important consideration has to do with your contributions. If you borrow, it may be difficult—if not impossible—to continue con-

**Figure 8.6**   Percent of 401(k) Plans Offering a Loan Feature

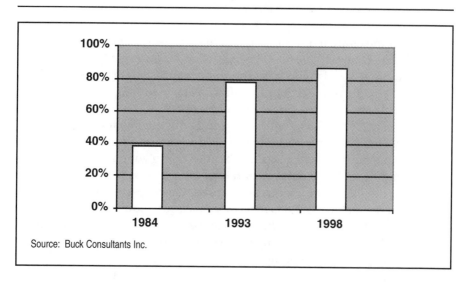

Source: Buck Consultants Inc.

tributing to your account while you're paying on your loan at the same time, or you may not be able to contribute as much as you did before. If your plan allows for matching contributions by your employer, you may wind up missing out on some—or all—of those matching contributions for the entire time that your loan is outstanding. This can amount to a lot of money.

Suppose your employer kicks in 50 cents for every dollar you contribute to your account. As a rule, you contribute $2,000 a year. This means that your employer kicks in an additional $1,000 a year. While you pay back your loan over five years, you decide you can't afford to contribute anything to your plan. As a result, you miss the opportunity to earn $1,000 each year for five years in employer-matching contributions.

## What "Lost" Contributions Can Cost

If your account typically earns an average of 8 percent a year, you pass up a chance at getting an extra $5,867 into your plan over that time, because that's what a $1,000 lump-sum annual matching contribution from your employer would total after five years, earning 8 percent a year.

It doesn't stop there. If you still have another 25 years before retirement, and your account continues to earn an average of 8 percent a year, that $5,867 in "lost" money could have earned enough to total more than $40,000 at retirement time—a nice little addition to your retirement nest egg. This figure doesn't include the amount you would have continued to contribute if you hadn't decided to focus your efforts solely on repaying the loan. Take a look at the total you would have missed out on in this example:

- For the entire five-year term that the loan is outstanding, you decide not to continue contributing your usual $2,000 a year to your account. In other words, you miss the opportunity to add a total of about $11,733 to your account over five years, assuming an 8 percent annual rate of return.
- Because you don't contribute, you're not eligible for your employer's matching contribution of $1,000 a year. As a result, you miss the opportunity to add a total of about $5,867 to your account (again assuming an 8 percent annual rate of return).
- At the end of the five-year loan repayment period, you've missed out on a total of $17,600 that could have been added to your account. Let's assume you still have another 25 years to go until retirement. Had that $17,600 been in your account and earning 8 percent for the entire time until retirement, it would have grown to about $120,532. That's what the experts mean when they talk about lost opportunities.

## Tax Consequences of Borrowing

Don't forget, too, that you use after-tax dollars to pay back your loan. In other words, you get no federal income tax break for borrowing from your 401(k) plan (as you generally would through a home equity loan). This is true even if you borrow from your 401(k) plan to help pay for buying a house.

In order to claim a federal income tax deduction for the interest you pay on a home mortgage loan (or a home equity loan), you must use "secured debt." In other words, you must put your house up as collateral for the loan; from the lender's standpoint, your loan is "secured" by the house. That's usually not true for 401(k) loans; your 401(k) loan is typically secured not by your house, but by the terms of the account itself. Except in the rarest of circumstances, then, you can't claim a tax break on a 401(k) loan that you use to help buy a house. (If you're considering a loan to help buy a house, check whether your plan administrator will let you add your house as security for your 401(k) loan. If you can add your house as security, you'll probably be able to claim a federal income tax deduction for the interest you pay on your 401(k) loan, assuming you meet the other requirements under federal tax law; for example, you must itemize your deductions).

There's another tax point to consider here, too. If you can't afford to continue contributing to your 401(k) plan when you take out a loan, you'll miss the opportunity to lower your adjusted gross income for tax purposes.

Why is this important? Some important federal income tax breaks (and some state income tax breaks, too) are keyed to your adjusted gross income, or AGI. The lower your AGI, the greater your chances of qualifying for these breaks.

For example, in general, the lower your AGI, the more likely you'll be to qualify for some education tax breaks, including the Hope Scholarship or Lifetime Learning credits. By lowering your AGI, you may also be eligible to claim a deduction—or more of a deduction—for such things as unreimbursed medical expenses.

# If You Lose Your Job Before You Pay Off Your 401(k) Loan

If you're still thinking about borrowing from your 401(k) plan, there's an even bigger tax issue to think about: What happens if you can't repay the loan? Indeed, this may be the most important factor in your decision.

Ordinarily, you pay back a 401(k) loan through payroll deduction. In other words, each pay period, your employer automatically deducts a certain amount from your paycheck, after taxes, to cover the principal and interest on your 401(k) loan installment. As long as you're employed, you make the payments each pay period until the loan is paid in full.

The key to this, however, is your continued employment. As long as you keep the job and keep making payments, you're all set. But what happens if you lose your job? You trigger all sorts of messy problems, including some potentially painful tax consequences.

First, when you leave your job, your loan typically comes due in full. More than two-thirds of all 401(k) plans require outstanding balances to be paid in full when a worker leaves his or her job, according to Buck Consultants. (Only about 17 percent of plans let you continue to make loan payments outside of payroll deduction; 16 percent of plans allow for other arrangements.)

If you have the financial resources to pay the loan off on the spot, you're all set. (Some employers will give you a brief grace period to pay off the loan, perhaps 30 days.) Chances are, however, that you won't have enough ready cash available to pay off the loan (which is probably why you had to borrow in the first place).

## When a Loan Becomes a Withdrawal

If you can't pay off your loan in full immediately—or within a brief grace period—after you leave your job, things can get complicated pretty quickly. The IRS will treat the entire outstanding balance as a taxable distribution. In other words, from the standpoint of the IRS, it'll be as if you've withdrawn a sum from your account equal to the amount that remains outstanding on your loan.

As a result, you'll have to pay federal income tax on the entire amount, plus a 10 percent early withdrawal penalty (unless you qualify for one of the few exceptions under penalty rules—you're 59½ or older, or you're disabled, for example).

Why not just use the rest of the money in your 401(k) plan to pay the outstanding balance on the loan? You may have that option, depending on how soon the plan lets you have the rest of your money once you leave work (some plans make you wait awhile). This strategy, however, will only trigger more tax problems. In general, if you don't roll over plan balances directly to an IRA or another plan that accepts rollovers, your employer must—by law— withhold 20 percent of the payout.

Why? The government assumes in these cases that you're not going to roll over the money; you're going to spend the money, so you're going to have to pay a federal income tax on it (even if you use it to pay off the outstanding balance on your 401(k) loan). Therefore, the government wants to be paid at least some of the tax up front, in the form of withholding.

You can see the mess you can wind up facing. To avoid tax problems resulting from the outstanding balance on your 401(k) loan, you use some or all of the rest of your 401(k) money to pay off the loan. This solves one tax problem but creates another. The second problem can be just as nasty as the first, even more so. From the government's standpoint in such cases, every dollar from your 401(k) that you fail to roll over, either to an IRA or to another employer's plan, is considered a taxable withdrawal.

To avoid the tax (and the possible 10 percent penalty on early withdrawals) in this situation, you must scramble to find enough money from other sources to put into an IRA or another employer's plan, and do it within the 60-day deadline required for rollovers. You must find enough money to cover not only the amount you actually used to pay off your loan, but also the 20 percent that your employer withheld. (If you complete this entire process, you'll get the withheld amount back at tax time as a refund.) Pulling all this money together is a tall order, however.

Can you afford to deal with these tax consequences, especially at a time when you're under a lot of financial and emotional stress from losing your job? Unless you can immediately find another job, odds are you'll have lots of other things to worry about, and lots of other demands for your money, besides dealing with an outstanding 401(k) loan.

If you fail to deal with these tax consequences quickly enough, you could face even more pressure: you may have to make an estimated tax payment quickly to cover your tax liability, or face interest and penalties. In other words, you may not be able to wait until tax-filing season to square your debt to the IRS; you may have to fess up immediately by filing a quarterly estimated tax payment with the IRS (and with your state, too, depending on where you live).

Borrowing from your 401(k) plan at work can be an easy procedure. The money's there, the paperwork required is minimal in most cases, you will probably receive your loan proceeds quickly, and you typically will get to pay the loan back through the convenience of payroll deduction.

Before borrowing, however, you have to think about what would happen if you lost your job because of a layoff, downsizing, a cutback, or any other circumstance. Would your employer require you to pay off the loan balance in full immediately? Most do. Would you have the financial resources to pay off the loan? If not, you'll face big tax problems.

How secure are you in your job? If you're confident that your job will be there for as long as it takes to pay off the loan, you needn't worry about the tax implications. Still, how many workers can say with certainty that their jobs are secure?

## How Hardship Withdrawals Work

Another way to pull money out of your 401(k) plan is through something the experts call an "in-service withdrawal." In other words, a plan may let you withdraw money from your account while you're still working.

Some plans let you withdraw money at any time for just about any reason. Your plan, however, may impose limits. For example, you may be eligible to withdraw money while you're still working only if you've been at the job a certain number of years. Or you may be able to make withdrawals while you're still working only if you've reached age 59½, because at that point your withdrawals won't be subject to the 10 percent early withdrawal penalty (although they will be subject to income tax).

The terms under which you may withdraw money from your 401(k) account while still working are spelled out in the booklet or brochure your employer gives you that describes how your plan works, known as the "summary plan description." By law, the only kind of in-service withdrawal that a pure 401(k) plan can offer is a hardship withdrawal; profit-sharing plans and "combination" type plans—those that combine a 401(k) and a profit-sharing plan—can offer other types of in-service withdrawals.

If your plan allows you to make a hardship withdrawal (technically called a "hardship distribution"), you'll have to find out exactly what your plan views as a hardship. There are some general rules that pretty much apply to all plans that allow hardship withdrawals. For example, a hardship withdrawal qualifies under U.S. Treasury regulations if it's made "on account of

**Figure 8.7**    Most Plans Allow Hardship Withdrawals

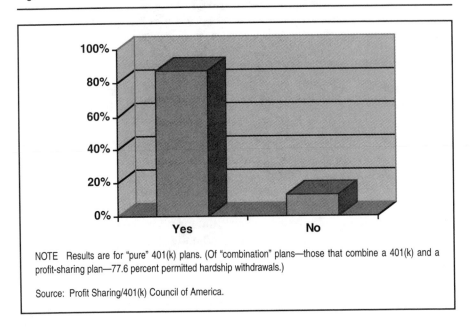

NOTE   Results are for "pure" 401(k) plans. (Of "combination" plans—those that combine a 401(k) and a profit-sharing plan—77.6 percent permitted hardship withdrawals.)

Source: Profit Sharing/401(k) Council of America.

an immediate and heavy financial need of the employee and is necessary to satisfy the financial need." What exactly does that mean? The government regulations generally say it depends on the facts and circumstances of each worker's situation. For instance, "the need to pay the funeral expenses of a family member would constitute an immediate and heavy financial need," according to the regulations. However, a worker's plan to use the money "for the purchase of a boat or television would generally not" count as "an immediate and heavy financial need," Treasury regulations say.

### You Must Exhaust All Options

To make a hardship withdrawal, you must show that you have no other financial resources to cover the need. In other words, you must first exhaust just about all other possible sources of funds before you can make a hardship withdrawal. These include insurance payments or reimbursements, liquidation of your assets, loans "from commercial sources on reasonable commercial terms," and loans or other withdrawals available from another plan at this or any other job.

You have to look not only at your own financial resources, but also at those assets that are "reasonably available" to you from your spouse or your minor children. (The Treasury regulations are fairly straightforward on this point. If you and your spouse have a vacation home, that counts as a financial resource; assets in an irrevocable trust or a Uniform Gifts to Minors Act custodial account do not count.)

## Reasons for Hardship Withdrawals

The government doesn't review each and every application for a hardship withdrawal. Instead, it generally leaves it to the plan itself to make the decision.

Still, Treasury regulations say that a plan may generally permit a hardship withdrawal to pay for these expenses:

- Medical care—for you, your spouse, or your dependents. (It can be for medical care that you or a family member has already received, or for care you or a family member needs to get.)
- Tuition, related educational fees, and room and board expenses for the next 12 months of "post-secondary" (college) education for you, your spouse, or your dependents.
- Costs directly related to your purchase of a "principal residence" (not a vacation home or second home).
- Payments that are needed to prevent your eviction from your principal residence, or to prevent foreclosure on the mortgage of that residence.

**Figure 8.8**   Hardship Withdrawals for Medical Care

The government generally lets you make a hardship withdrawal from your 401(k) plan for medical care for you, your spouse, or your dependents, for things such as

✓ the diagnosis, cure, mitigation, treatment, or prevention of disease;

✓ transportation that's mainly for (and essential to) medical care;

✓ lodging away from home (within limits), if it's related to care provided by a doctor in a licensed hospital or medical facility;

✓ qualified long-term care services; and

✓ insurance covering medical care, or a qualified long-term care insurance contract (within limits).

Sources: Internal Revenue Code; U.S. Treasury.

These are the main reasons for which 401(k) plans permit hardship withdrawals. There are also less common reasons, including expenses related to a divorce or adoption; payment of alimony, child support, or tax liens; and expenses involved in recovering from a natural disaster, according to a survey by Buck Consultants.

Although your plan may allow for hardship withdrawals, you can't just yank your money out; there are some important details you must consider. For example, you'll probably be prohibited from making contributions to your plan for at least 12 months after you've received the money from your hardship withdrawal.

Furthermore, your employer will probably require you to get your spouse's consent before you make the hardship withdrawal.

## Tax Impact of Withdrawals

There are taxes to consider, too. As a general rule, money that you contribute to a 401(k) plan isn't taxed on the way in; it's taxed on the way out, when it's withdrawn. This general rule applies to money you take out for your retirement, of course, but it also applies to hardship withdrawals. In other words, just because you face a hardship doesn't mean you can avoid the tax consequences of your withdrawal.

The amount you withdraw under your plan's hardship feature will be subject to federal income tax and may be slapped with state income tax, too, depending on your state's tax rules.

In addition, your withdrawal will be subject to a 10 percent early withdrawal penalty. You may be able to escape the penalty if you qualify for an exception under the penalty rules—you're 59½ or older or you've become disabled, for example. Otherwise you're stuck. Under a federal law passed in 1998, you can't roll over a hardship withdrawal to an IRA to escape the 10 percent penalty. There is, however, a silver lining in this rule: hardship withdrawals aren't subject to mandatory 20 percent withholding as other types of withdrawals are.

Once the money comes out of your account through a hardship withdrawal, the tax rules kick in. (Your employer may let you add enough money to your hardship withdrawal to pay any income taxes or penalties that you can "reasonably expect" to pay as a result of the withdrawal, government regulations say.)

# For More Information . . .

- The 401(k) Association, headed by R. Theodore Benna, the acknowledged "father" of the 401(k), publishes a quarterly newsletter about 401(k) plans, the *401(k) Update.* Among other things, the newsletter keeps track of tax law changes (and proposed changes) that could affect your 401(k) plan. For information, write to: 401(k) Association, 1118 Pine Hill Road, Cross Fork, PA 17729. Benna also is a regular contributor to a Web site that's devoted to 401(k) plans and which often tackles some of the thornier issues, including 401(k) loans and hardship withdrawals: <www.401kafe.com>.

# 9

# 401(k) Plans
# versus Roth IRAs

There's no doubt about it: using a retirement savings plan at work such as a 401(k) has lots of benefits. Still, it may not be your best option. In some cases, it may be better to invest outside your company's plan, either in a Roth IRA or in a regular taxable account (such as a regular brokerage account).

The decision to forego saving through an employer-sponsored plan is a big one. You shouldn't make it before you carefully consider all the benefits your plan may offer you, some or all of which you may have to give up should you decide to save elsewhere.

Because 401(k) plans are so popular and are in place at so many companies, this chapter compares 401(k) plans to some alternatives outside the work place, such as the Roth IRA and the regular taxable account. Nevertheless, the principles that apply to 401(k) plans also apply to other company-sponsored plans that work in much the same way, such as 403(b) plans (used by many schools, hospitals, and nonprofit organizations); Section 457 plans, (used by many government agencies); and SEP, SIMPLE, Keogh, and other retirement plans (offered mainly by small businesses).

## Advantages of 401(k) Plans

By saving through a 401(k), you may be eligible for a bunch of benefits. For instance:

- You contribute pre-tax dollars.
- Your employer may contribute an additional amount on your behalf.
- You may be able to contribute conveniently through payroll deduction.
- You may like the investment options your plan provides, options that may not be available to you outside the plan. (For instance, the mighty Fidelity Magellan mutual fund—and some other funds—are generally closed to new investors, but continue to accept money invested through retirement plans, including 401(k) plans.)

- You may be able to borrow from your account, if your plan allows. (This can be a convenient way to borrow, often requiring little paperwork and providing a quick turnaround for processing and a reasonable interest rate, and you can pay the loan back with the convenience of payroll deduction.)
- Your plan may allow for "hardship" distributions. This means you may be able to withdraw at least some of the money in your account if, according to your plan's rules, you face an "immediate and heavy financial need."
- Because of tax rules, 401(k) plans generally "lock in" your money. They offer a kind of forced savings program, which may be especially appealing if you lack the discipline to save on your own.
- Although you must withdraw money from your plan at some point, the rule is generally more liberal for 401(k) plans than for traditional IRAs. In general, you must begin withdrawing from an IRA by April 1 of the year following the year in which you reach age 70½. That used to be the rule for company-sponsored retirement plans, too, including 401(k) plans, even if you kept working. But in 1996, Congress changed the rule. As a result, if you keep working, you can now postpone required withdrawals until April 1 of the year following the year in which you retire from employment with the company that has your plan. (The more liberal requirement for most employer-sponsored plans does not apply to people who own 5 percent or more of their company. For them, the age 70½ rule remains in effect—even if they keep working.)

## Disadvantages of 401(k) Plans

With all these benefits, why bother looking elsewhere? There can be lots of reasons.

For instance, you may have no choice in the matter; you may *have* to look for alternatives, especially if you've reached the limits of your 401(k) plan.

One of these limits has to do with the amount you may contribute. The limit was set at $10,000 for 1999 and at $10,500 for 2000. (Late each year, the Internal Revenue Service posts the limit that will apply for the following year. To find out the current limit, call the IRS at 1-800-829-1040.)

There's another, lesser-known limit you may be bumping up against, too. It's an overall limit on the amount that can be funneled into your account each year.

This cap restricts the so-called "annual additions" that can be made to your account each year. It applies to the total of your contributions, your employer's contributions, any after-tax contributions you may be allowed to make, and any "forfeitures" that may be credited to your account. (A forfeiture may occur because other plan participants leave before they've earned the right to take their employer contributions with them; these leftovers are split up among other plan participants, including you.)

The limit on annual additions is generally 25 percent of your compensation or $30,000, whichever is less.

Therefore, if you're one of those rare supersavers who stashes away every possible penny in your 401(k) plan, you may "max out" your plan; then you must look at other options.

Even if you haven't reached your plan's limits, your particular plan may simply be a poor one for any of a variety of reasons. For example:

- Although the number of investment options offered by the average plan has grown in recent years, the number offered by your plan may be too few to suit you.
- The funds you have to choose from may be lousy performers.
- Your employer may contribute very little—if anything—to your plan.
- The fees and expenses your plan charges may be too high, eating away year after year at your nest egg.
- The material your plan provides may not disclose enough information about your investment options. You may not receive the official offering document, called a prospectus, for each of the mutual funds offered through your plan.
- You don't get account statements often enough, or the account statements you do receive are too hard to understand.
- The plan may have too many restrictions on how you can access your money.

For these and other reasons, your 401(k) plan may not appeal to you, and you may be better off looking elsewhere, not just for financial reasons, but for practical reasons, too. You may simply feel more comfortable saving *your* way, not according to the limits imposed by somebody else.

## Roth IRAs

What should you do if you choose not to invest in your company's 401(k) plan? One alternative is the Roth IRA. Although Roth IRAs are fairly new—the law creating them was passed in 1997, and Roth accounts first became available in 1998—they have a lot of nice features, chief among them your ability to make tax-free and penalty-free withdrawals.

The Roth has its own restrictions, of course. Here are some of the limits and potential drawbacks:

- Contributions to your Roth IRA are not tax deductible, but earnings accrue tax-free.
- The most you may contribute in any year is $2,000 or all of your compensation, whichever is less.
- You may contribute only if your income is less than $110,000 (if you're single) or $160,000 (if you're married and filing a joint federal income tax return).
- Although you may withdraw your contributions at any time without penalty or tax, there are restrictions on the withdrawal of earnings. In general, earnings may be withdrawn free of tax and penalty only if you've had the account for at least five years *and* the withdrawal occurs under any of these circumstances: you've reached age 59½, you're disabled, you've died, or you use the money (up to a $10,000 lifetime limit) to pay for first-time homebuyer expenses.

What's the big deal about Roth IRAs? The potential benefits are almost astounding. Again, you may withdraw your contributions whenever you want, for whatever reason, without tax or penalty. And although there are restrictions on the withdrawal of earnings, the rules may not pose a problem for you because of your circumstances (you plan to buy a house, for instance, or you're already 59½).

Don't forget, too, that Roth IRA withdrawals that meet the rules—and the rules aren't all that hard to meet—will come out entirely free of tax and penalty.

Compare that with your 401(k) plan, or even with a traditional IRA: in general, money you withdraw from those accounts is treated as ordinary income and is subject to federal income tax. As a result, withdrawals may face federal tax rates as high as 39.6 percent, depending on your circumstances.

The tax treatment of withdrawals isn't the only benefit that the Roth IRA offers. One of the Roth's most talked-about features is its extraordinary flexibility: almost every bank, savings and loan, credit union, mutual fund company, brokerage, and insurance company offers Roth IRAs, so you have lots of investment options from which to choose—probably far more than your 401(k) plan offers you.

## Directing Roth Investments Yourself

You may also open a so-called self-directed Roth IRA at a brokerage. This puts you in charge of all the investment decisions. You can pick and choose the types of investments you want—certain stocks, for instance, or certain bonds. You'll face commissions and fees on your trades, of course, and the more you trade, the more you'll generally pay. Nevertheless, this type of account can offer you maximum control over exactly how your dollars will be put to work.

In addition, there are literally hundreds of companies in which you can invest directly, buying your first and later shares from the company itself. With these direct share purchase plans, sometimes called no-load stock programs, you bypass brokerages and save on commissions, and some of these plans let you set up a Roth IRA directly with them (or their intermediaries, known as transfer agents). Many of these direct share purchase plans charge fees, but you'll generally pay less than if you invest through a brokerage.

Another advantage to Roth IRAs is their accessibility: you generally can get access to the money in your account (particularly your contributions) whenever you like. This is in stark contrast to the typical 401(k) plan, which may give you access only when you retire or lose your job (although some plans allow for loans and hardship withdrawals).

**Figure 9.1**  Direct Share Purchase Plans

---

You may buy your first and subsequent shares directly from these companies, bypassing brokerages and saving on commissions. These plans also let you set up an IRA to hold your shares.

| Company | Phone Number |
|---|---|
| Bell Atlantic | 1-800-631-2355 |
| Exxon Mobil | 1-800-252-1800 |
| Fannie Mae | 1-888-289-3266 |
| Ford Motor Company | 1-800-955-4791 |
| Lucent Technologies | 1-800-774-4117 |
| McDonald's | 1-800-228-9623 |
| Philadelphia Suburban | 1-800-774-4117 |
| Sears | 1-888-732-7780 |
| Wal-Mart | 1-800-438-6278 |

The phone number may connect to the company, its transfer agent, or a clearinghouse. Ask for a prospectus and enrollment information, and compare fees.

Source: *No-Load Stock Insider* newsletter.

### Withdrawals Aren't Required

You need never withdraw money from your Roth IRA if you don't want to; you may leave the money in your account as long as you like—even until you die, after which your beneficiaries may pull out the money in a lump sum, free of tax and penalty, or make periodic withdrawals, also free of tax and penalty, while allowing the balance to continue to grow.

Compare that advantage to your 401(k) plan, which generally requires you to start making withdrawals (probably all of them taxable) at about the time you reach age 70½ (unless you continue working and are not a 5 percent owner of your company).

True, contributing to a Roth IRA gives you no immediate tax benefit because your contributions aren't tax deductible as they are with a 401(k) plan or a traditional IRA. Still, the tax deduction that a 401(k) offers may not be such a big deal if you're not in a high income tax bracket.

# Comparing 401(k)s with Roth IRAs

Comparing these options from a tax perspective can be tricky business, because there are all sorts of variables to consider. But there are some rules-of-thumb that can help.

For instance, if you expect to be in the same federal income tax bracket when you retire as you are when you contribute, a 401(k) and a Roth IRA leave you in pretty much the same financial condition.

Let's assume you're in the 15 percent tax bracket now and you'll be in the same bracket when you retire. You contribute $2,000 a year (pre-tax) to a 401(k), and $1,700 a year (after tax) to a Roth IRA. You earn an average of

**Figure 9.2**   The 15% Federal Income Tax Bracket

| Filing Status | Taxable Income |
|---|---|
| Single | up to $26,250 |
| Married (filing jointly) | up to $43,850 |
| Married (filing separately) | up to $21,925 |
| Head of household | up to $35,150 |

Note: Figures are for the 2000 tax year.

Source: Internal Revenue Service.

8 percent a year in each, contribute for a total of five years, and are in the 15 percent federal tax bracket.

At the end of the period, you wind up with $11,733 in the 401(k), but after withdrawing the money (in a lump sum) and paying the tax, you're left with about $9,973.

What about the Roth IRA? The answer's the same: $9,973. That's because you put after-tax dollars into your Roth IRA, and you won't be taxed again on the money when you withdraw. (You'll never be taxed or penalized for withdrawing your contributions, and you may avoid tax and penalty for withdrawing earnings if you meet the rules—if you're 59½, for example.)

Purely from a tax standpoint, the 401(k) is a winner in some cases; in other cases, the Roth IRA has the advantage.

## When a 401(k) May Be Best

Here are some instances in which contributing to a 401(k) plan may be best:

- If you figure you'll be in a lower federal income tax bracket when you retire than when you contribute, the 401(k) can be a better deal. (You'll get a big tax break for contributing, and you generally won't have to pay much tax when you withdraw.)
- If you need other tax breaks, the 401(k) may be better. That's because when you contribute, you lower your adjusted gross income. The types of deductions, credits, and other benefits you may claim is generally tied to the amount of your adjusted gross income. If you can cut your adjusted gross income, you may be able to claim more itemized deductions, be in a better position to take advantage of benefits like the Hope Scholarship and Lifetime Learning tax credits, and be eligible for the $500-per-child tax credit.

## When a Roth IRA May Be Best

In some cases, the Roth IRA may be a better deal. Here are some examples:

- If you figure you'll be in a higher tax bracket upon retirement than you are when you contribute, the Roth IRA generally makes more sense (because if you meet the rules, Roth IRA withdrawals aren't taxed, whereas 401(k) withdrawals are).
- If you expect to withdraw money in retirement, and your financial circumstances are such that you'll be triggering a tax on your Social

Security benefits, the Roth IRA may be a better choice. That's because withdrawals from a 401(k) add to your income for purposes of calculating tax on your Social Security benefits; Roth IRA withdrawals don't.

- If you don't expect to need your IRA money in retirement, and you plan to use your account mainly as a way to build wealth and pass it along to the next generation (or to some other beneficiaries), the Roth IRA is the better choice. That's because withdrawals from 401(k) plans are mandatory after a certain point; withdrawals from Roth IRAs aren't.
- If you don't want to deal with the various formulas and calculations you'll face when you must start taking mandatory withdrawals from a 401(k), the Roth IRA wins easily.

Even if the Roth IRA doesn't appeal to you, a regular taxable account may be more attractive to you than your 401(k) plan—especially if you want some control over your tax destiny.

The 401(k) and Roth IRA certainly have their attractions, and the ability to accrue earnings on a tax-deferred or tax-free basis can be hard to beat. Because of their tax features, their broad appeal, and even their complexity, 401(k) plans and Roth IRAs get lots of attention in the media.

Don't forget about investing directly in stocks, however. They offer lots of flexibility and other features, not to mention some seldom-publicized tax benefits.

## Investing in Individual Stocks

When you invest in individual stocks, the world is literally within your reach. You can choose from thousands of domestic stocks and from equities of thousands more foreign companies.

There are all sorts of ways to invest, too. If you use a full-service brokerage, for example, you'll generally pay the most in commissions and other fees, but you're also typically entitled to a broker's recommendations and other advice, as well as to the brokerage's research and other services. If you use a discount brokerage, you'll typically pay somewhat less in commissions and fees, and you may be entitled to a limited amount of research and other services. With a deep-discount brokerage, you may be charged the lowest commissions and fees, and you'll typically get the least amount of services. There are also hundreds of companies in which you can invest directly instead of going through a brokerage.

You may invest by visiting a brokerage office in person, by using a toll-free phone number, or by trading online—with a computer and modem for Internet access. It all depends on what type of investor you are and what your needs are.

## Diamonds and Spiders

If you like to invest in stock market indexes instead of holding a bunch of individual stocks, you don't have to go through an indexed mutual fund; you can invest in individual stocks that represent an underlying portfolio of shares in an index (see Figure 9.3).

For example, one of the most actively traded stocks on the American Stock Exchange is the Standard & Poor's Depository Receipt, also known as the SPDR, or "Spider." Each share represents one-tenth of the S&P 500, the well-known stock market barometer that indexes 500 of the largest and best-known common stocks. When you invest in a Spider, you hold a piece of a trust that, in turn, owns shares of all of the stocks that make up the S&P 500 index.

You may also buy shares (known as Diamonds) in a trust that holds shares of the 30 blue-chip stocks that make up the Dow Jones Industrial Average. World Equity Benchmark Shares (WEBS) are another option. WEBS are shares in trusts that hold the stock of companies that make up the index of stocks in another country, such as Canada or the United Kingdom.

## Hidden Tax Benefits

By investing in individual stocks, you may also take advantage of tax benefits that aren't publicized as much as those for 401(k) plans and IRAs.

When you buy stocks, you don't get a tax deduction for the amount you invest, of course, but any increase in the value of your holdings won't be taxed until you sell. In other words, investing in stocks gives you automatic tax

**Figure 9.3**   Investing in Indexes

Instead of investing in indexed mutual funds, which track well-known stock market benchmarks such as the Dow Jones Industrial Average or Standard & Poor's 500 Index, you can invest in individual stocks that do the same thing.

| Stock | Symbol |
|---|---|
| **Diamonds:** Shares that are invested in a portfolio of stocks that represent the Dow Jones Industrial Average | DIA |
| **Spiders:** Shares that are invested in a portfolio of stocks that represent Standard & Poors 500 Index | SPY |
| **WEBS:** Shares that are invested in a portfolio of stocks that represent a stock index in a foreign country | (Varies) |

deferral. Of course, a stock may pay dividends, and dividends are taxed as ordinary income at rates as high as 39.6 percent.

Still, most people don't invest in stocks only for income; they're looking for growth, for something the experts call "price appreciation." You want the market value of your shares to increase so you can profit. There's a big difference, however, between paper profit and taxable profit.

If the price of your shares increases while you hold them, you have what's known as paper profit—your gain is all on paper, either on your account statement or on records you keep yourself. It is only when you sell some or all of your shares that you record an actual profit, and it is then that the IRS becomes interested because it wants a piece of your profit. Just remember that you can sit on your paper profits as long as you want to—you need never cash out if you don't want to.

If you do sell, your profit will generally be the difference between the price you paid and the price at which you sold. You may qualify for favorable tax treatment of your profit, known as "capital gains" treatment. Whether you do depends on your "holding period," or how long you've held your stock.

In general, if you sell shares you've held for one year or less, your profit will be treated as short term and will be taxed as ordinary income, at rates as high as 39.6 percent.

If you sell shares you've held for more than a year, however, your profit will be considered long term, and you'll qualify for what's known as long-term capital gains treatment. In other words, you'll be taxed at lower rates. This is one of the big benefits to selling stock you've held for a long time.

- In general, if your federal income tax bracket is 28 percent or higher, the most you'll pay in long-term capital gains tax is 20 percent. Starting in 2001, the maximum capital gains tax rate falls, but there's a twist. The top rate will be 18 percent on stock you've held more than five years, but this treatment is generally available only for stock you bought in 2000 and held five years. (In other words, you won't be able to take advantage of the 18 percent rate until 2005.)
- If you're in the 15 percent federal income tax bracket, the most you'll pay on long-term capital gains is 10 percent. Starting in 2001, this maximum rate drops to 8 percent on stock you've held more than five years, and doesn't matter when you bought the stock.

## Claiming Your Losses

Another key advantage to investing in stocks outside a 401(k) plan or an IRA has to do with losses.

Let's face it: stock prices don't always go up. Even if there are increases in the barometers that investors use to measure the market's direction—the Dow Jones Industrial Average, for instance, or a Standard & Poor's index—it doesn't necessarily mean that your stock will increase in value, too. Your stock may rise and fall independently of what the market averages indicate.

What if your stock falls in value from the time you bought it to the time you sell? In that case, you can claim what's known as a capital loss. Why is that important? In general, you may use all of your losses to offset all of your gains. If you have a profit from the sale of one stock, but a loss on the sale of another, you may use the loss to offset the gain for tax purposes.

What if you have some loss left over? You may use it to reduce your ordinary income for tax purposes (up to $3,000 in any given year), and you may also carry forward any "excess" loss to future years to offset gains or reduce ordinary income. You can't do this with a 401(k) plan or a Roth IRA. Getting a tax benefit for losses you suffer on an investment is a big selling point for investing in stocks outside a tax-sheltered plan such as a 401(k) or Roth IRA.

## The Stepped-Up Basis

Another tax benefit comes when you die. It has to do with something called "basis," which you must use in figuring out your taxable profit. Ordinarily, your basis is whatever you paid for your stock. If you originally invested $1,000, and you sell the stock many years later for $10,000, your basis is $1,000. To see how much profit you've made for tax purposes, you subtract your basis ($1,000) from the price you got when you sold ($10,000). The answer, in this example, is $9,000.

What if you hold the stock until your death? What basis will your heirs get in the stock? It's generally the market value of the stock on the date of your death. Suppose, then, that your heirs receive the stock in the example above, then immediately sell it for $10,000. They'll pay no tax, because their stepped-up basis ($10,000) is the same as their selling price ($10,000).

That's not true for 401(k) plans. Someone who inherits your 401(k) plan uses your original basis; they don't get a stepped-up basis. And because you probably didn't contribute any after-tax dollars to your 401(k) plan (although some plans do allow after-tax contributions), your beneficiaries will pay tax—as ordinary income—on the amounts they withdraw. (Roth IRAs work differently: in general, your beneficiaries will pay no tax on money they withdraw from an inherited Roth IRA.)

Here's another way to look at it: By investing in stocks outside of a 401(k) plan or an IRA (whether a traditional IRA or Roth IRA), you still get tax benefits, without all of the rules and other complications. In addition,

**Figure 9.4**   Comparing Investment Options

| | 401(k) | Roth IRA | Individual Stocks |
|---|---|---|---|
| Tax-deductible contributions | Yes | No | No |
| Tax-deferred growth | Yes | Yes | Yes |
| Withdrawals taxed | Yes | Maybe | Yes |
| Capital-gains tax treatment | No | No | Yes |
| Tax-free withdrawals possible | No | Yes | No |
| Stepped-up basis for heirs | No | No | Yes |
| Includable in your taxable estate | Yes | Yes | Yes |
| Many investment options | Maybe | Yes | Yes |
| Limits on annual contributions | Yes | Yes | No |
| Contributions limited by income | Maybe | Yes | No |
| Limits on access to money | Yes | No | No |
| Protection from creditors | Yes | Maybe | No |

Note: 401(k) plans allow for matching contribution by employer. Your contribution—and overall contributions—may be limited by your plan or by law. Certain types of favorable tax treatment may be available for 401(k) withdrawals, within limits. Contributions to Roth IRAs may be withdrawn at any time without tax or penalty, although withdrawn earnings may be taxed and penalized if you don't meet the rules. Stocks held more than a year qualify for favorable capital gains tax treatment when sold; otherwise, profit from a sale is generally treated as ordinary income. Only Roth IRAs allow for possible tax-free and penalty-free withdrawals. Annual contributions to 401(k)s are generally limited to $10,500 a year; Roth IRA contributions are generally limited to $2,000 a year (and are not allowed if you have no earned income, or if your modified adjusted gross income exceeds $110,000 if you're single, or $160,000 if you're married.)

you have far more control over your tax situation: whether you pay a tax depends on whether you sell your stock.

## Investing in Mutual Funds

The benefits of investing in individual stocks outside of a 401(k) plan generally apply to mutual funds, too.

Mutual funds are really investment companies that pool the money they get from you and other investors and use it to buy stocks, bonds, and other investment vehicles. Mutual funds are popular in part because investors are generally assured that their money is being invested by professionals, and because they automatically get what's known as diversification. In other words, investors are not putting all their money into just a few stocks; mutual funds use investor money to buy lots of individual stocks, more than each investor could probably afford to buy on his or her own. This

**Figure 9.5**    401(k) Assets in Mutual Funds

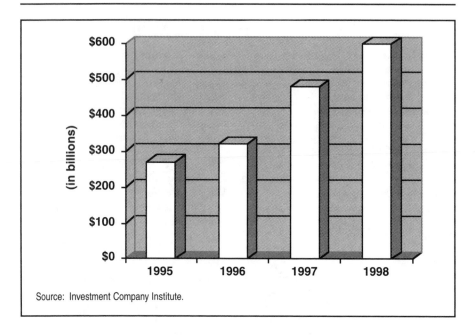

Source: Investment Company Institute.

is one reason why mutual funds are such a popular investment option for 401(k) plans.

There are thousands of mutual funds available, and there's also plenty of help at hand to guide you through the maze and help you choose one or more funds that may suit you best. Magazines such as *Money, Kiplinger's,* and *Consumer Reports* devote lots of coverage to mutual funds. In addition, libraries and bookstores carry many books—sometimes entire sections—on mutual funds and investing. Your local public library's reference section may also offer well-thumbed guides on mutual funds, such as *Morningstar* and the *Value Line Mutual Fund Survey,* which can help you pick and keep track of funds.

Many funds allow you to invest directly, simply by contacting them directly. You may also invest through brokerages or other intermediaries. In addition, mutual funds are often offered through banks, insurance companies, and other financial institutions.

You may get many of the same tax advantages from mutual funds that you can get with individual stocks. For instance, you may be eligible for favorable tax treatment of any profit you make or losses you suffer when you sell shares you've held more than a year. And your heirs may get a stepped-up basis on shares they inherit from you upon your death.

However, the tax treatment of mutual funds differs from the tax treatment of individual stocks in at least one key way: capital gains distributions.

With individual stocks, you generally trigger tax consequences only when you sell. (If your stocks pay dividends, the dividends are taxable, but dividends are usually fairly low, and you can avoid them altogether simply by investing in stocks that do not pay dividends.)

With mutual funds, however, you may face some unexpected tax issues. When a fund's portfolio manager buys and sells stocks at a profit, the fund typically passes these profits along to you, the shareholder, through what are known as capital gains distributions. The fund may parcel the money out late each year, and it'll be included in your Form 1099 that the fund mails you early the following year.

Capital gains distributions are taxable, and because the payouts can sometimes be huge, your tax liability can be significant, too. The bottom line is that you may wind up paying tax on money you didn't expect to receive, and you have to pay the tax even if you reinvest the money in the fund to buy more shares for your account.

Some mutual funds generate bigger payouts than others. Actively managed mutual funds, for instance, typically buy and sell securities in their portfolios more often than do indexed mutual funds—funds that try to follow the fortunes of a well-known stock market index. Still, even indexed funds can generate substantial capital gains distributions, especially in a down market, when the portfolio manager can be forced to sell long-held securities to cover shareholder redemptions.

The point to keep in mind is that mutual funds can be a great way to invest, too, as long as you're aware of the possibility that you'll have to pay more in tax each year than you would if you held individual stocks.

## Variable Annuities

One other alternative is the variable annuity. In general, variable annuities are offered by insurance companies, and your money is invested in mutual funds, but you aren't taxed each year on any dividends or capital gains distributions that are credited to your account. The tax is deferred until you cash out.

Variable annuities come in many varieties. One typical feature is a life insurance aspect: the insurer pledges to pay your beneficiaries a minimum amount in the event of your death. The problem is that the cost of the insurance can cut into your profits. Variable annuities may also levy various other fees and expenses, which, when added together, can make this investment option an expensive one.

If you're interested in a variable annuity, look closely at the expenses you may be charged. You typically won't pay these expenses up front, but your account will get hit with them, and you may wind up paying for them year after year.

## Look at All the Options

This raises another key point: You shouldn't look at any of these options in isolation; rather, you should keep the big picture in mind.

The truth is that this isn't an either/or situation. Each option has its own attractions, and you can easily take advantage of all of them. For instance, you need not invest only in a 401(k) plan or other retirement savings program offered at work; you may also invest in Roth IRAs, individual stocks, mutual funds, variable annuities, or other investment vehicles available outside the workplace.

There is a rule of thumb here: If your employer offers you a way to save, and you can get it through payroll deduction and with tax benefits, take advantage of it—especially if your employer is willing to kick in a little bit extra as an incentive to get you to save more. Try to save at least enough in your employer's 401(k) plan so that you'll qualify for the maximum employer match you can get. In other words, if your company is willing to chip in to your plan, don't ignore the opportunity; that money's just sitting on the table waiting for you to claim it. Once it's inside your account, it can grow there year after year on a tax-deferred basis.

You may choose one option over another out of necessity. For instance, if you've just begun a new job, you may have a waiting period before you can join your company's 401(k) plan. In that case, you may be able to continue to save by using a Roth IRA.

You may not be eligible for a Roth IRA. Remember the general rule: To contribute, you must have earned income (money from a job) and a modified adjusted gross income that does not exceed $160,000 (if you're married and filing a joint federal income tax return) or $110,000 (if you're single). If you're unemployed, you generally won't be able to contribute to a Roth IRA, and if you have a job, but you earn more than the income limits, you won't be able to contribute.

Even if you do have the opportunity to invest through a 401(k) retirement savings plan at work, keep in mind that you have lots of other options that may offer you flexibility, more investment options, and tax benefits, too. In other words, your company's 401(k) plan isn't your only option. The same principle holds true for the 403(b) plans that are offered to employees of many schools, hospitals, and nonprofit groups; the Section 457 plans that are offered to many government workers; and SEP, SIMPLE, and other retirement savings plans that are often available to workers in small businesses.

True, some employer-sponsored plans offer lots of attractions, including the convenience of being able to save through payroll deduction and the ability to borrow from your plan, to withdraw money in the event of financial hardship, and to chat about a plan's features and options with colleagues at the water cooler or on the company bulletin board.

Just remember that employer-sponsored plans aren't the only ways for you to save. There are other options—including Roth IRAs and individual stocks or mutual funds held in regular taxable accounts—that themselves may offer features that you find more attractive, such as a greater choice of investment options. These alternative ways to save require discipline, of course; it may be harder for you to invest on your own instead of through comparatively painless payroll deduction.

Whether these or other alternatives are well-suited to you depends on lots of factors, including your personal goals, your ability to save on your own, and exactly what features your company plan does—and does not—offer you.

## For More Information . . .

- For a prospectus on Diamonds and Spiders, call the American Stock Exchange at 1-800-843-2639, or contact the exchange's Web site: <www.amex.com>.
- For a free copy of the *No-Load Stock Insider* newsletter, which includes a master list of companies that offer no-load stock plans, write to: No-Load Stock Insider, 7412 Calumet Avenue, Suite 200, Hammond, IN 46324. For a master list of direct share purchase plans, call 1-800-774-4117, or visit the newsletter's Web site: <www.noloadstocks.com>.
- First Trust (1-800-525-8188) serves as a custodian for investors who want to direct their own IRA investments.
- The Strong group of mutual funds has lots of material on Roth IRAs, Roth IRA conversions, and retirement savings options. For information, write Strong Funds, P.O. Box 2936, Milwaukee, WI 53201, call 1-800-368-3863, or contact the company's Web site: <www.estrong.com>.
- Ed Slott, a certified public accountant in Rockville Centre, New York, is also editor of *Ed Slott's IRA Advisor,* a monthly newsletter that's devoted to tax and estate planning for your IRAs and other retirement savings vehicles. The newsletter also regularly provides clearly written answers to reader questions about IRAs. If you're serious about IRAs, including Roth IRAs, this newsletter is essential reading, especially if you're among the thousands of people who

have substantial assets in IRAs and other retirement savings vehicles. An annual subscription is about $80. For information, write to: E. Slott & Company, 100 Merrick Road, Suite 200E, Rockville Centre, NY 11570. On the Internet, contact Ed Slott's Web site: <www.irahelp.com>.

- For more on IRAs, see my book *Maximize Your IRA* (Chicago: Dearborn, 1998), which is a plain-language guide to traditional, Roth, and Education IRAs.

# 10

# 403(b), 457, SIMPLE, SEP, and Other Plans

Millions of retirees rely on defined benefit pension plans as a key source of retirement income. Millions of workers are looking to their 401(k) plans to help supplement their Social Security when it's time to end their careers.

For many other workers, however, retirement savings plans have different names and different rules. If you work for state or local government, for a small business, or for a university or hospital, odds are that you're covered not by a defined benefit plan or 401(k) plan, but by a Section 457 plan, a Section 403(b) plan, or a SEP or SIMPLE plan.

This chapter focuses on these other plans, the ones that typically don't attract publicity, but that nevertheless provide an important source of retirement savings for lots of workers throughout the country. It's helpful to know what these plans are and how they work.

## 403(b) Plans

If you work for a college, university, or other school, for a hospital or medical research facility, or for a tax-exempt organization, you probably know all about 403(b) plans, which are sometimes also called tax-deferred annuities, or TDAs, tax-sheltered annuities, or TSAs.

The giant in the field is TIAA-CREF, of New York, the largest private pension organization in the country. It has been running 403(b) plans for college professors, teachers, nurses, and others for decades. Many insurance companies and mutual fund companies offer these plans, too.

In effect, 403(b) plans are the nonprofit world's equivalent of 401(k) plans, and they work pretty much the same way. You typically set aside part of your pay into a mutual fund or annuity, usually through payroll deduction. The savings go into the account before taxes are applied. In other words, you get a tax break up front. (Your employer may contribute to your account, too, depending on how the plan is set up.)

Another tax benefit involves tax-deferred growth. In other words, your account grows on a tax-deferred basis, just like a 401(k) plan or an IRA. The

**Figure 10.1**　403(b) Plan Assets

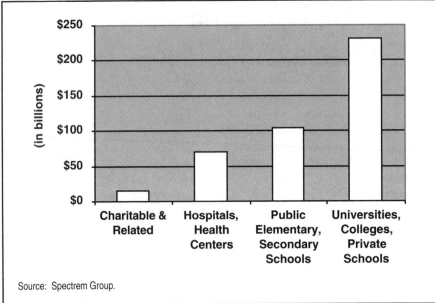

Source: Spectrem Group.

only time you pay tax on the money is when you withdraw it. Some plans also allow you to borrow from your account, on terms similar to those for 401(k) loans.

## Maximum Contribution

For 2000, the limit on employee contributions to 403(b) plans was set at $10,500. However, these plans also come with special "catch up" provisions that allow workers to contribute more in certain cases. If you didn't contribute the maximum allowed by law in earlier years, you may be eligible to contribute more than the limit in the current year to catch up.

A 1996 survey by Buck Consultants, an international human resources consulting firm, found that 56 percent of organizations offering 403(b) plans allowed participants to invest in mutual funds, sometimes called "custodial accounts" in the 403(b) industry, as well as in annuities.

Some school systems and other organizations have been slow to adapt to the increasing presence of mutual funds in the industry, and have been reluctant to expand the investment choices available to workers, usually out of habit or ignorance. If you want to invest your 403(b) dollars in mutual funds instead of annuities, lobby your union or plan administrator.

### Transferring to Mutual Funds

Even if your employer refuses to allow you a choice of investments and continues to require that your money be placed in an insurance company's annuity plan, remember that you have the right to transfer money out of your 403(b) annuity and into a 403(b) mutual fund of your choice, but only after the money has been deposited into your account. Most mutual fund companies offer 403(b) plans. Contact a fund for help in making the transfer.

Although 403(b) plans are "portable," they're not as portable as some other types of retirement savings plans. For instance, you typically can transfer, or "roll over," money from one 403(b) account to another, or from a 403(b) account to an IRA. However, because of the strange system of rules that dominate the pension world, you cannot move money from a 403(b) plan to another type of employer-sponsored retirement savings plan. (Congress and the White House have repeatedly tried to change this limitation, but haven't succeeded so far.)

### Withdrawing Money

In general, the only time you can withdraw money from your 403(b) is when you reach age 59½, you "separate from service" (leave your job), you become disabled, or you die.

Most workers begin withdrawing money as soon as they retire, to help supplement their income in retirement. However, the law lets you postpone withdrawals until April 1 of the year following the year in which you retire. (For money that went into your account before 1987, you may have to begin withdrawals "no later than the end of the calendar year in which you reach age 75," the IRS says. Check with your plan administrator, human resources department, or benefits section to find out how these withdrawal rules apply to you.)

Keep in mind that the IRS has been focusing more attention on 403(b) plans in recent years to try to correct alleged abuses: some plans haven't been following the rules, sometimes out of ignorance or because the rules are so complex.

## Section 457 Plans

Employees of state and local governments throughout the country have their own version of the 401(k)-type plan, called a Section 457 plan (it's named after a section of federal tax law).

About 90 percent of local governments nationwide, and all 50 state governments, provide their employees with access to Section 457 plans, according to Spectrem Group, a national consulting firm. In 1998, the plans held about $80 billion in assets.

A Section 457 plan is a kind of supplemental pension plan. Some workers refer to it as a "deferred compensation" program. You contribute money to an account on a pre-tax basis, typically through payroll deduction. The money doesn't get taxed on the way in; it's taxed only when you withdraw it.

The maximum allowable contribution can change from year to year depending on inflation. For 2000, the limit was generally set at $8,000 or one-third of your overall compensation, whichever was less. (The government sets the limit late each year to apply to the following year.)

You typically get to choose how your Section 457 contributions are invested. Mutual funds or insurance company investments may be among the options, depending on how the plan is set up.

The world of Section 457 plans has improved in recent years, thanks mainly to a big change in federal law. At one time, money you saved through your plan was technically viewed as your employer's money. As a result, your employer technically had the right to use it for things other than your retirement. Furthermore, the money in your plan was subject to the claims of your employer's creditors. If your employer ran into financial problems and filed for bankruptcy protection, creditors could use the money you saved in your Section 457 plan to pay their claims.

**Figure 10.2**   Growth in Section 457 Plan Assets

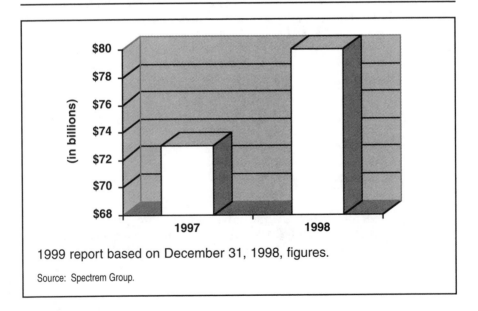

1999 report based on December 31, 1998, figures.

Source: Spectrem Group.

Because of these factors, a study by the U.S. General Accounting Office in 1996 concluded that people who took part in Section 457 plans were "exposed to greater risk than . . . participants in section 401(k) and 403(b) plans."

Changes in federal law have now brought protection to those who take part in Section 457 plans. Your contributions and earnings must now be held separately, in trust, for the benefit of you and your beneficiaries, under the same sort of rules that apply to 401(k) and 403(b) plans.

Section 457 plans still have some drawbacks, however. They aren't as portable as 401(k) plans and some other employer-sponsored retirement plans. For example, you generally can roll over money from one Section 457 plan to another, but not from a Section 457 plan to an IRA. In addition, you typically can't contribute as much to a Section 457 plan as you can to a 401(k) or 403(b) plan.

# A SIMPLE Solution

A survey conducted in 1999 by the Employee Benefit Research Institute, a nonprofit group in Washington, D.C., yielded a startling discovery. The institute, a highly regarded organization devoted to the study of employee benefits in the workplace, surveyed small businesses to find out, among other things, which retirement savings plans were the most popular.

Taking top honors was the 401(k) plan. No surprise there. Profit-sharing plans were also popular, finishing second in the survey. Which plan captured third place? The SIMPLE plan. Why is that so surprising? SIMPLE plans were almost brand-new in the world of employer-sponsored retirement plans.

## A Hot Plan

The survey confirmed what people in the industry already knew: the SIMPLE plan is one of the hottest retirement savings plans in the world of small business. It's worth getting to know a bit more about how this plan works, how it can benefit you, and why it's become so popular so quickly.

In 1996, there were many retirement savings plans available in the workplace, but they were burdened by lots of rules, some of them extremely complicated. As a result, many small businesses weren't eager to establish plans.

"Retirement plan coverage is lower among small employers than among medium and large employers," according to a congressional committee report issued at the time. "The Committee believes that one of the reasons small employers do not establish tax-qualified retirement plans is the complexity of rules relating to such plans and the cost of complying with such plans."

**Figure 10.3**  Retirement Plans Used by Small Businesses

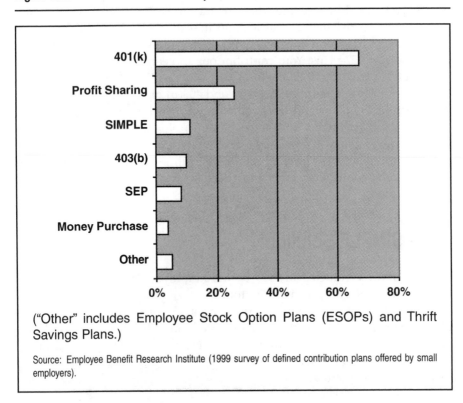

("Other" includes Employee Stock Option Plans (ESOPs) and Thrift Savings Plans.)

Source: Employee Benefit Research Institute (1999 survey of defined contribution plans offered by small employers).

So Congress came up with a simpler retirement plan that would appeal to small businesses. To drive home the point, Congress even gave the plan an uncomplicated name: the SIMPLE plan. Since SIMPLE plans first became available in January 1997, they've taken off. The plans are simple to understand and simple to operate. This makes them appealing to employers and employees alike.

### Linked to an IRA

Your employer may set up a SIMPLE plan in concert with either IRAs or a 401(k) plan. The IRA type is the most popular. It's called—you guessed it—the SIMPLE IRA.

Here, in a nutshell, is how the SIMPLE IRA plan works:

Your employer sets up a plan, and you set up your own SIMPLE IRA. You and your employer can both contribute money to your account. If you change jobs, you can take the money with you. When you retire, you can take the money out.

**Figure 10.4**   A SIMPLE Quiz

---

**Q:** What do the letters SIMPLE, as in SIMPLE retirement savings plan, stand for?

**A:** The Savings Incentive Match Plan for Employees.

Source: Congressional Committee Report accompanying the Small Business Job Protection Act of 1996.

---

Those are the basics. There are some other important details you should know about, however.

To be eligible for a SIMPLE plan, you generally must clear just two hurdles:

1. You have to have received at least $5,000 per year in overall compensation from your employer during any two prior calendar years.
2. You must reasonably be expected to earn at least $5,000 from your employer during the current calendar year.

That's all there is to it.

The idea behind this eligibility rule is pretty basic. The law lets companies exclude from the plan people, such as seasonal employees, who work relatively few hours and earn relatively little pay. Keep in mind, however, that these are the strictest eligibility requirements allowed by law. A company needn't impose the restrictions. A company can allow workers who earn less than $5,000 to participate.

Whatever the requirement your particular employer has regarding the amount of compensation you must earn, once you've cleared the hurdle, you're in. In other words, you immediately become eligible to take part, regardless of your age or years of service. There's no "waiting period." This point alone sets the SIMPLE plan apart from many other types of company-sponsored retirement plans, which may require that you be a certain age and work a certain number of years before you can be eligible.

## SIMPLE Benefits

Contributions to SIMPLE plans are tax deductible—whether they're made by you or your employer. In other words, there's a tax break for putting money into the plan. In this respect, the SIMPLE plan operates like its cousin, the traditional 401(k) plan, but with far fewer complications and with fewer set-up, administrative, and other costs. In addition, like money in a 401(k) plan, money in a SIMPLE plan grows on a tax-deferred basis.

Once contributions are made to your account—whether the money comes from you or your employer—it's yours; there are no complicated vesting rules to worry about.

## SIMPLE Flexibility

Another nice feature about the SIMPLE plan is its flexibility. You can open a SIMPLE account at a mutual fund company, a bank, a brokerage, a credit union, or another financial institution. (Some other types of company-sponsored retirement savings plans strictly limit how and where your money may be invested.)

Still another benefit of SIMPLE plans is that they are portable. If you change jobs, for instance, you can take the money in your SIMPLE plan—all of it—with you and invest it in another SIMPLE plan, or in a traditional IRA if you satisfy a two-year waiting period. With some types of company-sponsored retirement plans, the money must stay in your account with the company plan for a period of time—perhaps years.

## SIMPLE Restrictions

With so many benefits, are there any limits? Yes. The main one involves how much you may set aside in your own account. The most you may contribute is fixed each year by law and is indexed to rise with inflation. For 1999 and 2000, the limit on employee contributions was set at $6,000 a year. The most that can be contributed altogether to a worker's account each year is $12,000, including $6,000 in employee contributions and $6,000 from the employer.

If you're an avid saver, this rule can benefit you. Unlike some other employer-sponsored retirement plans, which limit your annual contribution to a percentage of your pay, the SIMPLE plan allows you to contribute the full dollar amount each year up to the limit set by law. With a SIMPLE plan, you may wind up being able to salt away more than you could under some other types of plans.

How much will your employer contribute to your account? It depends on which formula your employer chooses. Here are the basic options:

- If you contribute to your own account, your employer may match your contribution dollar for dollar within certain limits. The employer's total contribution for the year can't be more than an amount that equals 3 percent of your overall compensation for the year or $6,000, whichever is less. Suppose you were paid $25,000 in 1999, and you contributed 5 percent of your pay, or $1,250, to your SIMPLE IRA.

The most your employer could put into your account as a matching contribution in this example would have been $750 because 3 percent of your overall compensation of $25,000 is $750. (Incidentally, you qualify for these employer matching contributions only if you, too, contribute to your account.)

- As an alternative, your employer may contribute up to 2 percent of pay for all workers—regardless of which workers choose to contribute to their own accounts. In other words, under this option, the employer simply puts into each employee's account an amount equal to 2 percent of his or her pay. For example, suppose you earn $75,000 and decide to put 8 percent of your pay into your SIMPLE IRA. If your employer provides a 2 percent match for all workers, you'll get $1,500 (2 percent of your overall pay of $75,000).

- In rare cases, your employer can choose to contribute to your account an amount less than 2 percent of your overall compensation, but the amount of the contribution can't be less than 1 percent of your compensation, and there are restrictions on how often your employer can use this lower figure.

## SIMPLE Transfers

There's another key point you should know about. When a company sets up a SIMPLE plan, the company has the right to choose a single firm to handle the plan, *and to require all employees to set up their SIMPLE IRAs with that firm.* This rule could limit your investment options and your flexibility. (Although your company may not choose this option, many companies find it attractive, because it can limit their administrative and other expenses.)

Keep in mind, however, that your SIMPLE contributions must only initially flow to the institution that's designated by your company to handle the SIMPLE plan. By law, that institution must give you the option to transfer your SIMPLE IRA money to another institution, such as a bank, mutual fund company, insurer, or brokerage (generally without charging transfer fees or penalties).

This can prove a handy option, especially if you don't like the number or type of investment options available at the original institution, or if you feel the original institution charges too high an annual maintenance fee on your SIMPLE IRA account.

No matter where your SIMPLE IRA is located, however, remember that it can hold only contributions made by you or your employer through your company's plan. Your SIMPLE IRA is a vessel that's set up to handle only SIMPLE plan contributions; you can't throw in money from any other IRAs you have, or money or assets from other types of retirement plans.

## SIMPLE Withdrawals

How do you get the money out of a SIMPLE IRA?

Keep in mind that these plans are intended to help you save for your retirement. You can take the money out beforehand, but it may cost you dearly.

For instance, any amount you withdraw will be treated as ordinary income—it will be taxed at a rate as high as 39.6 percent, depending on your federal income tax bracket (most people are in the 15 percent bracket).

In addition, if you withdraw money within the first two years of taking part in the plan, you'll be hit with a whopping 25 percent early withdrawal penalty. After the first two years, the early withdrawal penalty drops to 10 percent—the same as for traditional IRAs.

You may escape the penalties altogether if the withdrawals are made under any of these circumstances:

- You've reached age 59½.
- The money is paid to your beneficiary or your estate after your death.
- You've become totally and permanently disabled.
- The withdrawal is part of a series of "substantially equal periodic withdrawals." (These withdrawals must be made at least once a year, and the amount of each must be based on your life expectancy, or on the joint life expectancies of you and your primary beneficiary.)
- You use the money to pay college expenses for you, your spouse, your children, or your grandchildren.
- You use the money to pay for a first-time home for you, your spouse, your children, your grandchildren, or your ancestors.
- You use the money to pay for health insurance premiums if you've also been receiving unemployment benefits for at least 12 consecutive weeks.
- You use the money to pay for medical expenses for which you can't be reimbursed by an insurance plan. Medical expenses qualify only if they exceed 7.5 percent of your adjusted gross income and are "deductible" expenses—the kind you can normally claim on your federal income tax return if you itemize deductions. (You are eligible to make penalty-free withdrawals for qualified medical expenses even if you don't itemize.)

In other words, the penalty exceptions are generally the same for SIMPLE IRAs as those that apply to withdrawals from traditional IRAs. (For publications with details on how these exceptions work, see "For More Information . . ." at the end of this chapter.)

Remember that you have the right to move money from one SIMPLE IRA directly to another at any time. (If your employer uses a particular financial institution to handle the company's SIMPLE IRAs, that institution must notify you, in writing, of your right to transfer your balance to a SIMPLE IRA at another institution without cost or penalty.)

In addition, you have the right to roll over your SIMPLE IRA to a traditional IRA after you've taken part in your SIMPLE IRA for at least two years. You'll then be subject to the normal IRA rules.

Once the money is in a regular IRA, you can convert the regular IRA to a Roth IRA, but you'll pay income tax on the amount you convert. Why would you want to do that? Even though you contribute after-tax dollars, the money your Roth account earns won't be taxed each year, according to the same rules that apply to regular IRAs. Unlike with regular IRAs, however, you may withdraw your contributions from your Roth IRA free of tax and penalty at any time. And you can withdraw your earnings without tax and penalty, too, as long as you meet the rules (generally, your Roth IRA must be open at least five years and you must be 59½ or older at the time of withdrawal).

Roth IRAs offer another special feature. With regular IRAs, you generally must start making withdrawals at about the time you reach age 70½. With a Roth IRA, however, you need never withdraw money if you don't want to. You can let the money stay in the account and continue to earn money tax-free. After you die, your beneficiaries can withdraw money from the account free of tax and penalty.

## More SIMPLE Points to Remember

Keep in mind that SIMPLE plans are intended for small businesses. A plan can be established only by an employer with 100 or fewer employees who earned at least $5,000 each in compensation in the preceding year. (A company with more than 100 workers can establish a plan if many of those workers earn under $5,000 a year and only 100 or fewer exceeded the $5,000 mark.)

In addition, to make sure that the new plans would reach workers who aren't already covered by a retirement savings plan, Congress came up with this rule: In general, SIMPLE plans can be adopted only by employers who don't have another employer-sponsored retirement plan. An employer can set up a SIMPLE plan at any time between January 1 and October 1 of a given year.

Here are some other SIMPLE points to remember:

- Technically, SIMPLE plans may be set up in one of two ways: as a SIMPLE-IRA plan, or as a SIMPLE-401(k) plan. Because the rules for the 401(k) version are somewhat more complicated, the IRA version has proven to be the most popular.

- Although the focus here has been on SIMPLE plans for small businesses, SIMPLE plans may also be offered by nonprofit organizations and can be an attractive way to save if you're self-employed.
- As an employee, you have at least a 60-day window each year during which you must decide whether to contribute to a SIMPLE plan. (The window typically is open from early November to late December of each year, letting you make decisions about your SIMPLE contributions for the coming year.) Your employer must formally notify you, before the 60-day period starts, about your chance to contribute to the plan on a pre-tax basis or to change the amount you want to contribute. The company must also use the notice to let you know whether your employer will make matching contributions to your account or simply give the same amount to all employees. The financial institution that handles the plan also must give you a brief description of the plan and where it's located.

## SEPs and SAR-SEPs

Another retirement savings plan created for small businesses was a kind of forerunner of the SIMPLE plan. It's known as the Simplified Employee Pension, or SEP, and it's been around since the late 1970s. A SEP is also linked with an IRA, and is sometimes referred to as a SEP-IRA.

Just about all workers at participating companies are eligible for a contribution to their plan account. In general, you qualify as long as you clear these hurdles:

- You must be 21 or older.
- You must have worked for your employer for at least three of the last five years.
- You must receive a minimum amount of compensation for the year during which a contribution is made to your account. (For 2000, the minimum amount of compensation was set at $450, up from $400 in 1999.)

In general, the employer contributes either a percentage of a worker's pay or a fixed dollar amount, to his or her IRA. Only employers may contribute to a SEP; employee contributions aren't allowed. Once the money is in the account, the account essentially operates as a traditional IRA. Contributions and earnings are not taxed until withdrawal.

Your employer may decide to have all employee accounts at a single location, such as a bank or a mutual fund company. Still, you may have some choice as to how the money in your account is invested. In addition, once the

**Figure 10.5**   Where Employer-Sponsored IRAs Go

About 9 percent of all U.S. households own an employer-sponsored IRA. The money is invested in a variety of places:

| | |
|---|---|
| Mutual funds | 56% |
| Bank money market deposit accounts, CDs | 20 |
| Individual stocks | 20 |
| Variable annuities | 14 |
| Individual bonds | 9 |
| Fixed annuities | 8 |

Includes SEP-IRAs, SAR-SEP IRAs, and SIMPLE IRAs. Survey included multiple responses because households can own more than one IRA.

Source: Investment Company Institute.

money is in your account, you can decide whether to transfer it to another financial institution.

## The Money Is Yours

Once the money is contributed to your SEP-IRA account, it's yours. You're immediately vested in the money your employer contributes. The money your account earns also belongs to you immediately. In addition, the SEP is portable; you can move it to another plan if you leave your job.

As with traditional IRAs, in exchange for the benefit of tax-free saving, you're expected to keep your money in your account until you retire. (This is, after all, a retirement savings account.) If you make an early withdrawal, you'll have to report it as income on your tax return and pay federal income tax on it (and state income tax, too, depending on where you live). You may also owe a 10 percent federal tax penalty on the amount you withdraw, unless one of the exceptions listed on page 174 applies.

## Employer's Advantages

SEP plans offer some benefits from the employer's standpoint, too. For instance, the employer gets a federal income tax deduction for the money contributed to workers' accounts. The employer also can decide how much to contribute each year, and the amount can vary from year to year. (With some other plans, the employer must contribute a fixed amount each year.) In addition, the employer generally has limited administrative and other expenses, unlike with a defined benefit plan or 401(k) plan, which can require lots of government paperwork and oversight by consultants and others.

SEPs can also be set up by self-employed people, and by unincorporated businesses, too. (Sole proprietorships are eligible, as are partnerships and firms that are organized as so-called Subchapter S corporations).

There can be a big bonus here, too: a lot of money can be socked away each year into the boss's account and into accounts of highly paid workers.

In general, an employer can contribute to a worker's account in a single year up to 15 percent of the employee's compensation, or $30,000, whichever is less. An employer can't take into account *all* of an employee's compensation for purposes of this calculation; a "compensation cap" is set by law each year. For 2000, the compensation cap was set at $170,000, up from $160,000 in 1999. As a result, the maximum contribution allowed for 2000 was set at $25,500. Because the limit is fairly high (and can go higher in future years), the SEP can be a good way for a boss to save for his or her retirement and to attract and retain key workers.

### The Salary Reduction SEP, or SAR-SEP

Before 1997, an employer could set up a SEP as a kind of 401(k) plan—allowing workers to contribute to the plan on a pre-tax basis through salary reduction. The plan became known as the SAR-SEP (the first three letters stand for "salary reduction").

When Congress created the SIMPLE plan, it decided to forbid companies to create any new SAR-SEPs as of January 1, 1997. However, SAR-SEPs that were already in place before that date can continue to operate, and workers can continue to contribute.

The chief benefit of the SAR-SEP is that you can decide in advance to set aside a certain amount of your salary or wages into your plan account. The money goes into the account before federal income taxes are applied. As a result, you get a tax break up front for the amount you contribute.

# Keogh Plans

For many years, medium and large businesses have had lots of options for establishing employer-sponsored retirement savings plans, but until recently small businesses had comparatively few. If a small business set up a retirement savings plan at all, it was typically a "Keogh" plan (named for former member of Congress from New York Eugene J. Keogh, who sponsored the legislation that created Keogh plans in the early 1960s).

Even though small businesses have a lot more options nowadays, the Keogh plan remains an alternative, and there are many of these accounts still around—held in banks, brokerages, and other financial institutions.

In general, a Keogh plan is more complicated than other types of small-business retirement plans. There can be a lot of paperwork and calculations involved, depending on the exact type of Keogh plan you have.

A Keogh plan can be established either as a defined contribution plan or a defined benefit plan. In practice, Keogh accounts are often created either as profit-sharing plans, money purchase plans, or defined benefit plans. The employer typically arranges the plan through a bank, savings and loan, credit union, mutual fund company, insurance company, or trade or professional organization.

As a general rule, employees must be allowed to take part in the plan if they're 21 or older and have put in at least one year of service (or two years in certain circumstances). Employers contribute and get to claim a federal income tax deduction. (Employees also may be allowed to make contributions and may be able to make them on a pre-tax basis, depending on plan rules.)

Keogh plans are mainly for the self-employed, for sole proprietorships. In other words, they're typically used by someone who owns his or her own business, has not incorporated the business, and accounts for business activity on Schedule C (filed as an attachment to U.S. Form 1040).

How does such a person account for contributions to a Keogh plan? Calculating this can be tricky and may require professional help. Why? Keep in mind that the amount of your deduction depends on the net earnings (net earned income) from your business. Your net earnings are generally your gross business income less allowable deductions, including the deduction you get for one-half of your self-employment tax, *and* the amount of your Keogh contribution. Here's the problem: You can figure the deductible amount of your Keogh contribution only if you know the amount of your net earnings. But you can't figure the amount of your net earnings unless you know the deductible amount of your Keogh contribution.

How can you resolve the problem? Here's rule of thumb: If the Keogh plan is a profit-sharing type of plan, your allowable deductible contribution is generally the smaller of $25,500 for 2000 (the figure adjusts annually) or 13.0435 percent of your earnings (after deducting one-half of your self-employment tax). If your Keogh plan is a money purchase plan, your allowable deductible contribution is the smaller of $30,000 or 20 percent of your earnings (after deducting one-half of your self-employment tax). Rather than struggle with these calculations, you can seek professional help or refer to the handy tables listed in IRS Publication 560. (To order your free copy of the publication, see the instructions at the end of this chapter.)

The rules for withdrawing money from a Keogh plan are generally the same as those for making withdrawals from 401(k) plans and similar defined contribution and defined benefit plans. You also can roll over money, tax-free, from a Keogh account to an IRA.

If you have a Keogh account, you must start making withdrawals by April 1 of the year following the year in which you retire. (Someone who owns 5 percent or more of the company, however, must start taking withdrawals by April 1 of the year following the year in which he or she reaches 70½—similar to the requirements for IRAs.)

## Other Retirement Plans

Here's a brief look at some other employer-sponsored retirement plans:

**Employee Stock Ownership Plans (ESOPs).** An ESOP allows a company to put shares of its stock into an account for an eligible employee. There are different types of plans with different names and rules, but they generally follow the same track. In effect, these plans give employees an ownership stake in their companies. The plans can help motivate workers and hold the promise of a big gain down the road if the value of the stock increases. In general, an employer contributes either shares of stock directly to your account or deposits cash that's used to buy shares for your account. (The company may be publicly held or privately owned. If the company is public, the shares give you voting rights that are usually associated with stock, such as the right to elect members to the board of directors. If the company is private, the shares may carry voting rights, depending on how the plan is structured.)

An ESOP is similar to other types of company-sponsored retirement savings plans, but there are key differences. For example, the employer generally gets to claim a tax deduction for the amount of the contribution, and you don't get taxed until you withdraw your shares (you generally get to withdraw shares—or cash, depending on how your plan is structured—when you leave your job or retire). However, if you receive the shares, you may be able to postpone tax on any additional increase in the value of your stock.

Another difference has to do with diversification. Because it's risky to focus too much of your retirement savings in just one investment—your company's stock—the law generally requires that, once you reach age 55, your company must give you the option to diversify at least part of your ESOP account. In other words, you can cash out a portion of your shares and invest the money elsewhere, either inside your ESOP account or outside (depending on how your plan is set up).

**Money purchase plans.** Under a money purchase plan, an employer must contribute money to an employee's account—typically a percentage of the worker's pay—at least annually. Employers don't have the option to skip one year and contribute the next; contributions are required. The money may be invested in a pooled account or trust fund and allocated to your individual account.

As with most of other types of company-sponsored accounts, your money can grow each year without tax; it'll be taxed only when withdrawn (typically when you leave your job or retire). The value of your benefits upon retirement is the total of all these contributions, including amounts the account has earned over the years. In other words, the value of your nest egg depends on how much your employer has contributed on your behalf and how well the plan's investments have performed over the years.

**Profit-sharing plans.** Profit-sharing plans allow employers to contribute company profits to employees' accounts. Profit-sharing plans typically give employers maximum flexibility because a company can make contributions even in an unprofitable year, and there's no requirement to make contributions in any given year. As a result, employees may also be allowed to contribute. These plans are often linked with 401(k) plans, which are described in detail in Chapters 7 through 9.

**Thrift plans.** Thrift plans are nothing more than savings plans. A worker contributes money, usually through payroll deduction and usually as a percentage of his or her pay. (An employer may kick in a matching contribution, too.) Because there are no tax advantages for employee contributions, these plans aren't as popular as 401(k)s and similar plans that offer tax breaks to encourage workers to save.

# For More Information . . .

The IRS offers a number of publications that will help you understand many of the features of the retirement savings plans described in this chapter. To acquire a free copy of one of these publications, visit your local IRS office, call the IRS at 1-800-829-3676, or contact the agency's Web site: <www.irs.gov>.

- For more details on SEPs, SIMPLE plans, Keogh accounts, and other retirement savings plans for small businesses, read IRS Publication 560, *Retirement Plans for Small Business.*
- To get more details on the exceptions to the early withdrawal penalties that apply to SIMPLE plans, see IRS Publication 590, *Individual Retirement Arrangements.* (This publication includes additional details on SEP, SAR-SEP, and SIMPLE plans, too.)
- To get more details on how withdrawals from pension plans are taxed, and how to avoid the penalty on early withdrawals not only

from IRAs but also from employer-sponsored retirement plans, see IRS Publication 575, *Pension and Annuity Income.*

- For information about Section 403(b) plans, including how to make additional contributions and how withdrawals are taxed, see IRS Publication 571, *Tax-Sheltered Annuity Programs for Employees of Public Schools and Certain Tax-Exempt Organizations.*
- Many mutual fund companies also offer retirement savings plans, and publish a variety of booklets and other materials to help you understand how the plans work and how to choose one that best suits you or your company. One good source for plain-language publications is the Vanguard group of mutual funds. For information, call 1-800-523-8552, or write to: Vanguard, P.O. Box 2600, Valley Forge, PA 19482. You may also contact the company's Web site: <www.vanguard.com>.

# 11

# Getting Your Retirement Plan Money

If you had a dollar for every newspaper or magazine story you've seen about 401(k) plans and similar retirement savings plans, you'd wouldn't need such a plan at all—you'd be rich.

The problem with all this publicity, however, is that it almost always focuses on how to put money into your plan and how to invest it. But if you take part in a 401(k) plan or other employer-sponsored retirement plan, it's just as important to know about when and how you can take your money out.

Can you grab the money whenever you like? No. A pension plan isn't a bank account; you typically don't get ready access to your funds.

Why? Technically, a pension plan is a "qualified retirement plan." In other words, because it meets certain rules, it qualifies for special tax treatment, the kind of treatment you can't get with a bank account.

For example, your company gets to claim a federal income tax deduction for the money it contributes to a plan on your behalf. If you contribute money too, you typically get a federal income tax deduction as well. In addition, the money the plan earns escapes tax year after year. In general, the only time your retirement plan money gets taxed is when you withdraw it.

## Limits on Access

Why do pension plans get such special tax treatment? Because Congress wants you to save for your retirement. The government offers tax breaks as a sweetener, an enticement, to encourage you—and your employer—to save. As part of this bargain, your pension money goes into a trust, a special place that is separate from your employer's other assets, and separate from your other assets, too.

There are lots of rules that determine exactly when, and under what conditions, the money comes out. True, it's a hodgepodge of rules, all of which are difficult to understand. The point to remember, however, is that the rules are there to protect your interests, and to ensure that the money will be there for you when the time comes.

In some cases, certain plans will give you access to the money that's in your account while you're still on the job—through so-called in-service withdrawals.

Even in these instances, however, there are restrictions. For instance, some plans may let you withdraw money for "hardships," but you generally must be ready to show you truly face a hardship. Your employer may require you to provide written evidence, for example.

Some plans allow you to borrow money in the form of a plan loan. Here, too, however, there are limits, and you must pay back the loan or face dire tax consequences.

Overall there are a few circumstances under which most plans permit withdrawals:

- If you leave your job
- When you die and the money is paid to your beneficiary or your estate
- If you become fully and permanently disabled
- When you reach normal retirement age
- If the plan itself is closed (or "terminated")

The rules and options for some of these so-called triggering events are fairly straightforward, but the rules for others can be complicated. It helps to know how they work.

## A Word about Vesting

First, however, a reminder about vesting, which is important because it may affect how much you get to withdraw. As you know, vesting simply refers to the time it takes for you to earn the unforfeitable right to the benefits in your plan. In general, the longer you work, the more you're vested. In other words, the more years of service you've clocked, the greater the chunk of your retirement plan benefits you're entitled to receive upon retirement.

You're always fully vested in any money you contribute yourself. But what about the money your employer contributes on your behalf? That's where the vesting schedule comes in. Some employers may let you vest immediately, but most employers require you to work a certain number of years before you win the unforfeitable right to receive full benefits from the plan.

For example, some plans may say that after a certain number of years, you become fully vested all at once. This is known as "cliff" vesting, and a company may require you to work no more than five years before you are fully vested. If you leave the job before you are vested, you get none of the money your employer contributed to the plan (although you do get to keep your own contributions). If you leave after you are vested, you get the right to all the benefits—both those that can be attributed to your contributions over the years, and those that can be attributed to your employer's contributions.

Other plans let you win the right to your benefits gradually, in stages. This method is known as "graded" vesting. An employer may require no more than seven years of service before you become fully vested in this case, and you do get partial credit if you leave earlier.

### One Man's Battle

In the late 1990s, a bus driver from Auburn, Maine, was preparing to leave one company to go to work for another. He studied his plan's documents and was aware of his rights. He intended to move the money from his 401(k) account to an IRA.

The problem was that his former employer wouldn't let him take all the money in his account. He could get access to the contributions he had made, of course. As for the money the company had contributed, however, he could get access to only a small percentage; the company said he hadn't worked there long enough to qualify for more.

In other words, the company said he wasn't fully "vested" in the company's contributions (and related earnings). He haggled with the company and went back and forth with the bank that was responsible for overseeing the plan, but he got nowhere. Although he could have hired a lawyer, he didn't have enough money, and the amount in question wasn't enough to justify the expense.

Eventually, the man was put in touch with a regional pension counseling service, funded in part by the U.S. Administration on Aging. The service convinced the bus company that it wasn't using the right formula to calculate how much the worker should receive. Because of the counseling service's efforts, the bus driver wound up getting about $23,000, which was about $6,000 more than the company was originally going to hand over.

## Leaving Your Job

If you leave your job—because you quit, you're taking a job elsewhere, or you've been fired or laid off—your employer may let you withdraw the money from your retirement plan. Whether you can depends on your plan's rules.

As a technical matter, an employer may hold on to the money until you reach normal retirement age—typically 65. In practice, however, most plans let you pull out your money within a short time after you leave your job.

In most cases, it depends on how often a plan fixes the value of all accounts in the plan. Some set the values daily. Others, however, do it less often—quarterly or even less frequently. It also can take some time to process checks, even after the plan fixes the value of your account.

To find out how your plan's rules work, take a close look at the booklet or brochure, called the "summary plan description," that your employer gave you. If your questions aren't answered there in enough detail, check the official "plan document." The rules about withdrawing money when you leave your job may be listed under a section entitled "Separation from service."

Consulting the rules is a critical step and can't be emphasized enough. Different types of pension and retirement savings plans have different rules about withdrawals. In addition, even plans of the same type—401(k) plans, for instance—may have entirely different rules.

It pays, then, to familiarize yourself not only with what type of plan you have, but also with the specific rules of your particular plan.

If your employer-sponsored retirement plan allows you to withdraw money when you leave your job, what should you do? You have four main options. You may

1. cash out,
2. transfer (roll over) the money directly to an IRA,
3. transfer (roll over) the money to a plan at your new job, or
4. leave the money in your old plan.

# Cashing Out

If you simply pull the money out of your plan, you'll be in big trouble. The problem, as always, is taxes. In general, the entire withdrawal will be treated as a distribution. In other words, it'll be taxed. If the amount is large enough, it could send you into a higher federal income tax bracket. You may also have to file a quarterly estimated tax payment. And you may face a 10 percent early withdrawal penalty (although you may avoid the penalty under certain circumstances, as Figure 11.1 shows.)

## Down Payment on Your Tax Bill

As if the tax and penalty weren't bad enough, there are added complications that the company is required to throw in. In general, if you accept the money from your plan, and the check is made out to you, your employer *must* withhold 20 percent of the money for taxes and ship it to the IRS. Your employer doesn't have a choice on this point. It's the law. The government assumes that you're going to spend the taxable money, so withholding is a

**Figure 11.1**   Avoiding the Early Withdrawal Penalty

If you withdraw money from your employer-sponsored pension or retirement savings plan, you may avoid the 10 percent penalty on early withdrawals. The exceptions are largely the same as for early withdrawals from IRAs, but there are differences.

| Pension Withdrawals Escape Penalty Under These Circumstances | IRA Withdrawals Escape Penalty Under These Circumstances |
|---|---|
| You're 59½ or older. | You're 59½ or older. |
| You die. | You die. |
| You become fully and permanently disabled. | You become fully and permanently disabled. |
| The withdrawal is part of a series of substantially equal periodic payments, and you leave your job (you "separate from service"). | The withdrawal is part of a series of substantially equal periodic payments. |
| You separate from service after reaching age 55. | N/A |
| The money is paid out under a "qualified domestic relations order" (divorce decree). | N/A |
| You use the money for medical expenses that exceed 7.5% of your adjusted gross income. | You use the money for medical expenses that exceed 7.5% of your adjusted gross income |
| N/A | You're unemployed and use the money to pay for health insurance premiums |
| N/A | You use the money for first-time homebuyer expenses |
| N/A | You use the money for college education expenses |
| You use the money to pay back taxes under IRS levy. | You use the money to pay back taxes under IRS levy. |

Source: Internal Revenue Service.

kind of prepayment on your tax bill. In other words, the government wants its piece of the pie up front.

What if you later decide to plunk your money into an IRA to avoid the tax consequences? You can do that, but you'll face some problems. First, you'll have to deposit or invest the money in an IRA within 60 days of receiving your retirement plan check. In addition, to make sure you escape tax (and possible penalty) in this situation, you must put into the IRA an amount that's equal to your total retirement plan withdrawal—including the amount that was withheld!

## An Example of Withholding

Yes, it's a weird and complicated rule. To see how it applies, consider this example:

You have $20,000 in your 401(k) account. This includes your pre-tax contributions, your employer's contributions, and earnings. (You're vested in your employer's contributions, so you can take the entire $20,000.)

You ask your plan administrator or trustee for a check for the entire amount, made out to you. What do you get? A check for $16,000. Why? Because the plan must withhold 20 percent of the withdrawal, and 20 percent of the withdrawal in this example is $4,000, which leaves $16,000 for you.

If you simply spend the money, you'll face a federal income tax on the entire $20,000 (and possibly a state income tax, depending on where you live and your state's rules). In addition, you'll face the 10 percent federal penalty on early withdrawals (unless you can qualify for an exception).

To avoid these problems, you decide to roll over the money into an IRA within the 60-day time limit. How much must you put into the IRA? The answer is $20,000. "But my company only gave me $16,000!" you say. "Where do I get the other $4,000?" You've got to find it someplace. Otherwise, the government will say you successfully rolled over only $16,000 and will tax you (and perhaps penalize you) on the remaining $4,000. That's right: You could face a tax and penalty on the amount your employer withheld!

If you put $20,000 into your IRA before the 60-day deadline, you won't be taxed or penalized. But what about the $4,000 that your employer withheld and shipped to the IRS? You'll get it back when you file your federal income tax return. This may take time, of course, and all the while, the government has enjoyed the use of that $4,000—your money.

Keep in mind that the 60-day rule on rollovers isn't flexible. Here's what the IRS says: "You must complete the rollover of an eligible rollover distribution paid to you by the 60th day following the day on which you receive the distribution from your employer's plan."

Incidentally, the 20 percent withholding rule generally doesn't apply to small amounts. Your employer won't have to withhold 20 percent of your withdrawal if the withdrawal—and all previous eligible rollover withdrawals you may have received during the year from the same employer—come to less than $200, the IRS says.

# IRA Rollovers

One way to avoid tax problems is to tell your employer (or plan administrator or trustee) to transfer the money from your account directly to an IRA. (Technically, this is called a "direct rollover.") If you do this, you will experience no tax consequences: no withholding, no taxes, and no penalty.

Unless it is a Section 457 plan, your plan *must* give you the direct rollover option. It's the law. If the plan administrator or trustee forgets to mention it (as sometimes happens), you should demand the option because it can save you taxes and headaches. (Congress keeps trying to change the law that won't let you roll over money from a Section 457 governmental retirement plan to an IRA.)

The IRA rollover option can be attractive, especially if you can't keep money in your old plan, you don't like your old plan, or you can't immediately put the money into another employer's plan.

## IRAs Offer Many Investment Choices

One benefit of the IRA is its flexibility. Most mutual fund companies, credit unions, banks, brokerages, insurance companies, and other institutions offer IRAs. As a result, your investment options are almost unlimited—unlike your options with a typical 401(k) plan or similar retirement savings plan.

Here are some other potential benefits of moving the money to an IRA:

- Once the money is in an IRA, you can move it freely from one IRA to another without triggering tax consequences. Fed up with the fees and expenses one IRA trustee or custodian is charging you? Transfer the money directly to another IRA trustee or custodian. You can have an unlimited number of such direct transfers. Just watch out for any maintenance, account-closing, or other fees that IRA trustees or custodians may charge.
- You'll be able to give yourself short-term loans if you need money. How? Instead of doing a direct transfer from one IRA to another, you can roll over the money yourself. When you do this, you have 60 days to complete the rollover. You can use that 60 days to give yourself a short-term loan. Just remember to complete the rollover within the 60-day deadline to avoid tax and potential penalty. Keep

in mind, too, that you're generally allowed only one such rollover in every 12-month period. Watch out, too, for any fees that an IRA trustee or custodian may charge.

- You can convert some or all of the money in your traditional IRA to a Roth IRA (if your modified adjusted gross income is $100,000 or less for the year in which you convert). Converting will cost you money in taxes, but Roth IRAs offer special benefits that may appeal to you. You can make tax-free and penalty-free withdrawals (if you meet the rules), or you can choose to never make withdrawals yourself, instead passing the entire amount on to your beneficiary, who will then be eligible for tax-free and penalty-free withdrawals. (You generally can't convert money directly from an employer-sponsored retirement plan to a Roth IRA.)
- If you wind up withdrawing money from your IRA before you reach age 59½, you will face a penalty unless you qualify for an exception. However, the penalty exceptions for IRAs are a bit more flexible than for employer-sponsored retirement plans. For instance, you'll escape the penalty if you use the money for college education expenses for you, your spouse, your children, or your grandchildren; for the cost of buying a first-time home for you, your spouse, your children, your grandchildren, or your ancestors (a $10,000 lifetime limit applies); or for health insurance premiums (if you're unemployed and receiving unemployment benefits).

Keep in mind that you can roll over to an IRA only the pre-tax contributions that were made to your employer-sponsored plan. If you made any contributions on an after-tax basis, as some plans permit, you'll have to withdraw them (there are no tax consequences for doing so because you already paid tax on this money), or keep them in the plan if the plan permits.

## Conduit IRAs

If you choose the IRA rollover option, consider using only a special kind of IRA called a "conduit" IRA to hold the money from your employer-sponsored retirement plan. This will give you maximum flexibility. You may later want to move the money to another employer-sponsored plan, one that accepts rollovers. However, you'll be able to move the money to the new plan only if it comes from a conduit IRA, not a regular type of IRA.

To ensure that yours is a conduit IRA, talk to the IRA's trustee or custodian, and be sure to keep inside that IRA only the money from your employer-sponsored retirement plan. In other words, don't "taint" the IRA with other money, such as new contributions or transfers from other IRAs.

This may not seem important to you now, but there's always a chance that in the future you'll take another job with a pension or retirement plan that has a lot of features that appeal to you and that will accept rollovers.

By moving your money to an employer-sponsored retirement plan later on, you may be able to take advantage of certain tax and other benefits that you can't get from an IRA (these benefits are described in more detail later in this chapter). In addition, there's a lot of convenience in having most or all of your retirement savings in just one place, instead of having to track different accounts in different places (and potentially with different rules).

If you choose the IRA rollover option, just remember to have the money transferred directly from your employer-sponsored retirement plan to the IRA to avoid potential tax problems. If the employer gives you a check, make sure it is made out to your IRA trustee or custodian. Your name can be on the check, but only as a beneficiary. The check should read something like this: "To XYZ Co., IRA Trustee, for the benefit of (f/b/o) Maria Employee, beneficiary." If the check is made out to you alone, your employer will have to withhold money, and you'll face the tax hassles described earlier in this chapter.

### Employer Stock

If your plan holds company stock, think carefully before rolling it over and consult a tax advisor about your options because if you hang on to the stock you could save a lot in taxes later on. Suppose the stock increases in value while it is in your plan. In general, if you take the stock out in a lump sum, that increase in value—technically called "net unrealized appreciation"—won't be taxed immediately. It'll be taxed only when you sell the stock, and at that point, the gain will qualify for favorable income tax treatment.

In other words, you'll get to treat it as long-term capital gain income, not as ordinary income. This means that the rate you use to figure your tax will be lower than it would if it were ordinary income.

In addition, if you sell the stock, any increase in the value of the stock after you took it out of the plan will receive favorable long-term capital gain treatment, depending on how long you held the stock after taking it out of the plan.

Why not roll this stock over into an IRA? When you eventually withdraw it, it'll be treated as ordinary income, at rates as high as 39.6 percent.

## Plan Rollovers

Most employers let you to transfer money from a retirement plan at one job to a retirement plan at another job. A survey by Buck Consultants, a

**Figure 11.2**   Most 401(k) Plans Accept Rollovers (Though Some Require a Waiting Period)

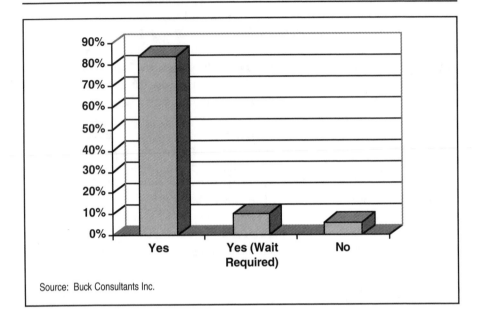

Source: Buck Consultants Inc.

human resources consulting firm, showed that 94 percent of 401(k) plans offer this feature.

Some employer-sponsored plans make you wait before doing the rollover, however. The survey showed that while 84 percent of plans accept rollovers immediately after you begin working, 10 percent require a waiting period.

If the plan at your new job requires a waiting period, you may either let the money sit in your old plan or transfer it to a conduit IRA in the meantime.

Should you bother to roll over your money into your new employer's plan? That depends. You first must carefully study the features and options your new plan offers. Does it have more or better investment choices than your old plan? What about expenses? If the new plan is more costly, it may be better to keep the old money in the old account because expenses can eat away at returns, especially over time.

## Advantages of Plan Rollovers

There can be some big benefits to rolling over your money directly to the plan at your new job. For example, in certain states, employer-sponsored plans typically get better protection from creditors than do IRAs. If you have a substantial sum to deal with, and you fear that creditors may try to come after you—particularly if you're in a profession that's prone to lawsuits—check with a lawyer to find out where your state stands on protection from creditors.

In addition, having all your retirement savings in one plan can be convenient. It's easier to keep track of the money, and you receive just one periodic account statement.

The plan at your new job may also offer a loan feature. Borrowing from your retirement savings is seldom a good idea. Still, it's good to know you can use the option as a last resort.

In addition, moving the money to an employer-sponsored retirement plan instead of an IRA may let you postpone withdrawals longer. With traditional IRAs, you generally must start withdrawing money at about the time you turn 70½. With a company-sponsored retirement plan, however, you generally don't have to start withdrawing until the time you retire— which could be later than age 70½. In the meantime, your money can continue to grow on a tax-deferred basis.

## Ten-Year Averaging

If you were born before 1936, you may be eligible for another potential bonus for investing your money in your new employer's plan. It's something called ten-year averaging, and it applies to a lump-sum withdrawal from most types of employer-sponsored retirement plans.

What's the big deal about that? Ordinarily, a lump sum would push you into a much higher income tax bracket, and you'd wind up facing a potentially huge federal income tax bill.

With ten-year averaging, however, you may use a special tax-rate schedule that can cushion the overall tax blow. In the end, you pay a tax as if you had received the money in ten equal annual installments. (You pay the tax only once; you don't pay it over ten years. Still, you can wind up paying less tax overall by taking advantage of the ten-year averaging treatment.)

As a Congressional Committee report put it, "The original intent of the income averaging rules for pension distributions was to prevent a bunching of taxable income because a taxpayer received all of the benefits in a qualified plan in a single taxable year."

You can find the special tax-rate schedule in the instructions to Form 4972, "Lump-Sum Distributions from Qualified Plans," which can be filed with your federal income tax return.

If you roll over the balance from your employer-sponsored plan to an IRA, however, you may lose this option (unless you roll it into a "conduit" IRA, take a new job later on, and move the money from the conduit IRA to the retirement savings plan at your new job).

At one time, you could have chosen another method to cushion the tax blow on lump-sum withdrawals, known as five-year averaging. This method was available to just about anybody, but it's been repealed. The last time you could have used it was for lump sums received in 1999.

# Leaving It in Your Retirement Plan

If you're interested in letting your money stay put after you leave your job, find out first if your plan allows for it. If your account balance is more than $5,000, your employer *must* let you keep your money in the plan until retirement. If it's $5,000 or less, your employer has the option of cashing you out—even if you want to leave the money in.

Also, consider whether your old plan has restrictions you find unattractive. For instance, your old plan may limit the number of times you may switch among investment options, or it may levy various types of fees and expenses that you could otherwise avoid.

If your plan permits you to leave your money in your plan account, this option has some benefits worth considering. For instance, you may find it appealing if you like the investment options and other features your old plan has or if you simply cannot decide what to do with the money or other assets in the old plan.

On the other hand, there's convenience and paperwork to consider. If you have two employer-sponsored plans running at once in two different locations, you could face a recordkeeping nightmare.

There are practical problems, too: You may not be able to keep as close a watch on your old plan as you could when you worked at your former company (you won't be able to pick up the tips you once got by checking the bulletin board or talking with colleagues, for instance).

What's more, you'll have to make sure your former employer (or your former employer's plan administrator) is kept posted on your current address so that you'll be sure to get notices of any important changes to the plan. (Keep in mind, though, that most employers won't let you borrow from a 401(k) plan once you've left that job and moved on.)

# When You Must Withdraw

No matter how much you love your employer-sponsored plan, no matter how much you like to save in your account and watch your money grow, there comes a time when you have to take the money out. It can't stay in there forever. After all, retirement plans are like traditional IRAs: the government gives you a tax break for putting money into your account and keeping it there over the long term, but the government wants to get some tax revenue from your account at some point.

Keep in mind that the law that governs required withdrawals from employer-sponsored retirement plans has changed in recent years. If you decide to keep working beyond the normal retirement age, you generally don't have to make your first withdrawal from your employer-sponsored plan until April 1 of the year following the year in which you retire. (This is in sharp contrast to the rules for IRAs, which require you to begin withdrawing at about the time you reach age 70½.)

To postpone your first withdrawal until retirement, you must be working at the same job where the retirement plan is in place. In addition, if you're an owner of the business (you hold a 5 percent or greater interest in it) you can't take advantage of this rule; you must begin withdrawals at about the time you turn 70½.

### Payment Choices

What payment options you will have generally depends on what your plan permits. Which option is best for you will depend on such factors as taxes and your personal financial situation.

Nearly all plans give you the option of taking your balance as a lump sum. This could give you the chance to manage your own money in retirement. For example, after taking a lump sum and paying the tax, you could buy stocks, mutual funds, and other securities, then tap these accounts for income as the need arises.

If you were born before 1936, you may qualify for a tax benefit with a lump-sum withdrawal, as outlined earlier in this chapter. Through this benefit, known as ten-year averaging, you could wind up with more money

**Figure 11.3**    You Have Choices When You Leave Your Plan

---

401(k) plans have a variety of payment options available to workers when they leave the job. Some options are offered by most plans; others are less common.

| Form of Payment | Availability |
| --- | --- |
| Lump Sum | 99% |
| Installments | 40 |
| Partial withdrawals | 24 |
| Plan-purchased annuity | 21 |
| In-kind distribution of company stock | 20 |
| Transfer to company's defined benefit plan | 11 |
| In-kind distribution of other investments | 4 |

Note: Survey respondents were permitted to select more than one item.

Source: Buck Consultants Inc.

than you would get to keep if you had to calculate the tax in the usual way after taking a lump-sum payment.

One problem with lump sums, however, is temptation. You may withdraw your plan's assets with good intentions, but once you get the money, you might be tempted to spend it all at once, leaving you little if any money to help supplement your other sources of income throughout retirement.

## Choosing an Annuity

The desire to avoid the temptation to spend retirement savings too quickly is one reason that many workers instead choose to receive their payments according to the installment method, often in the form of an annuity.

In general, to establish an annuity your employer uses the amount that's in your account to buy an annuity contract with an insurance company. The insurer pledges to pay you a certain amount of money at regular intervals—monthly, for example—to help supplement your pension, Social Security, or other sources of income in retirement. Some people feel more secure with the annuity option because it generally delivers a regular monthly check throughout their retirement.

No matter which option of payment you eventually choose, bear in mind that your decision will have far-reaching consequences. There are tax and other considerations to weigh.

For this reason, it's best to consult a certified financial planner, accountant, or other advisor before making your choice. That way, you can find out in detail about the potential benefits and drawbacks of each choice.

A financial planner, lawyer, or other professional can also help you with selecting a method to use for calculating withdrawals and with properly choosing beneficiaries—either for your employer-sponsored retirement plan or for your IRA. The choice of beneficiaries can have far-reaching tax implications and other effects on your overall financial and estate plan, especially if you have a substantial amount of money socked away in a plan or IRA.

In addition, if you can afford to keep your assets in your retirement plan or IRA until the last minute before you must start making withdrawals, you'll have to decide which method to use for calculating your withdrawals. There is no easy answer; which method you pick depends on your personal circumstances. Don't make this decision quickly and don't take it lightly, because it could have big implications for you, your beneficiaries, and your estate down the road. A financial planner, accountant, lawyer, or other professional can explain the benefits and drawbacks of each method, and which method may be best for you.

### Your Spouse Has a Say

If you're married, keep in mind that federal law generally requires that you get your spouse's approval for your choice of a payment method.

Congress was hearing lots of sad stories from people whose spouses withdrew lump sums without their knowledge and left them virtually penniless later on, at just the time they needed the money most.

In response, Congress passed a law that generally requires you to get your spouse's consent before you take a payout from your employer's pension plan. In other words, your spouse has to sign off on your decision. This law has two key results: (1) your spouse receives formal notice that you have a pension benefit coming, and (2) your spouse has a say on how the money will be paid out.

The standard "joint and survivor" annuity pays a certain amount of money each month while you're alive, and a reduced benefit to your spouse after you die. (This is the annuity method that most beneficiaries choose, because it makes some provision for the spouse after the owner of the annuity dies.)

Your employer will spell out the requirements for you when it's almost time for you to decide how to receive your money.

Here are a few other key point to bear in mind:

- Pension plans also typically offer a preretirement survivor annuity. This gives a benefit to a surviving spouse if the worker should die before reaching retirement.
- If you get divorced, keep in mind that your pension benefits may be part of the divorce agreement. An official document called the qualified domestic relations order, or QDRO (pronounced "Quadro"), may require that some percentage of your pension benefit go to your ex-spouse. Whether your ex-spouse gets the money immediately or only after you retire depends on the plan.

## For More Information . . .

- Fidelity Investments, the Boston-based mutual fund giant, has free kits available that offer details on transferring—or rolling over—money to an IRA from an employer-sponsored retirement plan. The kits include the *Fidelity Retirement Planning Guide* and another booklet, *Investing Your Retirement Plan Distribution*. For a free copy of these and similar publications, call 1-800-544-4774. If you have access to a computer, contact the company's Web site: <www.fidelity.com>.

# 12

# Finding a
# Lost Pension

When it's time to retire, will your pension be there for you? When you change jobs, you can take some types of retirement savings plans with you, such as 401(k) or SIMPLE plans. If you have another type of plan, such as a defined benefit plan (the traditional pension plan), it will generally stay where it is unless your account is small and your employer takes the option of simply cashing you out. In many cases, however, your pension stays at your old job. You typically get to claim your benefits in such a plan only when you retire, and that's where the problem of lost pensions arises.

## How Pensions Get Lost

You can generally lay claim to your pension benefit only if you re-member that you're owed a benefit in the first place. The trouble is that most workers change jobs frequently, and it's easy for them to forget about a pen-sion benefit that accrued while they were at an old job.

But that's not the only cause of lost pensions. Many companies get taken over. As ownership passes from one hand to another, the administration of pension benefits changes hands, too. In fact, your old company may wind up disappearing altogether.

Your pension records typically don't disappear. Remember that pen-sion benefits are usually held in a trust, separate from an employer's general business assets. Even if a company enters bankruptcy proceedings, your benefits are supposed to be protected and the records held intact.

Eventually, however, your pension records may wind up in a deposi-tory far from where you originally worked. And you may change addresses several times during your working career. The new administrator of your pension plan may have no way to get in touch with you.

For these or other reasons, you may reach retirement with a pension benefit owed you, but you may have no easy way to get it. This happens to thousands of American workers. They—or their survivors—are entitled to a pension benefit, but they don't claim it because they don't know where to look.

**Figure 12.1**  Your Pension Rights

---

Although your pension rights are protected under landmark federal legislation enacted in 1974—the Employee Retirement Income Security Act (ERISA)—there are some exceptions:

✓ Only private-sector workers are protected by the law, not employees of the federal government or of state or local governments.

✓ The law's provisions do not apply to workers who left their companies before the law took effect—in 1976 for most pension plans, and possibly later for some union plans.

✓ The Pension Benefit Guaranty Corporation insures only private-sector defined benefit pension plans.

Source: Pension Benefit Guaranty Corporation.

---

## Searching for a Lost Retirement Benefit

In 1998, a woman in New Jersey was looking for her pension benefit but couldn't find it. The company she worked for, Fleischmann Distilling, had been sold to a British firm. Later the company was sold again, this time to another British firm, Allied Domecq.

She had long before lost track of the various mergers and acquisitions, and she didn't know whom to contact.

Fortunately, Allied, which had inherited responsibility for her old pension plan, hired a firm in California to track down former participants who were eligible for benefits. The California tracking firm eventually got in touch with her by mail, seeking to confirm her current address and certain other details. She filled out the form and sent it back. As a result, Allied was able to bring its file up-to-date and keep her on its list of people who would be paid a pension benefit at retirement.

She was lucky. You may not be. What should you do? First, figure out whether you're actually entitled to a benefit. This means digging through your records—and your memory—to figure out whether a former employer offered a retirement savings or pension plan and what its rules were.

Keep these points in mind:

- You may not be eligible for a pension benefit. Pensions nowadays are governed by a landmark piece of legislation enacted in 1974, the Employee Retirement Income Security Act, sometimes called ERISA (pronounced er-RISS-uh). However, you—or your spouse—may have worked before ERISA took effect. If so, you may not be entitled to a benefit, no matter how many years of service you (or your spouse) put in. For example, at one time some companies in the jewelry industry in Rhode Island required employees to work until age 65 before they would be eligible to receive pension benefits. However, just before workers reached the magic age, they were fired, and they were unable to claim benefits.

- You (or your spouse) may not have been vested in a pension plan. Nowadays, you generally earn the right to a full pension benefit if you work a certain number of years: no more than five under some plans, no more than seven under others. At one time, however, companies could require employees to work 10 or 15 years—or more— before they could earn the right to a full pension benefit.
- If you're looking for a survivor's benefit from a pension plan that covered your late spouse, keep in mind that spouses have generally been automatically entitled to benefits only since a 1984 law, the Retirement Equity Act, or REA, took effect. Under this law, most plans are required to offer a "joint and survivor" payout option, which generally requires that benefits paid to married workers will be somewhat smaller during their lifetime, but that they will continue after a worker's death, to be paid to the worker's spouse. By law, a worker must choose this payment method unless the spouse signs a waiver. Before the law took hold, a worker could choose a pension payment option that provided benefits only for him or her until death, leaving nothing for the worker's spouse.

## Your Earnings Record Has Clues

As you search your files, take a close look at your official earnings record. This is the information that the Social Security Administration compiles over the years to figure out how much of a Social Security benefit you are entitled to receive.

You may already have your official earnings record in your file. In 1995, the Social Security Administration started mailing benefits statements each year to older workers. In 1999, the government expanded this program and started mailing annual statements to just about every worker.

The statement gives you an estimate of how much you and your family members can expect to get—now and in the future—in Social Security retirement, disability, and survivors benefits.

Altogether, Social Security now mails about 125 million such statements a year, as required under 1989 legislation that was sponsored by U.S. Senator Daniel Patrick Moynihan (D-N.Y.), who closely monitored the Social Security program and its impact on workers.

The statements are sent to nearly every worker age 25 and older. (Younger workers aren't included because most haven't yet qualified for benefits.) If you don't have your current earnings record, you can simply wait a bit. The government sends your statement about three months before your birthday. (If you were born in November, for example, your statement will be mailed to you in August.)

If you don't want to wait and can't find your most recent statement, you can fill out a form to request one. You can get the form by visiting your local Social Security office or by calling the Social Security Administration toll-free at 1-800-772-1213.

When you read your statement, you'll find a section that shows a year-by-year listing of your earnings history, naming each company. The government puts this listing together based on the information supplied to the Social Security Administration by your employers throughout your working career.

## Other Steps in Searching

The goal is to find a paper trail that will lead you to the people responsible for your retirement plans—and for any assets that the plans may still be holding for you.

Pore through your files at home to see whether a former employer supplied you with an account statement, a benefits booklet, a summary plan description, or other types of information about retirement or pension benefits at your old job.

If the company still exists, you can write to the human resources department or plan administrator to find out whether you're entitled to a benefit, and how to go about claiming it.

Even if the company has moved or otherwise closed its doors, you can check with former coworkers to see whether they're receiving pension benefits and where the plan's administrator is now located. Try to find any company officials who still live or work in the area. If a union represented workers at the company, contact union officials. (They may be willing to offer information even if you weren't part of the union.)

You may also contact the city or town hall in the community where the company was located to find an address for the company or its successor. If that doesn't work, try the secretary of state's office for the state in which the company did business.

Once you've found a person or organization you believe has some authority over your pension benefits, write a letter. Explain that you were a participant in the plan and that you believe you are owed a benefit.

Include your dates of employment and enclose a copy of any account statements or benefits documents you have. Ask how much money the plan holds on your behalf, how and when you may be eligible to claim it, and what steps you must take.

Make a copy of the letter to keep for yourself, then send the original letter by certified mail. Ask for a return receipt so you can make sure the letter was delivered and that someone formally accepted delivery.

If you're not satisfied with the company's response, there are some other steps you may take.

# Using Government Agencies

There are several government agencies and related services you can tap into to try to find a missing pension or to resolve a dispute over your pension rights.

### Department of Labor

One place to start is the Pension and Welfare Benefits Administration, which is part of the U.S. Department of Labor. This agency is generally responsible for enforcing federal pension laws and for protecting the interests of participants and beneficiaries of private-sector employee benefit plans, including retirement plans.

The Pension and Welfare Benefits Administration operates regional offices throughout the country. Contact the one nearest you. (To find the address and phone number for the nearest regional office, see the list in Appendix C.) Start with a letter that includes as many details as you can provide, including copies of any plan booklets, documents, or account statements from your files. Using the information you provide, the agency can investigate your claim, try to find your retirement plan, and check the plan's status.

The Pension and Welfare Benefits Administration doesn't keep specific records for everyone who's ever been involved in a retirement plan. However, it does keep records of the plans themselves. As long as you're vested in a plan, the plan is obligated to pay you a benefit at some point—even if your company is sold and ownership winds up overseas. (This isn't uncommon, especially nowadays, as corporations expand and global mergers and acquisitions become routine.)

### Pension Counseling Agencies

During the 1990s, the U.S. Administration on Aging awarded grants to a number of agencies throughout the country so they could offer pension counseling services free of charge. Many of these agencies, often called "pension counseling projects," work on difficult cases that cannot be easily resolved elsewhere—including lost pension cases.

Pension counseling agencies can help answer many of the pension-related questions you have, including questions about lost pensions:

- How can I find out if I'm entitled to a pension?
- What should I do if I think I'm entitled to a pension but my employer or former employer says I'm not?
- How do I find out who manages a company's pension plan?
- Will I receive payments under my former spouse's pension?
- What happens to my benefits when I die?
- How does my Social Security benefit affect my pension?
- What happens to my pension plan when I change employers?
- Will my benefits be paid if my employer goes bankrupt? Are my benefits insured?
- Should I take early retirement?
- Should I take a lump-sum payment?

See Appendix C to find the address and phone number of the pension counseling service nearest you.

## The Pension Benefit Guaranty Corporation (the PBGC)

By contacting the PBGC, you may be able to find out whether there's a pension benefit owed you. You can call or write the agency or contact its Web site at <www.pbgc.gov>. The agency has a computerized list of thousands of people who are entitled to benefits, and the list is available on the Internet.

The PBGC is responsible for insuring most types of defined benefit pension plans. It currently guarantees payment of basic pension benefits earned by about 42 million American workers and retirees who are participants in more than 44,000 plans.

As part of its mission, the PBGC operates a pension search program. The program tries to locate people who are owed benefits from certain types of defined benefit plans because they were either participants in or beneficiaries of an underfunded pension plan that was taken over by the agency. The PBGC also can help people whose plans were essentially shut down by their employers.

When an employer wants to end a fully funded pension plan, it must distribute all the plan's benefits to workers and retirees before the procedure can be completed. Employers may run into trouble if they can't find some people who are owed a benefit. Employers must make an effort to find each beneficiary, using a professional locator service if necessary.

If its search is unsuccessful, the employer may turn to the PBGC program, providing it with detailed information on the beneficiary and the benefit that's owed. The agency has been able to find many beneficiaries, but not all of them. As of mid-1999, the PBGC was trying to reach nearly 10,000 people who were owed more than $19 million in pension benefits.

To improve its search effort, the PBGC launched the *Pension Search Directory* several years ago. It lists the names of the people the agency is seeking, the companies where they earned their pension benefits, and the dates their pension plans ended. The directory is updated from time to time and is available, free of charge, on the Internet at <search.pbgc.gov>. If you have Internet access you can view the site and send an e-mail message to: missing@pbgc.gov. (Even if you don't have access to the Internet, you probably know someone who does, or you can ask for assistance at the reference desk at your local public library or community college.) You may also write to: PBGC Pension Search Program, 1200 K Street NW, Washington, DC 20005.

When writing the PBGC, try to include as much detail as possible, including your name, address, daytime phone number, Social Security number, date of birth, and the names and locations of employers that might be holding pension benefits for you. Try also to include other details, if available, such as the name of the pension plan, the nine-digit Employer Identification Number, and the three-digit Plan Number.

## Claiming Abandoned Property

Keep in mind, too, that some employers buy annuities from insurance companies to provide pension benefits to workers who have earned them. These annuity payments may operate independently of your employer. Some plans turn over pension benefits to a bank or mutual fund. If these institutions are unable to find a person who's owed a benefit, they may turn the benefit over to a state unclaimed property agency.

By law, states must try to locate the owners of such "abandoned property." However, their efforts aren't always successful. Some private firms use the states' lists to try to locate you, then charge you a fee to put you in touch with your money. Unfortunately, the fees charged by some locator firms are excessive, and some "tracer" firms demand payment up front as part of a scam.

You're better off trying to locate such assets yourself. Contact your state's unclaimed property division for help. The division may be an independent agency, or it may be part of your state's treasury department, attorney general's office, revenue department, tax commission, or other branch of state government.

The appropriate state agency can search its database for you and give you an idea how to contact other states that may be holding unclaimed assets for you. Many states have moved at least part of their vast databases onto computers, and many unclaimed property lists are now available on the Internet.

The umbrella group for these agencies, the National Association of Unclaimed Property Administrators, has a Web site that offers information about each state agency, including Internet links where available. If you have access to the Internet, contact <www.unclaimed.org>.

## Avoiding Future Problems

To make sure you don't miss out on a pension benefit, keep your past employers informed when you change your address. In addition, make sure you keep a file in a safe place that includes any information you've received from employers over the years about pension plans and your pension benefits. If you can, make a separate list to keep on file that includes each employer's name, nine-digit employer identification number (or EIN), and three-digit plan number, and the name and address of each plan administrator, trustee, or other plan representative.

## For More Information . . .

- The Pension Benefit Guaranty Corporation publishes *Finding A Lost Pension*, a 34-page booklet that offers tips on how to find a lost pension and explains what to do if you find one. For a free copy, write to: Pension Benefit Guaranty Corporation, Communications and Public Affairs Dept., 1200 K Street NW, Washington, DC 20005. You may also read or download the booklet by contacting the PBGC Web site at: <www.pbgc.gov>.
- The U.S. Department of Labor's Pension and Welfare Benefits Administration publishes *Pension and Health Care Coverage: Questions and Answers for Dislocated Workers,* which discusses health and pension benefits for workers who've lost their jobs through plant closings or layoffs, and another booklet, *What You Should Know about Your Pension Rights.* It also publishes *Protect Your Pension,* a 77-page booklet that helps you find out who manages your pension money, outlines basic plan rules, helps you read and understand a plan's annual financial report, and explains the general rules about plan contributions and investments. For a free copy, call the agency's toll-free publications hotline at 1-800-998-7542. You may also write to: U.S. Department of Labor, Pension and Welfare Benefits Administration, 200 Constitution Avenue NW, Washington, DC 20210. If you have

access to the Internet, you may read or download a copy by contacting the agency's Web site: <www.dol.gov>.

- The Pension Rights Center is a nonprofit group that fights for workers' pension rights and publishes booklets and brochures about them. For more information, write to: Pension Rights Center, 1140 19th Street NW, Suite 602, Washington, DC 20036.

- The New England Pension Assistance Project, one of the pension counseling agencies that operates in various parts of the country, operates a Web site that offers helpful pension information, links to other sources of information, and details about the National Pension Lawyers Network, a national referral network of lawyers in all states who specialize in pension cases and can handle pension claims. Here's the address: <www.pensionaction.org>.

- The American Academy of Actuaries has a list of actuaries who are willing to volunteer to help people check the accuracy of pension calculations. For information, write to: American Academy of Actuaries, 1720 Eye Street NW, 7th floor, Washington, DC 20006.

*3*

# *OTHER BENEFITS*

The two most important elements of an employee benefits package are health insurance and retirement plans. There are lots of other benefits that employers may offer as well, and some of them may be even more important to you.

For example, more and more companies reward their workers by granting them stock options. Indeed, for some companies, especially start-up and high-tech companies, stock options are one of the most important ingredients in a worker's compensation and benefits package because they have the potential to generate great wealth.

The following section focuses on stock options and other types of benefits you may already have or would like to have, including educational assistance and group life insurance. These benefits may not form the bedrock of a typical employee benefits package, as health insurance and pensions do, but they are important nonetheless, and they can be a critical factor in helping you decide whether to keep your current job or move to another.

# 13

# Group Life Insurance

If employee benefits were a meal, life insurance would be a side dish.

You'd probably focus first on the meatier items on the plate—health insurance and pension plans. Only when you'd filled up on them would you turn to life insurance.

That would be a mistake, however. Life insurance is an important part of your personal financial picture, especially if you have a family. Coverage may not mean much to you (after all, you won't be the one who's collecting the proceeds), but it could make all the difference for your spouse and children. Just knowing that it will help them can give you peace of mind.

If you have group life insurance at work—as millions of Americans do—it pays to understand exactly what it is, how it works, and how it can best work for you.

## How Group Life Insurance Evolved

When you take part in a group life insurance policy at work, you're engaging in a practice that reaches back toward the beginnings of civilization. As early as 2500 B.C., Egyptians developed benevolent societies: members contributed to a pool out of which their burial expenses would be paid. Guilds in ancient Rome offered life insurance contracts to their members.

The principle behind your group life insurance benefit at work is essentially the same: Your death could plunge your family into severe financial hardship, perhaps bankruptcy, so why not pay a little something—a premium—into a pool, and have the pool pay off upon your death.

In a sense, group life insurance is like regular life insurance: instead of shouldering the risk yourself, you transfer it to a group, so that the group bears the burden. With an individual life insurance policy, you agree to a certain small loss (the premium) now, in order to avoid a big loss later on (the financial hardship caused by your death). Group insurance applies this theme to a master policy that covers a large group—typically the workforce of a company.

The first known group life insurance policy in the United States was offered in 1911 by a company in Passaic, New Jersey, Pantasote Leather Co., but it wasn't until the 1940s that group life insurance policies became a mainstay of employee benefits programs. They became popular in the 1940s because of a wage freeze that was in force after World War II. Workers understood that they couldn't get regular pay hikes, so they sought better benefits, and life insurance was one of them.

Today group life insurance is one of the most widely offered employee benefits in the United States. In fact, about 40 percent of all the life insurance in force in the United States is group insurance, which offers a total of about $5.3 trillion in coverage.

A study in the mid-1990s by the Employee Benefit Research Institute (EBRI) showed that nearly 90 percent of full-time workers at large and medium-sized companies and in state and local government were covered. Life insurance was common but not as widespread at smaller firms, where about 61 percent of full-time workers were covered.

# How Group Policies Work

Your employer buys a policy—a group policy—from an insurer. (Unions and professional associations may offer policies, too.) The company holds the master policy, and you typically get a certificate that shows you take part in the group plan.

Group life insurance policies are generally intended to replace the income that your family or other beneficiaries would lose if you died. Although your employer holds the policy, you get to choose your beneficiary or beneficiaries, who can be someone other than a spouse or children. (For this reason, group insurance appeals to many single people as well as married employees.)

If your death occurs while you're covered by the policy, the insurer pays the death benefit directly to your beneficiary or beneficiaries. The benefit may be paid in the form of a lump sum, but many insurers allow beneficiaries to receive the money in installments, or as an annuity, providing income for the rest of each beneficiary's life. (You may have the option to choose how your beneficiary is to be paid.)

Most employers pay for the entire cost of their employees' policies, although in some cases employees contribute—especially when a company offers life insurance as part of a cafeteria-style benefit package.

If you have a plan at work, odds are you're covered by term insurance. In other words, you're covered only while you're employed; coverage typically stops after you leave your job or you retire.

Your coverage may be broader than that, however, and you may have different options, depending on the policy your company has. For instance:

**Figure 13.1** Workers with Group Life Insurance (Large and Mid-sized Firms)

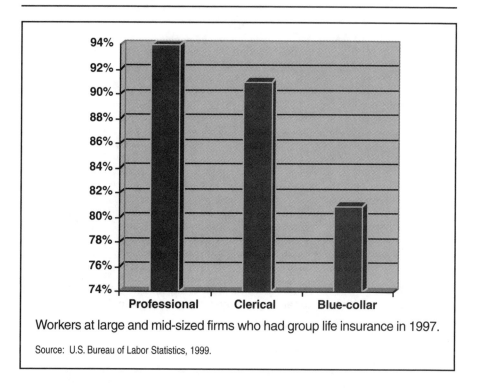

Workers at large and mid-sized firms who had group life insurance in 1997.

Source: U.S. Bureau of Labor Statistics, 1999.

- Some plans continue coverage after you retire, although the coverage you get under such a provision is often sharply reduced, mainly because the cost of covering older people can be especially expensive.
- Even if your employer doesn't automatically continue coverage for you after retirement, you generally can continue coverage by paying the premiums yourself, directly to the insurance company.
- If you're disabled, your coverage may continue at no cost to you.
- Some plans offer "living benefits," which let you receive a portion of the benefits while you're alive, under certain circumstances. These benefits, also known as viatical settlements, may be available if you're terminally ill, and if your policy allows you to claim a reduced benefit (often paid to a third party, who gets the death benefit when you die).
- Some plans give you the option of covering your dependents. The amount of such coverage is usually small, and companies typically require you to pay the premiums.
- Many plans also include accidental death and dismemberment insurance, which generally kicks in if you die or lose an eye or limb in an accident.

**Figure 13.2**   Workers with Group Life Insurance (Small Firms)

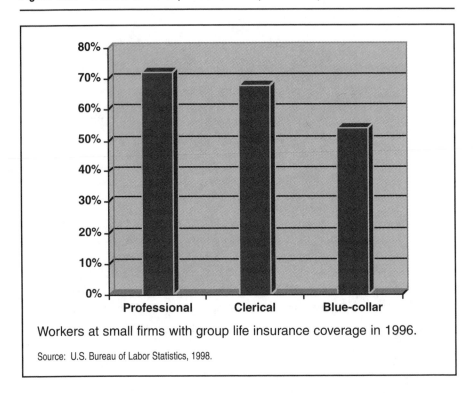

Workers at small firms with group life insurance coverage in 1996.

Source:  U.S. Bureau of Labor Statistics, 1998.

- Some employers also offer some type of travel accident insurance, which pays if you die while on company business.

Companies routinely use life insurance for a variety of reasons—to reward executives, for example, or to provide a partner with enough cash to buy out another partner's interest following his death.

Group term life is the form of life insurance businesses use most widely today, and while sales of individual life insurance policies have been flat or have fallen in recent years, sales of group policies have risen.

Companies often base the amount of coverage you'll get on how much money you earn. The experts call this the "multiple of earnings" method. More than half of full-time workers at large and mid-sized firms with group insurance had coverage based on a multiple of their earnings, according to a 1995 EBRI study. For other workers, benefits were figured differently. Some companies provided a flat dollar amount, for example.

At most companies, coverage begins as soon as you're hired, but some companies require a brief waiting period. The amount of coverage is typically equal to or double the amount of your annual earnings.

**Figure 13.3** Group Life Insurance

---

Facts at a Glance

✓ More than 163 million workers and family members are covered by group life policies.

✓ About 87 percent of workers at large and medium-sized firms are covered.

✓ Sales of individual life insurance policies have been flat in recent years, but sales of group life policies have increased.

✓ More than 640 insurance companies sell group life insurance.

✓ Up to $50,000 in group life coverage per worker is tax-free; the worker pays federal income tax on coverage above this threshold.

Source: American Council of Life Insurance, U.S. Bureau of Labor Statistics.

---

To find out exactly how your group insurance plan works, contact your company's human resources department or the person in charge of employee benefits. Remember that group term life insurance is a benefit that must meet strict federal disclosure rules. As a result, your employer is required to provide you with a "summary plan description," which sets out how the plan works and what coverage you have.

## Tax Troubles

Somewhere beneath our nation's capitol, deep underground, is a top-secret chamber. There, a group of sadistic gnomes toil to produce bizarre and complex tax rules. From time to time, in the dead of night, usually toward the end of a session of Congress, the gnomes gleefully stuff a fresh batch of tax complexities into a pneumatic tube and fire it upstairs. Out it pops, onto the tail end of a new piece of legislation, which tired lawmakers swiftly approve as they hasten toward adjournment.

Don't believe it? How else can you explain the tortuous tax rules that govern group term life insurance. Need proof? Ask someone who has more than $50,000 of coverage.

It is likely that most or all of the group term life insurance your employer provides will be free of tax to you. As long as your company's plan meets certain rules, the first $50,000 of coverage is free for you, and your employer will be able to claim a federal income tax deduction for the premiums, too.

To get this favorable tax treatment, your employer can't pick and choose which employees to cover. In other words, the plan can't discriminate; in general, the plan has to cover most of the workforce and provide pretty much the same type and level of benefit to everybody. (Technically, the plan has to pass some tests that are spelled out in Section 79 of the Internal Revenue Code. Among other things, these rules say that a group term life plan can't discriminate in favor of the bosses.)

However, even if your employer pays for all your group term life insurance, it may still cost you. Here's where one of the strangest provisions of tax law applies:

- If you have more than $50,000 in group term life insurance coverage, the cost of providing the insurance that exceeds the $50,000 threshold will be considered income—to you! It's part of your gross income. You must include it on your tax return—and pay tax on it, even though you don't receive the money on your paycheck. (The gnomes have a special phrase for this—it's called "imputed" income.)
- To figure exactly how much of this income you'll have to report on your tax return, don't use the true cost of your insurance coverage above the $50,000 threshold. That would make too much sense. You (or your employer) must look instead at a special table the IRS publishes, a table of so-called uniform premiums. (The gnomes call it Table I. And if you don't believe this, you can look it up yourself under Section 79 of the Internal Revenue Code.)

## A Change in IRS Rules

For most people, the tax on premiums is small. It can sting a bit, however, if you have a large amount of coverage, especially if you're older.

Fortunately, the IRS changed the rules in 1999 to make the tax less onerous. How much you'll save because of that change depends on your age, tax bracket, and how much coverage you have. (See Figure 13.4.) Why the rules change? Mainly, it's because the American Council of Life Insurance, a trade group for the life insurance industry, persuaded the IRS to update its mortality tables, which show death rates by age. The trade group wanted the IRS to take into account the facts that people are living longer and that more women are in the workforce (women tend to live longer than men).

By acknowledging this, the IRS in effect accepted that the cost of group term life insurance policies has dropped. As a result, the IRS couldn't assign people in certain age bracket's the same amount of imputed income as it did before.

**Figure 13.4**

| Age | Death Benefit | Imputed Income (Old Rules) | Imputed Income (New Rules) | Annual Savings |
|---|---|---|---|---|
| 24 | $ 75,000 | $ 24 | $ 15 | $ 9 |
| 34 | 100,000 | 54 | 48 | 6 |
| 44 | 250,000 | 306 | 180 | 126 |
| 54 | 300,000 | 1,440 | 690 | 750 |
| 64 | 350,000 | 4,212 | 2,376 | 1,836 |

Note: Annual savings is the reduction in the amount of taxable income you must report. Actual tax savings depends on your tax rate.

Source: American Council of Life Insurance.

Under the old rules, if you were 24 years old with $75,000 of coverage, you had to pay tax on $24 a year of extra income.

Under the new rules, you pay tax on $15 a year of extra income. That's a savings of $9 a year. If you're in the 15 percent federal income tax bracket, that savings will cut your taxes by about $1.35 a year—enough, perhaps, to buy a cup of coffee.

If you're older, however, and you have more coverage, the savings you reap could be bigger—enough, say, to buy a cup of coffee every day of the year!

For example, under the old rules, if you were 64 years old with $350,000 of coverage, you had to pay tax on $4,212 in extra income each year. Under the new rules, you'll pay tax on only $2,376 in extra annual income.

That's a savings of $1,836 a year. If you're in the 28 percent tax bracket, you'll cut your annual federal tax bill by about $514.

The savings don't stop there. A drop in your imputed income from group term life insurance premiums can also cut your Social Security tax. Why? The government says that any amount of employer-sponsored group term life insurance above the $50,000 threshold is income to you, and this extra income must also be treated as "wages." As a result, it's subject to the Social Security tax ("FICA" tax), typically levied on you at a rate of 7.65 percent.

Because of the change in the IRS rules, however, the additional income you must report for employer-sponsored group term life insurance coverage above the $50,000 threshold will be lower than it used to be. As a result, the amount of Social Security tax you'll have to pay on it will be lower, too (although the exact amount of the savings depends on how much you earn overall).

The rules change may also cut your state and local income tax, depending on where you live.

The change took effect July 1, 1999, so the savings applied for only half of the 1999 tax year. It wasn't until 2000 that the first full year of savings came about. Exactly how you'll see this savings depends on your employer: some companies withhold the tax every pay period, others once a year. This means you may see the savings in your paycheck every pay period, or in a lump sum at year end in your W-2 wage statement.

# Determining Your Imputed Income from Employer-Paid Premiums

To figure exactly how much extra income you'll be liable for under the new formula, see Figure 13.5. Next to your age bracket, you'll see the *monthly* cost per $1,000 of insurance above the $50,000 tax-free threshold. To get the *annual* cost, multiply the monthly cost by 12, then multiply the annual figure by the number of thousands by which your coverage exceeds $50,000.

For example, suppose you're 52 years old, you earn $50,000 a year, and your group term life insurance policy provides for coverage at three times earnings. This means you have $150,000 in coverage. To calculate how much in extra income you'll have to report on your federal income tax return, you need only do some quick arithmetic.

Figure 13.5 shows that if you are 52 years old, your cost per $1,000 in coverage is 23 cents per month. Multiply that by 12 months to find the annual cost per $1,000 of coverage. The answer is $2.76.

Next you need to know by how many thousands of dollars your coverage exceeds the tax-free threshold of $50,000. The answer is 100. Your final step, then, is to multiply 100 by $2.76 (which is your annual cost per $1,000 above the $50,000 threshold).

The answer is $276. That's how much extra taxable income you'll have to report on your federal income tax return because your group term life insurance coverage is over the $50,000 tax-free threshold. (Under the old rules, by the way, you would have had to report $576. As you can see, the change in the IRS rules made a big difference in this example—a drop of more than 52 percent.)

## A Twist in the Rules

There is a twist to the rules that'll affect you if you have group term life coverage at two jobs. Even if neither policy's coverage exceeds $50,000, you

**Figure 13.5**  Determining Your Imputed Income

| Age Bracket | Monthly Cost per $1,000 of Insurance above $50,000 |
|---|---|
| Under 25 | $0.05 |
| 25 to 29 | 0.06 |
| 30 to 34 | 0.08 |
| 35 to 39 | 0.09 |
| 40 to 44 | 0.10 |
| 45 to 49 | 0.15 |
| 50 to 54 | 0.23 |
| 55 to 59 | 0.43 |
| 60 to 64 | 0.66 |
| 65 to 69 | 1.27 |
| 70 and above | 2.06 |

Note: To find your total annual cost, multiply the figure in the second column by 12, then multiply the result by the number of thousands by which coverage exceeds the $50,000 threshold.

Source: American Council of Life Insurance.

may wind up paying a tax. That's because the tax is applied to your *total* group term coverage, not just to your coverage at one job.

Keep in mind, too, that this is one tax rule that's hard to enforce. Employers aren't required to find out if you have group term life insurance at another job (or through your union or professional association).

If you have less than $50,000 in group coverage at one job, and less than $50,000 at another job, it won't show up on your W-2 wage statement from either employer—even if your *combined* coverage exceeds the $50,000 threshold. It's up to you to keep track of it; there's no real way for the IRS to track it. In other words, it's the honor system and you're on your own.

### If You Pay Premiums

What if your coverage exceeds the $50,000 threshold but your employer doesn't cover the entire cost of it, requiring you to kick in some money to help pay for it instead? Figure your tax by subtracting the amount you paid out of pocket from your total amount of imputed income. Report the net result on your income tax return.

For example, suppose you're 52 years old and have $150,000 in coverage. By checking the table in Figure 13.5 and doing some quick calculations, you find that your total amount of imputed income would be $276 for the amount of coverage beyond $50,000 if your employer paid the entire premium.

But what if you paid $75 for your group coverage out of your own pocket? Then your net amount of imputed income is $201 ($276 for coverage exceeding $50,000, minus the $75 you paid out of pocket). As a result, you'll report only $201 in imputed income on your federal income tax return.

### You May Not See Savings

Some workers will not see the savings at all. That's because some companies are taking advantage of the rules change by increasing the amount of coverage they offer their workforce. In other words, your employer may either pass the savings directly along to you in the form of lower tax, or use the savings to buy you more coverage: you may be able to get more coverage for the same amount of imputed income.

(Keep in mind that the savings relates only to employer-paid group term life insurance. If you pay all the premiums yourself, the change probably won't affect you. If you pay some of the premiums, you should see some of the savings.)

# Don't Ignore Group Term Benefits

One of the chief benefits of group term life insurance coverage is that it's convenient. Even if you have to pay for a part of the coverage, you probably will do so by payroll deduction.

Group term life is also usually inexpensive. In fact, it may be far less expensive for you to get coverage under a group plan than under an individual plan because the insurer saves the cost of writing a bunch of individual policies and saves on other administrative expenses as well.

If you're in poor health or otherwise uninsurable, your group coverage can be especially crucial because you may not be able to get life insurance on your own, or if you can, the cost might be prohibitive. Furthermore, unlike individual policies, group plans typically don't require you to undergo a physical or to submit to other such tests. You're often covered automatically just by virtue of your employment.

Another nice feature of group plans is that you get to pick your beneficiary and can change your beneficiary if you like—even though you technically don't own the policy. And the death benefits can pass directly to the beneficiary; they typically don't have to go through the probate process first, so the courts usually don't have to get involved.

**Figure 13.6** Survivor Income Benefits

Although they're not strictly considered group insurance plans, "survivor income benefits plans" are related to them and may also be part of your benefits package. Here's a general look at how survivor income benefits plans work:

✓ They pay benefits to your dependents—even if you haven't named them as beneficiaries of your other employee benefits plans. Benefits typically go to your spouse and any unmarried dependent children under a certain age.

✓ These plans are generally intended to supplement government-paid Social Security survivor benefits.

✓ Survivor income insurance plans are far less common than life insurance as a benefit. Only 5 percent of workers at large and mid-sized firms, and 1 percent of workers at small firms, had such coverage, according to a government survey of 1993–1994 data.

✓ Monthly payments may be a fixed amount or a percentage of the deceased worker's pay (for example, 20 percent for a surviving spouse, 10 percent for each dependent child).

✓ Companies usually pay these benefits to survivors for a limited time (typically 24 months), but may pay them until a surviving spouse marries or reaches age 65, or until a dependent child reaches a certain age.

✓ Survivors may also be eligible for payments from a worker's other benefit plans, such as a defined benefit pension or long-term disability plan.

Source: U.S. Bureau of Labor Statistics.

Just make sure to pick at least one beneficiary. If you don't, the proceeds will be paid to your estate, they'll be routed through the probate court process and will be handed out either according to the terms of your will or according to the terms of your state's probate laws if you don't have a will.

Some group plans provide an added bonus if the insurer decides to go public. In late 1999, industry giant MetLife (Metropolitan Life Insurance Co. of New York) officially launched a plan to convert to a stockholder form of ownership. MetLife had been a "mutual" company, owned by its policyholders. It decided to try to become a publicly held company, owned by its stockholders. According to MetLife's preliminary proposal, holders of MetLife's group insurance policies were to benefit from the conversion, perhaps through lower premiums or greater coverage.

# Don't Rely Only on Group Coverage

Although group term life insurance can be a great fringe benefit, don't rely on your group policy alone. Remember that it's only part of your overall financial picture, and there are lots of reasons to get an individual policy on your own.

For example, if you lose your job, you could lose your life insurance, too, at a time when your family may need it most. True, you probably have the option to continue coverage after you leave your job by agreeing to pay the premiums directly to your insurer. (You're generally able to convert your group coverage to an individual policy within 31 days after you leave your job.) However, you may not be able to afford to pay the premiums—especially if you leave your job because of a layoff, plant closing, or other unforeseen event.

It's also possible that the amount of coverage your employer provides won't be enough. If you're single, have no dependents and no debts, and are in good health, the coverage you get from your plan at work may be all you need—at least for now.

If you're married and have children, however, you may need more coverage—perhaps far more—than you can get at work.

Your employer may give you the option to buy additional coverage, especially if your coverage is offered through a cafeteria plan. But the premiums for the extra coverage may be unnecessarily high. It makes sense to shop around. This may be true especially if the premiums at work are high to begin with because of the kind of job you have. Think about it: An insurer may charge relatively low premiums for a group plan that covers office workers, but higher premiums for a group plan that covers utility workers.

Keep in mind, too, that the premiums an insurer charges your employer are blanket rates. They are intended to cover a wide swath of the workforce, including those in good health and in bad, smokers as well as nonsmokers—another reason that group premiums may be higher than you could get on your own with an individual policy.

Of course, you may not even be eligible for your employer's plan. If you're a part-timer or a temporary worker, you probably won't be covered by a plan that is available only to full-time workers. You also may not be covered by a group plan if you have less than three years of service, even if you're a full-time worker. Or the company may exclude you from its group plan if you're in a union and your union hasn't obtained life insurance coverage for its members through collective bargaining. Any of these factors is reason for getting coverage on your own.

# Shopping for an Individual Policy

Before you make a decision about individual coverage, do some comparison shopping outside your company. And when you get price quotes, don't take them on face value. Some prices may appear extremely low at first glance, but if you investigate a bit, you'll find they apply only if you're young and in excellent health, if you work at a relatively safe job, and if you have no habits or hobbies an insurer may consider risky. An insurer may require you to pass a health exam and may ask you to provide a detailed history of your family's health. Any red flags may disqualify you, at least from the insurer's lowest-cost policy.

No matter how you get your insurance, it's a good idea to check on the insurer's financial health: a low-cost policy is no good if the insurer won't be around to pay off.

Another factor to consider is so-called permanent insurance. Why? Remember that most group plans are "term" plans: you're typically covered only for a certain time. Coverage may end when you leave your job or when you retire, for example. Term policies are typically offered for only one year; it's up to the employer whether to renew. For some people, it makes sense to get a permanent, or "whole life," policy. In general, as long as you pay the premiums, you're covered—no matter how old you are, and whether or not you're employed.

Premiums for whole life policies are typically higher than for term policies. However, policies for permanent insurance also have a so-called cash value, or investment, feature. As time goes on, the amount of this cash value builds up, and it can provide extra income to you in retirement.

To find out whether your premiums may be lower for an individual policy, start with your insurance agent. The company that provides you with auto, homeowners, and other basic insurance coverage may be able to offer you a deal on life insurance, too, as part of a broad package of coverage.

You may also belong to a union or a professional, trade, or other membership organization that offers at least some life insurance benefits.

Here are some other places to check for information, policy types, and price quotes:

- Insurance Information Inc. doesn't sell insurance, but provides price comparisons. For a flat $50 fee, you'll get the five lowest-cost term life policies available, based on your age and other factors. Call 1-800-472-5800.
- Quotesmith surveys insurance companies for low rates. Call 1-800-556-9393, or visit their Web site: <www.quotesmith.com>.

- SelectQuote also surveys insurance companies for low rates. Call 1-800-343-1985, or visit their Web site: <www.selectquote.com>.
- Savings Bank Life Insurance, which is available only in some New England states, can be reached at 1-888-438-7254.
- Ameritas Life Insurance Corp. sells directly to consumers. Call 1-800-649-5223, or visit their Web site: <www.ameritasdirect.com>.
- USAA Life also sells directly to consumers. Call 1-800-531-8000, or visit their Web site: <www.usaa.com>.
- Amica sells directly to consumers as well. Call 1-800-24-AMICA (1-800-242-6422), or visit their Web site: <www.amica.com>.
- Quicken's insurance Web site: <www.insuremarket.com>, and the Insurance News Network: <www.insure.com>, are also helpful.

## The Death Tax

One final point has to do with your estate. The death benefit paid by your group life policy is tax-free to your beneficiary. In other words, your beneficiary won't have to pay federal income tax on the money he or she receives under the policy after your death.

However, the death benefit *is* counted as part of your gross estate for the purpose of calculating any federal estate tax that may be due, and estate tax is a punishing tax: the rate can reach 55 percent or more.

Most people aren't affected by this so-called death tax. For example, if you're married and all your assets pass to your spouse, there's no estate tax. Even if you're not married when you die, your estate may not be subject to the federal estate tax because it may not be big enough. If the overall value of your estate falls below a certain threshold set by law, the tax doesn't apply. For 2000 and 2001, the law set the threshold at $675,000. For 2002, the law set the threshold at $700,000. (The threshold is scheduled to keep rising until it reaches $1 million for 2006 and later years, unless Congress repeals the tax, and there's been a lot of talk about that possibility lately).

Congress's Joint Committee on Taxation estimated in a 1999 report that of all the people dying in 2000, only about 2 percent would have enough in assets to trigger the tax.

Just remember that the proceeds paid out under the terms of your group policy are generally included in your gross estate for purposes of the tax, and if your coverage is large, it could be just the thing that would make your overall estate big enough to trigger the tax.

If you're worried that the death tax may affect you, contact a lawyer who has experience in dealing with estate-tax complexities, and who may be able to help you assign all of your "incidents of ownership" in your group policy to somebody else. This maneuver, if done properly, can remove the death proceeds from your estate and help you escape a death-tax problem.

## For More Information . . .

Whether group term life insurance is part of your fixed benefits package or it's an option in the benefits menu offered through your employer's cafeteria plan, check to see how it rates. The most important thing about a life insurance policy is the company that stands behind it: you need to know whether the company will be there when it's time for the policy to pay off.

To check how a life insurance company rates from a financial standpoint, start with your local library. Many libraries subscribe to publications from one or more ratings agencies. You may also contact the agencies directly. Here are a few to start with.

- **A.M. Best Co.** of Oldwick, New Jersey. By calling 1-908-439-2200 you can order a full financial report on an insurer for $19.95. If you contact Best's Web site, you can get ratings and a brief financial report on an insurer at no charge: <www.ambest.com>.
- **Standard & Poor's Corp.** of New York City. By calling 1-212-438-2400 you can check the rating on an insurer at no charge other than the price of the call. If you have access to the Internet, you can get free ratings at: <www.standardandpoors.com>.
- **Weiss Ratings Inc.** of Palm Beach Gardens, Florida. By calling 1-800-289-9222 you can get a rating over the phone for $15. For $25, you can get a more detailed one-page ratings report sent to you by mail. For more information, contact the firm's Web site: <www.weissratings.com>.

# 14

# Stock Options and Other Benefits

$S$uppose your employer gives you a key to a room, but you can't use the key immediately; you have to wait, maybe for a few years.

When the time finally comes, you insert the key, unlock the door, and find one of two things: untold riches or nothing at all.

This, in effect, is what employee stock options are all about. Your employer gives you the right to buy company stock at a fixed price at a later date. When the time arrives, you get to "exercise," or take advantage of, your options. In other words, you get to unlock the door.

What's behind the door? That depends on how your company's stock has performed since the options were issued. If the stock has risen in price, it can literally mean untold riches for you, especially if the price of your company's stock has risen sharply.

## How Workers Become Millionaires

When the stock price has risen significantly, your stock options allow you to pay a little bit for something that's worth a lot. This is what turned some average workers into millionaires in the roaring 1990s, especially workers at high-technology firms and other companies whose stock price soared in value.

These are the workers who were featured in magazine and newspaper stories, on TV shows, and on the Internet. They profited immensely, and they used their windfalls in any number of ways, buying new cars and big houses, launching their own businesses, becoming investment tycoons, or just retiring early and living the good life.

The point behind stock options is to motivate executives and rank-and-file workers, to get everybody working together, putting their shoulder to the wheel to improve the company's overall performance—and to increase the value of the company's stock.

# Disadvantages of Options

There is, however, another side of the story, one that gets comparatively little attention. For some workers, stock options are little more than scrip. They are pieces of paper that hold the potential for wealth, but deliver nothing.

Why? The workers receive stock options, sure enough, but the value of their company's stock may not rise, or may not rise much. When the time comes to exercise these options, there is no point. Workers are left holding a benefit that isn't worth much—if anything.

This is an important point to keep in mind regarding stock options. They may sound appealing, but they don't always pay off. Unlike most other types of benefits, their value is tied to something else, something over which you have little or no control—the value of your company's stock.

Jane Bryant Quinn, a syndicated columnist, once described employee stock options as a kind of lottery: they might pay off, but they might not.

If you're trying to decide whether to take a job at another company, or you're weighing an offer of a new job with your current employer, and stock options are part of the mix, you've got to figure out how important options are to you and what the chances are of a big payoff later on.

This isn't an easy task. At some companies, stock options are a large piece of the employee benefits package. The National Center for Employee Ownership estimates that at least 7 million employees nationwide are eligible to receive stock options. You may be offered options in place of a higher salary or broader package of benefits. If you are considering accepting a job with lower pay because you're attracted to the prospect of cashing in on your options down the road, you have to consider a company's prospects and whether its overall value on the stock market will rise over time.

Perhaps your best bet is to look at stock options as an extra, something that may pay off, but may not.

# How Employee Stock Options Work

First, some basics. A stock option gives you the right—but not the obligation—to buy a certain number of your company's shares at a fixed price at some time in the future. The fixed price is usually the per-share price of your company's stock at the time you're granted the stock options. (People sometimes refer to the fixed price as the "grant" or "strike" price.) If your company's stock increases in price over time, you can exercise your stock options and reap a profit.

Suppose, for example, that your company's stock is currently trading at $10 a share. Your company gives you one stock option. Its fixed price, or grant price, is $10. A few years later, the company's stock is trading at $35 a share. If you exercise your stock option at that point, you can get a profit of $25 a share.

How? Remember that the fixed price, or grant price, of your stock option in this example is $10. This means that your option gives you the right to pay $10 for a share of stock that's worth $35. The difference ($35 minus $10) is a profit of $25.

Is that what stock options are all about? A $25 profit? No. In the real world, you typically aren't issued just one stock option; your company may grant you hundreds or thousands of stock options, especially over time.

Suppose you hold 1,000 stock options, all with a fixed price, or grant price, of $10. You decide to exercise all of the options when your company's stock is worth $35 a share. In this example, your profit per share is $25, and you have 1,000 options, giving you the right to buy 1,000 shares. Your profit, then, isn't $25; it's $25,000!

That's what stock options are really all about—the opportunity to gain a lot of wealth. It's why top executives at many of America's largest corporations demand stock options—lots and lots of stock options—as part of their executive compensation packages. It's fine to get a big salary, bonuses, and a range of perks; it's the stock options, however, that can really deliver a huge payday—and a prosperous retirement.

## Plan Restrictions

There are some details you need to know about. First, a company usually places restrictions on options. This is true whether the options are going to the chief executive officer, a salesperson, or a worker on the shop floor.

The main restriction has to do with vesting. As described in Chapter 6, some retirement savings plans require you to work a certain number of years before you get the right to a benefit. Once you have completed those years of service, you are vested: the benefit becomes yours and you cannot be forced to forfeit it.

Stock option plans typically work the same way. Your employer may require you to work a certain number of years at the company—three to five years is fairly standard—before you can take advantage of your stock options by cashing them in.

As with some pension benefits, your stock options may "vest" all at once, or in stages over time. In other words, you may get to take advantage of them all at once, when you have become fully vested, or a little at a time.

An employer may require an executive not only to complete a specified vesting period, but also to achieve a set of corporate goals—including an increase in profits, for example—before the executive can cash in the options.

In other words, a company can link the executive's stock option package to the executive's—and the company's—performance. Experts in the world of executive compensation sometimes call this "pay for performance."

### Time to Exercise Your Options

When you're vested, you can take advantage of your options by exercising them to buy shares that have risen in value since the time the company granted you the options. You typically pay cash to buy shares.

Keep in mind, however, that you don't have to exercise them right away; you can hold onto your options in hopes that the value of your company's stock will rise even more. Just don't forget that your options will expire at some point, so you must keep careful track of them. For example, your options may have a "life" of ten years. If you don't take advantage of them before their term is up, you will lose them and the opportunity that comes with them.

If you do take advantage of your stock options and acquire shares of your company's stock, you can either sell the stock right away and lock in the profit you've made, or you can hold onto your stock, again in hopes that its market value will rise even more.

## Tax Treatment of Stock Options

Bear in mind that there are tax consequences when you exercise your options. The federal government wants a piece of the action (and your state or local government may, too, depending on where you live). Exactly how much tax you'll owe and when you'll owe it, depends in part on the type of stock options you have.

### Nonqualified Stock Options

With nonqualified stock options (sometimes called NSOs), you owe federal income tax on the difference between the fixed price of your options and the price at which you exercise them. For instance, if you were originally granted one option with a fixed price, or grant price, of $10, and you later exercise (take advantage of) that option by cashing it in when the company's stock is valued at $25 a share, you'll owe federal income tax on the difference: $15. It'll be treated as ordinary income, too. In other words, you'll have to pay tax at rates as high as 39.6 percent, depending on your federal income tax bracket (most taxpayers are in the 15 percent bracket).

By exercising your stock option in this example, you get one share of stock worth $25. You can sell it and get the cash, or you can hold it in the hope that its value will continue to increase. If you hold the share until it is worth $30, then sell it, you'll owe another tax, on the difference between the value of the share when you acquired it by exercising your stock option ($25) and the price at which you eventually sold the share ($30). In this example, then, you'll owe tax on a profit of $5. However, *this* profit will be treated as a capital gain. In other words, it'll receive favorable income tax treatment. In general, even if you're in the 28 percent (or a higher) federal income tax bracket, the most you'll pay in federal capital gains tax is 20 percent. If you're in the 15 percent federal income tax bracket, the most you'll pay in federal capital gains tax is 10 percent. Keep in mind that these are the capital gains rates for 2000; they're scheduled to be even lower in later years.

One interesting feature of nonqualified stock options is that the option can have a built-in discount. In other words, when your employer grants you the option, the grant price can be lower (or higher) than the prevailing market price of the stock at the time of the grant.

## Incentive Stock Options

With incentive stock options (often called ISOs), the tax rules can be more beneficial to you—and more complicated. The idea with these options is to get favorable capital gains tax treatment on your entire gain. Here is how it generally works:

Your employer grants you a stock option. (The fixed, or grant, price of the option must be at least as high as the market value of the stock at the time of the grant. In other words, you can't get a discount with this type of option.) Later on, the price of the stock increases. You exercise your option and acquire the underlying shares.

At this point, you pay no tax at all—even if the current market value of the stock is higher than the fixed price of the option. (With nonqualified stock options, you do pay tax at this point.) This tax-deferral feature is one of the highlights of incentive stock options.

Later you sell the stock and lock in your profit. It's at this point that federal income tax is due on the profit. However, you pay the tax at favorable capital gains tax rates.

Simple, right? The problem is that there is a holding period, a hurdle you must clear for this deal to work right. Here's what the IRS has to say: "If you hold the stock you buy under the option for more than one year after the stock is transferred to you, and more than two years after the option was granted to you, gain or loss from the sale of the stock is generally a capital gain or loss." The difference between the amount you pay for the stock (the option price) and the amount you receive when you sell it is a capital gain or loss reported on Schedule D and attached to your Form 1040.

You can see the impact. With nonqualified stock options, you pay tax at two points and in two different ways: once when you exercise your option (your paper profit at that point is treated as ordinary income), and again when you sell the stock that you acquired when you exercised your option (your profit at that point is treated as a capital gain).

With incentive stock options, you pay the tax once, when you ultimately sell the stock, and the entire profit—the difference between the fixed price you paid when you exercised your options and acquired the shares, and the price of the stock when you sold it—is treated as a capital gain, giving you more favorable tax treatment.

However, to get this favorable treatment, you've got to hold on to your shares awhile. Incentive stock options give you a tax break, but to get it you must agree to wait, and put up with all the gyrations in the stock price in the meantime. If you exercise your incentive stock option and sell your stock before you've cleared the two holding period hurdles—in other words, if you sell prematurely—your incentive stock option is, in effect, treated as a nonqualified stock option, and your profit is taxed accordingly. In other words, you lose the favorable capital gains tax treatment on the difference between the price of the stock when your employer originally granted you the option and the price of the stock when you exercised your option and acquired the actual stock. The remaining gain, based on the price at which you eventually sold your actual stock, gets taxed at favorable capital gains rates.

## Dealing with the Alternative Minimum Tax

Incentive stock options can trigger other tax complications. Although you may not know about it, there's a second income tax system floating around out there. It's called the alternative minimum tax. Some people call it the AMT or the Alt-Min tax.

The alternative minimum tax is a kind of backup to the regular federal income tax system. The AMT was created because some people, particularly wealthy people, were able to arrange things in such a way so as to pay little or nothing in income tax under the regular system. If you don't pay what the government considers to be your fair share of federal income taxes under the regular system, the backup system kicks in.

The backup tax system known as the AMT ignores a lot of the deductions you'd normally claim under the regular system. It also takes into account some items of income that you wouldn't normally have to report under the regular system. Incentive stock options are one of these income items that, in a sense, don't get fully reported under the regular income tax system, but they do have to be fully reported under the AMT system.

Remember that one of the key features of incentive stock options is tax deferral. When you exercise your incentive stock options and acquire actual shares of your company's stock, there's no tax due on your paper profit at that point. However, you must do a calculation when you acquire the shares to make sure you don't trigger the alternative minimum tax because you don't want to wind up facing a big federal income tax bill under the alternative minimum tax system. You can trigger the AMT if you have a lot of deductions—for mortgage interest, property tax, state income tax, and such—and you reap a lot of profit from such things as incentive stock options. (If you do have to pay the AMT, you can claim a credit for it later on when you sell the shares you acquired by exercising your option. That's of little use to you, however, in the year in which you have to fork over tax under the AMT calculation.)

Before you make a move with incentive stock options, be sure to visit your accountant, enrolled agent, or other professional tax advisor. Ask your advisor to run the numbers to see whether you'll be subject to the AMT. Congress and the White House keep talking about blunting the impact of the AMT, especially because it's come to burden middle-class taxpayers who weren't its original target. Even if the government changes the law, however, it's still worth checking with a tax professional to see if you may be subject to it—especially if you reap a lot of gains in a single year from incentive stock options.

## Other Employee Stock-Purchase Plans

You can acquire company stock through other employee benefits plans as well. In an employee stock-purchase plan, for example, you typically get to buy your company's stock at a discount—you pay a price for each share that's somewhat below the stock's prevailing market value. (Tax is due when you eventually sell the stock, and it's generally calculated in much the same way as in the open market: you subtract how much you paid for the stock from how much you received for the stock when you sold it and get favorable capital gains tax treatment.)

You may also acquire your employer's stock through an employer-sponsored retirement plan, such as a 401(k) plan. Here, too, your paper profit is protected from tax until you sell.

No matter how you acquire shares of your company's stock through an employee benefits program, be sure to consult a professional tax advisor. There are lots of rules and details for each type of plan and it's easy to trip up.

# Employee Education Assistance

Of all of the workplace benefits available to employees, the educational assistance plan is one of the oldest—and best. The general rule is that you can receive up to $5,200 a year tax-free from your employer to cover tuition, fees, books, and supplies toward your undergraduate education.

Different plans work in different ways. Your employer may pay for your educational expenses up front, or you may need to successfully complete a course of study (and perhaps achieve a certain letter grade or higher), then seek reimbursement from your employer.

However your company's plan works—or the plan at a job you're thinking about taking—this is simply a great benefit. College costs money, in some cases a lot of money. If your employer is willing to foot some or even all of the bill, this leaves you more time to focus on your studies.

Keep in mind, however, that educational assistance plans seem to be forever caught in a political tug-of-war between Congress and the White House. Washington can never seem to permanently adopt this important tax benefit; instead, it typically extends the availability of the benefit every one or two years. In addition, the government changes the nature of the benefit from time to time. Sometimes it covers graduate education; sometimes it doesn't. As of early 2000, tax-free reimbursement is allowed only for undergraduate expenses. Your employer can still reimburse you for educational expenses at the graduate level, but you have to report the reimbursement as income on your federal tax return.

It pays, then, to keep an eye on Washington to see which way the wind blows. Even if your reimbursement for education isn't tax-free, it's still a great benefit if your employer offers it.

# Childcare Assistance

Childcare assistance is one benefit that can truly help attract and retain workers. Parents who have problems with their childcare arrangements can lose a lot of work time to tardiness and absenteeism. Employers who offer a childcare program can boost productivity and improve employee morale.

Childcare assistance programs come in various forms. For example, some employers make childcare centers available to workers on-site or near the place of the business. The center may be operated by the company itself or run by an independent contractor. Workers may be guaranteed slots in such a center and may be eligible for reduced rates.

Other employers offer a referral network, helping parents get up-to-date information on available childcare resources near the workplace.

Still other employers may make the cost of childcare (or elder care) more affordable by linking it to a cafeteria plan, flexible benefits program, or flexible spending account. (See Chapter 5 for details on how these plans work.)

The rules for childcare plans vary. Under one model, you agree in advance to contribute a certain amount of your pay to an account. Your contributions are typically made through convenient payroll deductions, and the money goes into the account on a pre-tax basis. Because you get a tax break for contributing, each childcare dollar you contribute goes farther. As you incur expenses, you present your receipts to your benefits department, human resources administrator, or a third-party administrator. You then get reimbursed for your expenses.

No matter how an employer structures a childcare program, it can be a great financial and psychological benefit to workers and a productivity boost to the employer.

## Dental, Disability, and Long-Term Care Insurance

In addition to group health and life insurance, many employers offer a variety of other group insurance programs, including dental, disability, and long-term care insurance.

One or more of these group programs may be offered as a stand-alone benefit or as part of a flexible benefits plan or cafeteria plan. Sometimes employers pay the full premiums; in other cases, workers must foot some or even all of the bill.

No matter the arrangement, group insurance plans are worth a careful look, especially if you don't already have coverage on your own. Furthermore, coverage may be cheaper through a group plan than through an individual policy that you buy in the open market.

A group dental plan can be a boon to you and your family. As with group health plans generally, the terms can differ from plan to plan. Dental coverage may be offered as part of a broader health insurance package and may be made available through an HMO, PPO, or traditional plan. As with other health insurance, be sure to read the summary plan description and other materials your employer provides you so you'll understand fully how much you'll have to pay in out-of-pocket costs, and will know exactly what your plan will and won't cover.

The same principle applies to group disability and group long-term care insurance. If you don't have disability insurance on your own, strongly consider getting it through your employer. Keep in mind that you're more likely to become disabled than you are to die during your working years.

You'll need a source of income if you're out of work because of a disability, especially if Social Security won't cover you because of its strict definition of what a disability is.

Most employers offer some sort of short-term disability insurance program. (Indeed, as of 1999 five states operate mandatory state benefit funds that provide protection for workers against the loss of income due to disability: California, New Jersey, New York, Rhode Island, and Washington, according to the IRS.) Long-term disability plans aren't as prevalent. If a policy is available and offers fairly attractive terms, grab it.

Keep in mind that if you pay the premiums outright for disability insurance, the benefits you receive are free from federal income tax. However, if your employer pays the premiums, or if you pay them with pre-tax dollars—through a cafeteria plan or a flexible benefits program, for example—the benefits will be taxable.

Group long-term care insurance may also be worth a look because government programs typically don't cover the cost of long-term care unless you're indigent. If you need long-term nursing home or home-health care, you'll have to find a way to pay for it. Long-term care insurance can cover at least a significant portion of the expenses, allowing you to protect your other assets for your loved ones.

If you decide to acquire long-term care insurance, odds are that you'll be able to get coverage more cheaply through an employer-sponsored group plan than on your own. Bear in mind, however, that financial advisors aren't unanimously in favor of long-term care plans, in part because few if any plans guarantee a fixed rate of premiums for as long as you hold your policy. In other words, premiums can go up, sometimes sharply, in your later years, even if you began coverage while you were employed.

## Benefits Sold at Your Workplace

The focus of much of this book has been on employer-sponsored benefits—programs that an employer provides directly to workers.

Some benefits, however, are simply made available in the workplace. Some employers set aside space and time for you to get financial planning assistance. In other cases, employers allow insurance agents, banks, and credit unions to describe their financial services to workers on company time.

Some employers allow workers to buy products and services or to invest money through payroll deduction, making it more convenient to buy auto insurance or to contribute to bank accounts or state-sponsored college savings plans, for example.

# U.S. Savings Bonds

One of the most widely available programs allows you to invest in U.S. Savings Bonds directly through payroll deduction. About 45 million Americans can now buy savings bonds through payroll savings programs at work, according to U.S. Treasury estimates. This program is worth a close look because it can help you save.

Even if your employer doesn't offer savings bonds through payroll deduction, you can invest in them yourself through the government's new EasySaver plan. Under this plan, you agree to make periodic investments in savings bonds. To pay for the bonds, you authorize the U.S. Treasury to make periodic withdrawals from your bank account. (The minimum contribution is $25, and you must agree to invest at least twice a year, so the minimum annual investment is $50. The withdrawals from your bank account

**Figure 14.1**  Choosing a Savings Bond

---

You don't have to visit a bank or credit union to buy U.S. Savings Bonds; you can invest directly through a payroll savings plan at work or through automatic investments from your bank account using the government's EasySaver program.

Only two types of bonds are available for sale through these channels: Series I bonds and Series EE bonds.

**Series I Bonds:** The interest rate Series I bonds earn rises with the rate of inflation; the "I" stands for inflation. Therefore, these bonds are said to be inflation proof. Series I bonds bought from November 1999 through April 2000 earned interest at an annualized rate of 6.98 percent. I bonds are issued at their full face value (a $50 bond costs $50). The most you may invest in them is $30,000 a year. You can't swap Series I bonds for Series HH current-income savings bonds.

**Series EE Bonds:** The interest rate Series EE bonds earn is tied to the yield on five-year U.S. Treasury securities. If the yield on five-year Treasury notes rises, the interest rate for Series EE bonds rises, too; when Treasury yields drop, the rate on Series EE bonds drops. Series EE bonds bought from November 1999 through April 2000 earned interest at an annualized rate of 5.19 percent. Series EE bonds are issued at half their face value (a $50 denomination bond costs you $25). The most you may invest is $15,000 a year. These bonds may be exchanged for Series HH current-income bonds.

Source: U.S. Treasury, Bureau of the Public Debt.

**Figure 14.2** Buying Savings Bonds at Work

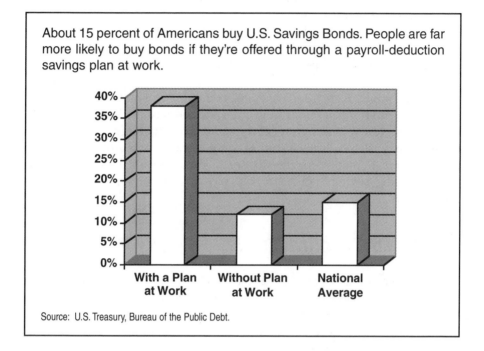

About 15 percent of Americans buy U.S. Savings Bonds. People are far more likely to buy bonds if they're offered through a payroll-deduction savings plan at work.

Source: U.S. Treasury, Bureau of the Public Debt.

are made either by the treasury's Bureau of the Public Debt or by the Federal Reserve Bank.)

Once the arrangements are made, the procedure is automatic: The treasury makes an electronic withdrawal from your bank account on the date and in the amount you choose; the treasury mails out the bonds about two weeks after making each withdrawal.

To get started, you fill out an enrollment form. (To order one, see "For More Information . . ." at the end of this chapter). On the form, you tell the government how much you want to invest, how often, how you want your bonds to be registered, and to whom the bond should be mailed.

You also list on the form details about your bank or credit union, and include the account number for whichever checking or savings account you want the withdrawals to come from.

Whether you use automatic withdrawals or payroll deduction, you typically get to choose whether to invest in Series EE bonds (minimum investment: $25 per bond) or Series I bonds (minimum investment: $50 per bond). The chief benefit of these plans is that you don't have to remember to buy a bond, and you don't have to visit a bank or credit union to make your purchase; it's all done electronically, automatically. And you'll pay no fees, commissions, or other charges.

Just remember that savings bonds are conservative investments. You typically won't get the kind of returns you might get by investing in stocks or stock mutual funds, for example.

However, you won't lose money, either. Savings bonds are backed directly by the U.S. government, which guarantees that you'll get back your original investment—plus interest—at the time you cash in, or "redeem," your bonds.

When you redeem your bonds, your interest will be subject to federal income tax, but it'll be exempt from any state and local income tax. In addition, the interest can escape federal income tax altogether if you use the money to pay for a college education and you meet certain rules, including income limits, to qualify for this tax break. To get details on the tax advantages of using savings bonds to help pay for education, see "For More Information . . ." below.

# For More Information . . .

- The National Center for Employee Ownership (NCEO), a nonprofit group, is widely regarded as the premier source of information about employee ownership and employee stock option plans. It's wide range of publications includes *The Stock Options Book,* which is written in plain language and explains the legal, tax, and other implications of stock option plans. For information on how to order this or other NCEO publications, or for details on membership, call the group at 1-510-272-9461; write to: NCEO, 1736 Franklin Street, 8th Floor, Oakland, CA 94612, or contact the group's Web site: <www.nceo.org>.
- For details on the tax aspects of stock options, read IRS Publication 525, *Taxable and Nontaxable Income.* For your free copy, visit your local IRS office, call the IRS at 1-800-829-3676, or contact the agency's Web site: <www.irs.gov>.
- For a good, clear look at the full tax implications of stock options (and for information about other tax issues), visit the Fairmark Press Web site: <www.fairmark.com>.
- For more information about employee educational assistance, read IRS Publication 508, *Tax Benefits for Work-Related Education.* It includes information about reimbursements from employers for education expenses. For your free copy, follow the instructions above for ordering from the IRS.
- To set up an account for automatically investing in U.S. Savings Bonds through the EasySaver program, order the brochure and enrollment form by calling toll free 1-877-811-7283. You may also read more

about the plan and download a copy of the enrollment form from the savings bond program's Web site: <www.savingsbonds.gov>.

- To check the current interest rates that savings bonds are earning, call 1-800-487-2663, write to: Savings Bonds, Parkersburg, WV 26106-1328, or visit the savings bond program's Web site: <www.savingsbonds. gov>.
- To find out more about how to qualify for the tax break offered through the educational feature of savings bonds, see IRS Publication 550, *Investment Income and Expenses,* IRS Publication 970, *Tax Benefits for Higher Education,* and Form 8815. For free copies, see the instructions above for ordering from the IRS.

# How Benefits Fit into Your Family Budget

To get an idea of exactly how and where your employee benefits fit into your financial picture, and to take better advantage of them, you must take an important first step: getting your household budget in order.

How can you decide what type of health insurance plan to get—or which health plan options to choose—if you don't know how you're going to pay for your plan? How can you contribute to your 401(k) or other retirement savings plans if there are gaps in your basic family budget that need to be filled first?

## Getting Your Household Budget in Order

The point is that you should put your finances in some order before making big decisions about your employee benefits package. This isn't a huge task. You may already have your financial affairs carefully sorted out. Perhaps all the information you need is up to date and you've listed it neatly using Quicken or another computer software package. Maybe you've hired a certified financial planner who's already crafted a comprehensive financial plan for you.

If you're like most people, however, you have a financial plan, but it isn't focused. You have a pretty good idea of what you own, what you owe, where the money comes from, and where it goes, and the evidence is scattered throughout your house—in your checkbook, in some file folders, in a strongbox.

If that's the case, all you need to do is some organizing. Your household financial picture may be like a big backyard garden—it's healthy enough, and there are things growing in it, but it needs some tending to: a bit of weeding, a bit of fertilizer, a bit of tender loving care.

Once your financial affairs are in better order, you'll be in a better position to make sound decisions about more effectively using the benefit plan you have at work. You will also gain peace of mind, and you will have a sound basis on which to make other important decisions about your financial affairs: how to best save for a house, for example, or how to invest for a child's college education.

Think of it this way: You spend a big chunk of your life trying to juggle work, family time, leisure time, and time for reflection and spiritual growth. Wouldn't it all go a little easier if you could get your money matters in better shape?

You owe it to yourself and to your loved ones.

Set aside some time, then, to get this basic job done. If you can't do it right now, then plan ahead: reserve a block of time (a few hours should do the trick) either this weekend or next week. You needn't be an accountant or financial expert to do the job. All you really need is a little time, a pencil, some paper, and ready access to your most important personal files. Shut off the TV, turn down the radio, and unplug the telephone. Clear a space on your desk at home or at the kitchen table. Pour a cup of coffee or iced tea. Then begin.

To make the work go more quickly and smoothly, collect all of the essential tools that help you keep track of your money matters: income tax returns, check registers, bank statements, and pay stubs; pension or profit-sharing statements, life insurance policies, mutual fund records, and charge account statements; and all the files that contain key financial documents.

Once you've assembled your documents, it's just a matter of finding the right numbers, jotting them down in the right places, and listening carefully to what they tell you.

You can begin by creating two helpful tools, the kind that many businesses use to keep track of their finances: a cash-flow statement, and a balance sheet.

## Creating a Cash-Flow Statement

Start with making what accountants often call a cash-flow statement, or profit-and-loss statement. For you, this simply means putting together a kind of giant checkbook, one that applies not just to your checking account at the bank or credit union, but to your entire financial picture over a year's time. You want to see exactly where the money comes from and where it goes.

The point here is to find out whether you have "positive cash flow"—with more money coming in than flowing out—or "negative cash flow"—with more money rushing out than coming in. Once you know this, you can do some fine-tuning.

The worksheet on page 240 shows a sample cash-flow statement. Feel free to fill it in, with your information or use it as a starting point to make your own statement, personalizing it as you go. Use plenty of footnotes to explain your entries if you feel the need.

**Worksheet**    Your Household Cash-Flow Statement

---

### For Year Ended December 31 (Insert Year)

**Money Flowing In:**

Salaries (before tax):
Interest from savings accounts, CDs:
Interest from money market accounts:
Dividends (from stocks, mutual funds):
Withdrawals from savings:

**Total inflows:**

---

**Money Flowing Out:**

Deposits to savings:
Investments:
**Total savings and investments:**
Fixed outflows:
  Mortgage payments:
  Car-loan payments:
  Real estate tax:
  Insurance premiums:
  **Total fixed outflows:**
Variable outflows:
  Federal, state, local income taxes:
  Social Security tax:
  Food, drink (including dining out):
  Utilities, other household expenses:
  Transportation (including gas, maintenance for car):
  Entertainment, vacations:
  Out-of-pocket medical, dental expenses:
  Clothing, shoes, haircuts, personal care:
  Charitable contributions:
  Hobby expenses:
  Miscellaneous:
  **Total variable outflows:**

**Total outflows:**

---

Note: Cash outflows and inflows must balance exactly. For "salaries" include gross amount of wages, salaries, commissions, bonuses, etc. For "savings and investments" remember to include deposits to bank accounts and money market funds, plus your own contributions to pensions, profit-sharing plans, and IRAs. The "mortgage payments" category is for principal and interest only. "Insurance premiums" are for car, home-owner, life, medical, disability, and other insurance policies. "Miscellaneous" includes all other items.

As you put your cash-flow statement together, consider taking these steps, or adding some of your own:

On one side of the sheet, show your cash inflows over the past year. In other words, list the sources and amounts of all the money that has flowed into your household over the past year, from salary, wages, commissions, tips, bonuses, interest from bank accounts, dividends from mutual funds, stocks, and bonds, and any other amounts—no matter how small they might seem—that you or any other members of your household have taken in. (For accounting purposes, be sure to include any withdrawals that you or other members of your household have made from bank accounts, mutual funds, certificates of deposit and the like.)

On the other side of the sheet, jot down all your cash "outflows" over the past year. In other words, enter here all of the places where your money has gone over the past year. List the big-ticket items, such as your rent or mortgage, car-loan payments, and student-loan payments. Make sure you also include the money you spend on such items as insurance premiums (life, health, homeowner, auto, and disability policies); utilities (electricity, heat, water, sewer, cable TV, and the like); taxes (federal income tax, state income tax, Social Security tax, property tax, excise tax); food (groceries, take-out, dining out); and all the other things on which you spend money, such as clothing, car upkeep, vacations, and entertainment. Be sure to list one of the big sinkholes in any household budget: "miscellaneous."

List as many separate categories as you can. This will make the last step—analysis—a lot easier.

## Creating a Household Balance Sheet

Once you've got your cash-flow statement done, you're ready for the second biggest recordkeeping task: building your own balance sheet.

This isn't as hard as it may sound. Your cash-flow statement shows where the money comes from and where the money goes over the course of a year.

A balance sheet, however, is a picture of your overall financial condition, focusing on a single point in time. It is truly the big picture. It doesn't involve how many checks you wrote, how many bank deposits you made, or how many withdrawals. It doesn't consider your salary or part-time job. It's just a list of all your assets and all your debts. As author Jordan E. Goodman puts it, a balance sheet "is a snapshot, not a motion picture."

In effect, a balance sheet answers this question: If you could freeze everything for a single moment in time, and put all the things you own (your assets) into one pile, and all the things you owe (your debts) into another pile, what would it all come to? Which pile would be bigger? In other words, what would your "net worth" be? (Net worth is the difference between your assets and your debts.)

By creating a balance sheet each year, you can find out what the result is of all of your financial activities during the year—all the money you made and all the money you spent. The annual balance sheet shows whether your overall financial picture—your net worth—has improved or worsened.

How can you put a balance sheet together? The worksheet on page 243 is a sample. You can fill it in as is, or just use it as a guide, personalizing it to suit your needs.

As you put your balance sheet together, consider taking the following steps or adding some of your own:

On one side of the sheet, jot down the dollar value of everything you own. For example, list the value of your big-ticket items, such as your house and car. Don't forget to include the market value of any investments you have, such as mutual funds, retirement savings plans at work, stocks, and bonds. Remember to list your "cash" assets, too. This includes not only actual cash you may have on hand—in a strongbox, safe, or safe-deposit box, for example—but also things that you could quickly convert to cash if you had to, such as a checking account, savings account, money market mutual fund account, and the cash value of life insurance policies. Remember, also, to list a value for all the other things you own, such as appliances, jewelry, coins, collectibles, art, antiques, furniture, and the like. Use current market values as of the date of your balance sheet. (For some things, such as a couch or a standard bookcase, make a reasonable estimate. In other words, it's okay to guess, but be consistent: If you knock 10 percent off of the price you originally paid for the couch for each year you've owned it, for example, do the same for the coffee table and refrigerator.)

On the other side of the sheet, list what you owe—the balance outstanding on all your debts. This is the place to list the balance you still owe on your home mortgage loan, car loan, credit card accounts, student loans, and the like. This may be the easiest part of all, because you've probably got the balance right at hand. (The most recent statement you received from your lender will probably show the balance that's outstanding on the loan).

## Figuring Your Net Worth

When you've finished crunching the numbers on your personal balance sheet, you can then take the significant but easy final step—figuring your net worth. To get this figure, simply subtract the total of the things you owe from the total of the things you own.

**Worksheet**   Your Household Balance Sheet

---

## As of December 31 (Insert Year)
**Assets:**                                        **Debts:**

**Cash and Cash Equivalents:**

Checking account:                          Balance on mortgage:
Bank savings account:                    Balance on car loan(s):
Money market fund:                        Balance on credit cards:
Life insurance cash value:

   **Cash and cash equivalents total:**

**Invested Assets:**

IRAs:
Pension plans:
Mutual funds:
Stocks:

   **Invested assets total:**

**Personal-Use Assets:**

House(s):
Car(s):
   **Personal-use assets total:**
      **Total assets:**                            **Total debts:**

---

**Your Household's Net Worth:**
**(Total assets minus total debts)**

Note: List fair market value of each asset as of the date of your balance sheet. List only the vested portion of your pension plans (the amount you've earned the right to receive). For "personal-use assets" use fair market value of all other assets you own, including furniture, jewelry, appliances, television and other electronics, camper and other recreational vehicles, and other items. (It may help to create a separate list of personal-use assets to use as a supplement.) List only the outstanding principal of mortgage loan, car loan(s), credit card debts, and other debts.

This is the heart of the entire exercise. It shows the true big picture, your actual bottom line. In other words, if you had to sell all that you own, and use the proceeds to pay off all that you owe, the amount left over would be your net worth.

# How to Cut Spending and Boost Savings

Congratulations! You've now completed a detailed picture of your household finances. Your next step is to look closely at the picture to see what belongs and what doesn't, where there are gaps that need filling, and whether or not the picture is in balance. In other words, you can now step back and look at the whole canvas to see what needs fixing.

The first place to look is your cash-flow statement. This is where the trouble lies for some households. If you're spending more than you're taking in, you have a problem to fix. However, because you have it all down on paper, it shouldn't be too hard a job.

Study each item carefully.

### Inflows

**Wages.** It's easy to conclude that your income is the source of the problem. If only you could earn a little more, you'd be all set. That's often a mistake, however. The source of household budget problems usually is spending too much, not earning too little. The key here is to live within your means. That takes discipline. It's hard to do, especially when it seems that all your neighbors, friends, and colleagues are in better financial shape than you are. The truth, however, is that most people are simply living beyond their means. They're spending more than they're taking in. Often, they're doing this magic trick by using credit: they borrow on credit cards and take out home equity loans, and when they've reached their limits on those sources of credit, they turn to others, digging themselves deeper into debt. Don't make that mistake. If you can increase your income, fine. If you or someone else in your household is about to get another job and boost your overall income, that's great. But you still need to learn the lesson of living within your means. You must spend less than what you take in; that's the way to really get ahead. However, even without a big jump in earnings (from a second job, for instance), there are some ways you can boost your income relatively painlessly. Keep reading.

**Interest.** Take a close look at where your short-term cash is parked. Do you keep a checking account at a large bank? If so, do you need to? Odds are you can get a better deal with a community bank or credit union. You may be able to earn more interest with a smaller balance. Even if you can't earn interest, at least you can find a bank or credit union that charges you less in fees. Remember that big banks are usually geared to serving big customers. If you're not a big customer, look for a bank or credit union that can better meet your needs.

While you're at it, look at what your savings are earning. Why park money in certificates of deposit (CDs) when you may earn more from a money market account? Shop around among some community banks and credit unions to see if your money can earn a higher rate. You can check the rate surveys published in newspapers and magazines and online, but keep in mind that these surveys typically aren't all-encompassing; they usually focus only on the largest institutions in the largest markets, and a few other institutions that are known to offer high yields, and they typically ignore small community banks and credit unions. Look in your own backyard before you go outside your region. You can often find good deals—including unadvertised special rates—simply by calling around to banks and credit unions in your area to compare terms on everything from checking and savings accounts to CDs and money market accounts.

**Withdrawals.** One of the key problems in almost everybody's budget has to do with withdrawals from savings. How often are you pulling money out of your savings account or money fund to pay for ordinary expenses? Try to use your savings only as a cushion, a reserve to be used only in emergencies. Here, too, the important thing is to live within your means. If you can't afford something, don't buy it. If it's not in your budget, skip it. If you really want to get something that's not essential, something that doesn't qualify as an emergency, try to trim your other expenses first, before you tap your savings.

## Outflows

**Savings.** If the line item for savings in your cash-flow statement is zero, you've got problems. You should dedicate part of your income every pay period to savings. The more the better, of course, but at least start with something. If you haven't the willpower to save on your own, ask your employer about payroll deduction. Odds are that your employer has an arrangement for taking money out of your paycheck each pay period and putting it directly into a savings account.

If payroll deduction isn't available, ask about a payroll savings plan. Many employers allow you to buy U.S. Savings Bonds on a regular basis through payroll deduction. This is a great way to save: the money comes right out of your paycheck before you see it, so in a sense you don't miss it. The bonds are mailed to you on a regular basis. Interest on the bonds is subject to federal income tax, but escapes state and local income tax. In addition, the savings bond program has been overhauled repeatedly in recent years so that the rules are now a bit easier to understand, and the rates bonds pay are often more competitive. (While you're at it, check out the new Series I bond, which earns more as inflation increases. These bonds offer you a hedge against inflation.)

**Mortgage.** Here's one of the places where you must ask a really big question: Are you living at too high a level? In other words, can you afford to pay the mortgage on the house you now have? This is a vexing question that can drive right to the heart of who you are and what your life's about. Some people's budgets are squeezed so tightly each month that they're miserable and cannot afford to spend time or money on some of the nice things that life has to offer. They work two and three jobs just to pay the mortgage. If they have children, the children are harnessed into day care—sometimes from early in the morning until late in the evening—just so the parents can have a big house in a fancy neighborhood. What's the point? Why not downsize—buy a smaller house (or at least a less expensive one) in another neighborhood?

If you're determined to stick it out, at least consider refinancing. Check the newspaper daily to track interest rates. If rates move down, think about trading in your higher-rate loan for a lower-rate loan. Here, too, big banks can often be beaten by community banks, credit unions, and specialized mortgage lenders. If you're comfortable with your house and your mortgage, why not think about trading in your existing mortgage for a shorter-term loan. That way, you'll pay off the loan sooner and you'll save yourself potentially thousands of dollars in interest.

**Car-loan payments.** Whether you read a newspaper or a magazine, watch TV, or listen to the radio, there's a steady drumbeat of car advertising. It doesn't matter the make or the model; the message is the same—you need a new car. This is one reason why so many family budgets are in turmoil. People spend a big chunk of their money paying for the latest car, truck, or sports utility vehicle. Do they need to? No. This is one area where you can save a lot of money if you're willing to use a little discipline. Can you get by with the vehicle you now have? Can you keep it running well beyond the time you've paid off your loan? Do you really need to own or lease a late-model vehicle? Would a good used car do the job just as well?

The issue is expectations. If your budget's in trouble—if you're spending more than you're taking in, or you're not saving enough—look closely at how much you're spending on transportation and consider cutting back. Keeping your older-model vehicle allows you to save not only on car payments, but also on auto insurance and on excise taxes if you live in a place that levies a separate tax on vehicles.

**Real estate tax.** If you're willing to lower your expectations about the kind of house you will live in, you can lower your real estate taxes and your premiums for homeowners insurance. If you decide to stay where you now live, you can keep your property tax bill under some control by holding off on major home-improvement projects that you can live without. Keep in mind that property taxes are typically based on the value of your house. If you move forward with major home improvements, the value of your house may increase, boosting the amount of property tax you have to pay.

Another way to monitor your property tax expenses is to keep a close watch on what other houses are selling for in your neighborhood, and asking neighbors and friends about the assessed value of their homes. City and town governments aren't perfect; their assessors sometimes make mistakes. If the government places too high a value on your property, you can file an appeal seeking what's known as an "abatement" on your property taxes. Businesses often do this, and you should consider it, too, especially if you can come up with sound evidence to support your claim for a lower valuation— and a lower tax.

**Variable outflows.** If there were ever a place to cut down on your spending, this is it: a grab bag of expenses that can quickly get out of control if you're not careful. Some things may be fairly obvious. For instance, to cut down on the amount of income tax you pay, be sure to claim all the deductions to which you may be entitled. (See "For More Information . . ." at the end of the chapter for more details.) Don't forget, too, that by contributing to a 401(k), SIMPLE plan, or other such employer-sponsored retirement plan, you can reduce the amount of federal and state income tax you pay. In addition, if you take part in a cafeteria plan or flexible benefits program at work, you can reduce not only your income tax, but your Social Security tax, too.

The key to saving money on variable outflows is self-discipline. Preparing meals at home can sharply reduce the amount of money you spend on food and drinks. If you are too busy to cook every night, you can buy in bulk, set aside one night for kitchen duty, and prepare a week's worth of meals in one cooking session. Cooking at home can cut way down on the amount you and others in your household spend on dining out. Try only visiting restaurants as an occasional treat. When you eat at home, shut off the radio, the television, and the ringer on the telephone, and use mealtime as an opportunity to focus more on your family members or others in your household. Take a few minutes each night to prepare lunches for the following day. This can add up to big savings every week. Consider bringing a Thermos to work each day filled with coffee, tea, or soup.

To save money on utilities, you can always cut back by turning off lights when you leave a room, lowering the thermostat in winter, and shutting off or lowering the air-conditioning in summer. If you have cable TV, cut back or eliminate premium services. If you travel, consider taking just one trip a year instead of two. If you gamble, cut back on bingo, or limit your visits to the racetrack or casino. When buying clothing, forget about the high-priced catalogs that come in the mail; they may look nice, but you can probably get the same thing in a discount store—and you'll save on shipping charges, too. Don't be addicted to the shopping mall, either; comb through thrift shops or consignment shops in your area for good deals and quality goods.

Are you carrying a big balance on your credit cards? If you pay off your balance in full each month, you'll save money in finance charges. If you can't swing that right now, at least shop around for a card that'll charge you a lower interest rate. (Check your daily newspaper, or such magazines as *Money* and *Kiplinger's*, for listings of the best low-rate and no-fee cards.) And if you have too many credit cards, get out the scissors and cut some—or all—of them into tiny pieces and toss them away. This will help you avoid the temptation to spend.

By now you get the idea. You're not going to save thousands of dollars in any single category; the point is to cut back a little bit in a number of areas to reap more savings overall so you can get your family's budget in better order.

Use the cash-flow sheet that you've put together to help you study carefully your saving and spending habits. Having all the numbers in front of you helps you see the picture more clearly, and it may give you the information you need to make some big decisions, especially those you may have been putting off.

Your next step is to take a close look at your balance sheet. This is where you can focus on the whole picture.

If you have more debts than assets, you're in big trouble, and you should look at taking some drastic steps. You may need to move to a smaller house to slash your mortgage debt, or sell one of your cars to eliminate a car loan, for instance. And if such drastic steps don't help much, you may have to seek court protection from creditors under federal bankruptcy law while you try to sort out your financial affairs. (Talk with a lawyer or debt counselor to review your options. See "For More Information . . ." for more details.)

## Looking at the Long Term

Your balance sheet can also help you make important long-term decisions about your household's financial situation. For example, if it shows that you have a lot of money salted away in retirement plans at work, or in stocks, bonds, and mutual funds, but that you have little cash available, you can reorganize your financial situation to reduce the amount you invest and raise more cash. No matter how appealing your 401(k) plan is at work, for example, it may be of little help if your hot-water heater breaks down or your roof starts leaking, and you don't have the cash to pay the repair bill.

Before you save any more money in retirement plans, college education funds, or the like, make sure you have cash set aside to handle emergencies.

Experts sometimes recommend having enough money to cover three to six months of expenses and keeping this money in short-term, conservative investments, such as bank accounts, money market funds, U.S. Treasury bills, or U.S. Savings Bonds.

## Your Investment Picture

Looking closely at your household balance sheet can also give you an indication of whether your investment program is out of balance. For purposes of this exercise, don't forget to consider all of your investments— including those in taxable accounts, and those in tax-deferred accounts, such as IRAs, 401(k) plans, and Keogh accounts. (It's crucial not to look at your employer-sponsored retirement plan in isolation; make sure you view it as part of your overall financial picture.)

When you look at the big picture, you may find that you have too great a portion of your overall assets invested in the more risky arena of stocks and stock mutual funds. Likewise, you may find your overall investment picture is weighted too heavily on the more conservative side, with money in bonds, bond funds, and such. The trick is to find some balance.

## Insuring against Risks

Planning for your retirement is important, of course. But don't overlook your health in the meantime. One of the most important benefits you can get is health insurance. Without it, you could face calamity.

If you're on the job hunt, try to find an employer that offers health insurance. If your current employer doesn't offer health insurance, ask some of your coworkers to join you in trying to persuade your boss to offer this benefit.

Health insurance is no small matter. Although most Americans have health insurance through an employer-sponsored group plan, working is no guarantee of being insured, according to a 1999 survey by The Commonwealth Fund.

"Despite the importance of ready access to health care for a productive and stable workforce, many employers do not offer health benefits to their employees, or restrict eligibility for benefits," the study found. "Nearly one-fifth of all workers . . . were not offered an employer-based plan, or were ineligible for coverage," according to the report.

In general, the lower the income, the more likely workers were to lack job-based health coverage. In addition, Hispanic employees were twice as likely as black or white workers to be employed by a company that didn't offer health insurance benefits.

Furthermore, the report found that a significant number of adults said that they lived from paycheck to paycheck, with little financial protection in the event of a major illness or injury.

One-third of all working-age adults surveyed said that, at best, they have just enough money or are not able to pay for the basic costs of living. This included poor families, but also revealed a trend among the middle class, the survey found.

In other words, these people couldn't afford to get sick.

Other studies have shown that small businesses, on average, are less likely to offer health coverage than are large and medium-sized businesses.

No matter how hard you must squeeze your budget, try to get health insurance.

Look carefully at the other risks you face in your daily life, too, and make sure you've got them properly covered. Do you have enough auto insurance? Are your household furnishings and belongings covered in addition to your house? If you have children, do you have enough life insurance to not only cover your debts, but also replace the stream of income that your family would lose out on upon your death? (See the discussion of group life insurance in Chapter 13.)

Don't forget about disability insurance, either. Remember that you stand a greater chance of suffering a serious disability—and missing work for a long period of time—than of dying during your working years. If you don't already have a disability insurance policy—either on your own or through work—consider getting one. Bear in mind that although coverage through work is better than no coverage at all, you may need separate coverage through an individual policy in case you lose your job and land another that doesn't offer a disability insurance plan.

## Developing a Financial Plan

Once you have your personal financial house in order, you can think about long-term goals and how to reach them, and how your employee benefits package fits in. Keep in mind that this process can be tricky. There are a lot of variables and a lot of tax, legal, and other complications. Consider enlisting professional help from an accountant, certified financial planner, or other advisor.

Start by writing down your goals and objectives. Would you like to save to buy a house, a vacation home, or a boat? Are you thinking about putting your children through college? Do you want to build a nest egg to help cover expenses during your retirement years? Whatever your goals are, write them down, then estimate how much each will cost.

Do you have enough money set aside to achieve your goals? If not, how much would you need to save and invest to meet them? Can you squeeze enough out of your existing budget, or do you have to make some cuts? Can you meet all the goals you've set, or just a few?

Ultimately, you'll probably have to set priorities. In other words, you may have to write down all your goals, then list which ones are the most important to you, and which can be realistically achieved given how much you've saved or invested, how much you can pull out of your budget, and how many years you have left to try to reach each goal.

## Building Your Nest Egg

If you're nearing retirement and you have little if any money set aside, then building a retirement nest egg may be your top priority. You must also search your soul to try to figure out how comfortable you are risking some of your money in various types of investments.

As you know, stocks (and stock mutual funds) generally offer the highest returns over the long haul, but they typically come with the most risk: The value of your investment could fall sharply at some point, so these types of investments are best only for long-term goals. Should a severe market downturn occur, your investment may need five to seven years or more to recover from the drop.

On the other hand, if you can't tolerate the risk and you're comfortable only with the safest investments, such as bank accounts, you may not be able to reach your goals; you may have to scale back your objectives, or find another way to pay for them, such as a second job.

Building a nest egg is where your employer-sponsored retirement plan can come in handy. If your employer offers a traditional pension, or defined benefit, plan, you can rest assured that you'll have at least some steady stream of income in retirement to supplement your Social Security benefits.

Odds are, however, that your pension won't be enough to cover your expenses. If that's the case, then you may want to take advantage of other retirement savings opportunities at work, such as a 401(k) plan, a SIMPLE plan, or something similar that lets you save regularly through the convenience of payroll deduction and lets you reduce your taxes, too.

Even if your employer offers you no retirement savings options (most small businesses do not), there are plenty of options available outside work. Consider contributing to a traditional IRA or a Roth IRA, for example. These can give you some tax benefits, and they offer a variety of investment vehicles for more flexibility.

# Social Security Benefits

Another key point to bear in mind is how soon you'll be able to retire. Most workers probably reckon that they'll be able to retire at age 65. This is changing, however.

Your "full retirement age" is the age at which you qualify for full Social Security benefits. Full retirement age used to be 65. Under a little noticed change in federal law, however, the full retirement age for Social Security purposes is later for people who were born after 1937. How much later depends on the year in which you were born. For example, if you were born in 1938, you'll have to work until you're 65 years and 2 months old to qualify for full Social Security benefits. If you were born in 1960 or later, you'll have to work until you're 67 to get full Social Security benefits. To find out exactly when you'll be able to retire with full Social Security benefits, see Figure 15.1.

**Figure 15.1**    Qualifying for Full Social Security

---

The later you were born, the longer you will have to work in order to qualify for full Social Security benefits. Under the old rules, you had to be 65 or older. In other words, 65 was the "full retirement age." Under the new rules, the full retirement age occurs later.

| Year of Birth | Full Retirement Age |
|---|---|
| 1937 or earlier | 65 |
| 1938 | 65 and 2 months |
| 1939 | 65 and 4 months |
| 1940 | 65 and 6 months |
| 1941 | 65 and 8 months |
| 1942 | 65 and 10 months |
| 1943 through 1954 | 66 |
| 1955 | 66 and 2 months |
| 1956 | 66 and 4 months |
| 1957 | 66 and 6 months |
| 1958 | 66 and 8 months |
| 1959 | 66 and 10 months |
| 1960 and later | 67 |

Source: Social Security Administration.

### Early Retirement

In addition, benefits will be reduced more sharply than before for people who take early retirement. In general, if you take early retirement, your benefits will be permanently reduced based on the number of months you will receive checks before you reach full retirement age. Here's how it works:

- If your full retirement age is 65, the reduction for starting your Social Security payments at age 62 is about 20 percent; at age 63, about 13⅓ percent; at age 64, about 6⅔ percent.
- Under the new rules, you'll still be able to retire early, but the reduction in benefits will be greater than it was. For example, if your full retirement age is 67 (in other words, if you were born in 1960 or later), the reduction for starting your benefits at age 62 will be about 30 percent; at age 63, about 25 percent; at age 64, about 20 percent; at age 65, about 13⅓ percent; at age 66, about 6⅔ percent.

### A Change in Outlook

These changes will have a big impact. Either you'll have to work longer in your job to qualify for full Social Security benefits, or you'll retire early and take a bigger cut in your benefits than you would have under the old rules.

This represents a major psychological and financial shift. You'll still have to save to help supplement your Social Security income in retirement. However, you may wind up working longer than you had originally planned. If you decide to take early retirement, you may have to save more than you originally planned, to make up for the shortfall in the Social Security benefits you'll be eligible to receive.

## Calculating Your Retirement Income Needs

To figure out how much you'll need to save for retirement, complete the worksheet on page 254. It will help you to estimate your income needs in retirement and to calculate how much you'll have to set aside now in order to reach your target.

Keep in mind that the worksheet isn't perfect; there are lots of variables to consider, and your circumstances may change in coming years. Financial planning is really a matter of substituting error for chaos, but don't let that stop you from at least coming up with an estimate.

**Worksheet**   How Much Must You Save toward Retirement?

---

Follow these steps:

1. How much annual income will you want in retirement?   $_____
   (Figure 70 percent of your current annual gross income just to break even.)

2. Subtract the income you expect to receive annually from

   a. Social Security. (If you make under $25,000,
      enter $8,000; between $25,000 and $40,000,
      enter $12,000; above $40,000, enter $14,500)   –_____

   b. a traditional employer-sponsored pension.
      (Ask your employer for an estimate, in today's dollars.)   –_____

   c. part-time income.   –_____

   d. other sources.   –_____

3. **This is how much you need to make up for
   each retirement year:**   = $_____

Now you need a ballpark estimate of how much money you'll need in
the bank the day you retire. (For convenience, this formula assumes
that you'll make 3 percent a year on your investments after inflation,
that you'll live to age 87, and that you'll start receiving Social Security
benefits at 65 or at full retirement age.)

4. To figure the amount you'll need to save, multiply
   the amount you need to make up for each year
   (number 3) by the factor below:   $_____
   
   | If you expect to retire at age: | 55 | ... your "factor" is: 21.0 |
   |---|---|---|
   | | 60 | 18.9 |
   | | 65 | 16.4 |
   | | 70 | 13.6 |

5. If you expect to retire before age 65, multiply your
   Social Security benefit from number 2 above by the
   factor below:   + $_____
   
   | If you expect to retire at age: | 55 | ... your "factor" is: 8.8 |
   |---|---|---|
   | | 60 | 4.7 |

6. Multiply how much you already have in savings by
   the factor below:   –$_____
   (Be sure to include savings in IRAs, 401(k)s, and all other savings plans.)
   
   | If you want to retire in: | 10 years | ... your factor is: 1.3 |
   |---|---|---|
   | | 15 years | 1.6 |
   | | 20 years | 1.8 |
   | | 25 years | 2.1 |
   | | 30 years | 2.4 |
   | | 35 years | 2.8 |
   | | 40 years | 3.3 |

**Worksheet**    Continued

---

7. **Total additional savings needed at retirement:**    =$_____

8. To figure out the annual amount you'll need to save,
   multiply the total in number 7 by the factor below:    =$_____

   | If you want to retire in: | 10 years | . . . your factor is: .085 |
   |---|---|---|
   | | 15 years | .052 |
   | | 20 years | .036 |
   | | 30 years | .020 |
   | | 35 years | .016 |
   | | 40 years | .013 |

Source: Adapted from the "Ballpark E$timate" worksheet from American Savings Education Council, <www. asec.org>.

---

# For More Information . . .

- The U.S. Department of Labor's Pension and Welfare Benefits Administration publishes *Top Ten Ways to Beat the Clock and Prepare for Retirement,* a brochure that offers retirement planning tips. For your free copy, write to: Pension and Welfare Benefits Administration, U.S. Department of Labor, 200 Constitution Avenue NW, Room N5619, Washington, DC 20210. You may also call the agency's toll-free publications hotline at 1-800-998-7542, or contact the agency's Web site: <www.dol.gov/dol/pwba>.

- For information about how your Social Security benefits are figured, call the Social Security Administration at 1-800-772-1213 or contact the agency's Web site: <www.ssa.gov>. You can order or download helpful publications, including *Social Security Retirement Benefits* and *Social Security—Understanding the Benefits.*

- The IRS publishes a number of booklets, many of them in plain language, that explain how the income tax system works and how you can cut down on the amount of taxes you pay. Start with Publication 17, *Your Federal Income Tax.* This is one of the best publications the IRS produces. It offers a handy overview of the tax system and how it affects you. It covers lots of details you may not be aware of about the federal income tax, including deductions you may be able to claim to reduce the amount of income you have to pay tax on. For your free copy, visit your local IRS office, call 1-800-829-3676, or contact the agency's Web site: <www.irs.gov>.

- Debt Counselors of America is a nonprofit group that offers tips on how to get your budget in better order and cut down on debt. The group also offers lots of resources to which people can turn when they are deeply in debt. For more information, contact the group's Web site: <www.getoutofdebt.org>.

- The T. Rowe Price group of mutual funds has published the "T. Rowe Price Retirement Planning Kit," designed for people who have more than five years to go before retirement. It includes a workbook to help you figure how much money you'll need for retirement and how much you need to save to reach your goal. It also offers tips on putting together a retirement investment strategy. Another publication, the "T. Rowe Price Retirees Financial Guide," is for those who are already retired or who are close to retirement. It includes a workbook to help retirees estimate how much money they can afford to spend in retirement so that they can maintain their standard of living. It takes into account taxes, inflation, and sources of retirement income, including Social Security. Both kits are available free by calling 1-800-541-8460, or by writing to: T. Rowe Price, P.O. Box 17302, Baltimore, MD 21297-1302.

### Suggestion Box

If you have questions, comments, or suggestions about this book, contact the author, Neil Downing, via e-mail at: <NDowning@msn.com>.

# APPENDIX

# *A*

# State Insurance Regulators

Here's how to contact the state insurance regulator near you.

**Alabama**
Alabama Department of Insurance
201 Monroe St., Suite 1700
Montgomery, AL 36104
1-334-269-3550

**Alaska**
Alaska Division of Insurance
Department of Community and
    Economic Development
P.O. Box 110805
Juneau, AK 99811-0805
1-907-465-2515

**Arkansas**
Arkansas Department of Insurance
1200 W. 3rd St.
Little Rock, AR 72201-1904
1-501-371-2600

**Arizona**
Arizona Department of Insurance
2910 N. 44th St., Suite 210
Phoenix, AZ 85018-7256
1-602-912-8400

**California**
California Department of Insurance
300 Capitol Mall, Suite 1500
Sacramento, CA 95814
1-916-492-3500

**Colorado**
Colorado Division of Insurance
1560 Broadway, Suite 850
Denver, CO 80202
1-303-894-7499

**Connecticut**
Connecticut Department of Insurance
P.O. Box 816
Hartford, CT 06142-0816
1-860-297-3802

**Delaware**
Delaware Department of Insurance
Rodney Building
841 Silver Lake Blvd.
Dover, DE 19904
1-302-739-4251

**District of Columbia**
Department of Insurance and Securities
    Regulation
810 First St., NE
Washington, DC 20002
1-202-727-8000

**Florida**
Florida Department of Insurance
200 E. Gaines St.
Tallahassee, FL 32399-0300
1-850-922-3101

**Georgia**
Office of Commissioner of Insurance
716 West Tower
2 Martin Luther King, Jr. Dr.
Atlanta, GA 30334
1-404-656-2056

**Hawaii**
Department of Commerce and
    Consumer Affairs
Insurance Division
250 S. King St., 5th Floor
Honolulu, HI 96813
1-808-586-2790

**Idaho**
Idaho Department of Insurance
700 W. State St., 3rd Floor
Boise, ID 83720-0043
1-208-334-4250

**Illinois**
Illinois Department of Insurance
320 W. Washington St., 4th Floor
Springfield, IL 62767-0001
1-217-785-0116

**Indiana**
Indiana Department of Insurance
311 W. Washington St., Suite 300
Indianapolis, IN 46204-2787
1-317-232-2385

**Iowa**
Division of Insurance
State of Iowa
330 E. Maple St.
Des Moines, IA 50319
1-515-281-5705

**Kansas**
Kansas Department of Insurance
420 SW 9th St.
Topeka, KS 66612-1678
1-785-296-7801

**Kentucky**
Kentucky Department of Insurance
215 W. Main St.
Frankfort, KY 40601
1-502-564-6027

**Louisiana**
Louisiana Department of Insurance
Attn: Craig Johnson
950 N. 5th St.
Baton Rouge, LA 70802
1-225-342-5423

**Maine**
Maine Bureau of Insurance
Department of Professional and
    Financial Regulation
State Office Building, Station 34
Augusta, ME 04333-0034
1-207-624-8475

**Maryland**
Maryland Insurance Administration
525 St. Paul St.
Baltimore, MD 21202-2272
1-410-468-2090

**Massachusetts**
Division of Insurance
Commonwealth of Massachusetts
One South Station
Boston, MA 02110
1-617-521-7794

**Michigan**
Michigan Insurance Bureau
Consumer and Industry Services
611 W. Ottawa St., 2nd Floor
Lansing, MI 48933-1070
1-517-373-9273

**Minnesota**
Minnesota Department of Commerce
133 E. 7th St.
St. Paul, MN 55101
1-651-296-6848

**Mississippi**
Mississippi Insurance Department
1804 Walter Sillers State Office Building
550 High St.
Jackson, MS 39201
1-601-359-3569

**Missouri**
Missouri Department of Insurance
301 W. High St., Room 630
Jefferson City, MO 65101
1-573-751-4126

**Montana**
Montana Department of Insurance
P.O. Box 4009
Helena, MT 59604-4009
1-406-444-2040

**Nebraska**
Nebraska Department of Insurance
Terminal Building, Suite 400
941 "O" St.
Lincoln, NE 68508
1-402-471-2201

**Nevada**
Nevada Division of Insurance
788 Fairview Dr., Suite 300
Carson City, NV 89701
1-775-687-4270

**New Hampshire**
Department of Insurance
State of New Hampshire
56 Old Suncook Rd.
Concord, NH 03301
1-603-271-2261

**New Jersey**
New Jersey Department of Banking
    and Insurance
20 W. State St. CN325
Trenton, NJ 08625
1-609-292-5360

**New Mexico**
New Mexico Department of Insurance
P.O. Drawer 1269
Santa Fe, NM 87504-1269
1-505-827-4601

**New York**
New York Department of Insurance
25 Beaver St.
New York, NY 10004-2319
1-212-480-2289

**North Carolina**
North Carolina Department of
    Insurance
P.O. Box 26387
Raleigh, NC 27611
1-919-733-7349

**North Dakota**
North Dakota Department of Insurance
600 E. Boulevard
Bismarck, ND 58505-0320
1-701-328-2440

**Ohio**
Ohio Department of Insurance
2100 Stella Ct.
Columbus, OH 43215-1067
1-614-644-2658

**Oklahoma**
Oklahoma Department of Insurance
P.O. Box 53408
Oklahoma City, OK 73152
1-405-521-2828

**Oregon**
Oregon Division of Insurance
Department of Consumer and Business
    Services
350 Winter St. NE, Room 440
Salem, OR 97301-3883
1-503-947-7980

**Pennsylvania**
Pennsylvania Insurance Department
1326 Strawberry Sq.
Harrisburg, PA 17120
1-717-783-0442

**Rhode Island**
Rhode Island Insurance Division
Department of Business Regulation
233 Richmond St., Suite 233
Providence, RI 02903-4233
1-401-222-2223

**South Carolina**
South Carolina Department of
    Insurance
1612 Marion St.
Columbia, SC 29202
1-803-737-6160

**South Dakota**
South Dakota Division of Insurance
Department of Commerce and
    Regulation
118 W. Capitol Ave.
Pierre, SD 57501-2000
1-605-773-3563

**Tennessee**
Tennessee Department of Commerce
    and Insurance
Davy Crockett Tower
500 James Robertson Pkwy.
Nashville, TN 37243-0565
1-615-741-2241

**Texas**
Texas Department of Insurance
P.O. Box 149104
Austin, TX 78714-9104
1-512-463-6464

**Utah**
Utah Department of Insurance
3110 State Office Bldg.
Salt Lake City, UT 84114-1201
1-801-538-3800

**Vermont**
Vermont Division of Insurance
Department of Banking, Insurance,
    Securities, and Health Care
89 Main St., Drawer 20
Montpelier, VT 05620-3101
1-802-828-3301

**Virginia**
State Corporation Commission
Bureau of Insurance
P.O. Box 1157
Richmond, VA 23218
1-804-371-9694

**Washington**
Washington Office of the Insurance
    Commissioner
14th Ave. & Water St.
P.O. Box 40255
Olympia, WA 98504-0255
1-360-753-7301

**West Virginia**
West Virginia Department of Insurance
P.O. Box 50540
Charleston, WV 25305-0540
1-304-558-3354

**Wisconsin**
Office of the Commissioner of
    Insurance
State of Wisconsin
121 E. Wilson
Madison, WI 53702
1-608-267-1233

**Wyoming**
Wyoming Department of Insurance
Herschler Building, 3E
122 W. 25th St.
Cheyenne, WY 82002-0440
1-307-777-7401

**American Samoa**
Office of the Governor
American Samoa Government
Pago Pago, AS 96799
011-684-633-4116

**Guam**
Dept. of Revenue & Taxation
Insurance, Securities, Banking & Real
    Estate Division
Government of Guam
P.O. Box 23607
GMS, GU 96921
1-671-475-1843

**Puerto Rico**
Puerto Rico Department of Insurance
Cobian's Plaza Building
1607 Ponce de Leon Ave.
Santurce, PR 00909
1-787-722-8686

**Virgin Islands**
Division of Banking and Insurance
1131 King St., Suite 101
Christiansted
St. Croix, Virgin Islands 00820
1-340-773-6449

Source: National Association of
Insurance Commissioners.

# Top-Rated Health Insurance Plans

The health plans listed in the following table qualified for the highest possible rating—"Excellent"—by the National Committee for Quality Assurance (NCQA) in October 1999. To qualify for this rating, health plans had to show "commitment to clinical excellence, customer service, and continuous improvement," according to the NCQA.

These plans have also generally achieved scores in the top 25 percent on a broad range of performance measures, such as mammography and immunization rates, beta blocker treatment after a heart attack, and overall satisfaction, according to the NCQA.

As you read the list, keep in mind that the NCQA accreditation process is product-specific. In other words, a health plan's Medicare, Medicaid, and commercial products may not all share the same accreditation status.

The NCQA, a nonprofit group, assesses, measures, and reports on the quality of care provided by the nation's managed care organizations. More than three-quarters of Americans enrolled in HMOs are in plans that have been reviewed by the NCQA.

## America's Highest-Rated Health Plans

| Health Plan | City | Product |
| --- | --- | --- |
| Aetna U.S. Healthcare, Inc. Southern New Jersey/Delaware | Wayne, Pa. | M |
| Aetna U.S. Healthcare, Inc. Southeastern Pennsylvania/Harrisburg | Blue Bell, Philadelphia, Pa. | C, M |
| Anthem BlueCross and BlueShield of Connecticut, Inc. | North Haven, Conn. | C |
| BlueCross and BlueShield of Maine | S. Portland, Maine | C |
| BlueCross and BlueShield of Massachusetts, Inc. | Boston, Mass. | C |
| Capital District Physicians' Health Plan, Inc. | Albany, N.Y. | C |

| Health Plan | City | Product |
|---|---|---|
| Capital Health Plan | Tallahassee, Fla. | C, M |
| ConnectiCare, Inc. | Farmington, Conn. | C |
| Excellus Health Plan, Inc.—Rochester Area Division | Rochester, N.Y. | C, M |
| Fallon Community Health Plan | Worcester, Mass. | C, M |
| Group Health Cooperative of Puget Sound | Seattle, Wash. | C |
| Harris Methodist Texas Health Plan, Inc. | Arlington, Tex. | M |
| Harvard Pilgrim Health Care | Brookline, Mass. | C, M |
| Health Alliance Medical Plans, Inc. | Urbana, Ill. | C |
| Health Alliance Plan of Michigan | Detroit, Mich. | C |
| Health Care Plan | Buffalo, N.Y. | C, M |
| Health Plan Hawaii | Honolulu, Hawaii | C |
| Health Plan of the Redwoods | Santa Rosa, Calif. | M |
| HealthPlus of Michigan | Flint, Mich. | C |
| Healthsource Maine, Inc. | Freeport, Maine | C |
| Healthsource New Hampshire, Inc./ Healthsource Preferred, Inc. | Concord, N.H. | C |
| HMO CNY - BC/BS of Central NY | Syracuse, N.Y. | C |
| HMO of Northeastern Pennsylvania - dba First Priority Health | Wilkes-Barre, Pa. | C, M |
| Independent Health Association, Inc. | Buffalo, N.Y. | C |
| Kaiser Foundation Health Plan of Georgia | Atlanta, Ga. | M |
| Kaiser Foundation Health Plan of Hawaii | Honolulu, Hawaii | C, M |
| Kaiser Foundation Health Plan of North Carolina | Raleigh, N.C. | C |
| Keystone Health Plan Central | Camp Hill, Pa. | C |
| Matthew Thornton Health Plan | Bedford, N.H. | C |
| Matthew Thornton Health Plan | Schenectady, N.Y. | C |
| Network Health Plan of Wisconsin, Inc. | Menasha, Wis. | M |
| PennState Geisinger Health Plan | Danville, Pa. | C |
| PersonalCare Insurance of Illinois, Inc. | Champaign, Ill. | C |
| Preferred Care | Rochester, N.Y. | C, M |
| Priority Health | Grand Rapids, Mich. | C |
| Rocky Mountain HMO | Grand Junction, Colo. | C, M |
| Sentara Health Management | Virginia Beach, Va. | C |
| Touchpoint Health Plan | Appleton, Wis. | C |
| Tufts Health Plan | Waltham, Mass. | C, M |
| United HealthCare of New England, Inc. | Warwick, R.I. | C |

Note:  "C" is for commercial product lines; "M" for Medicare.

Source:  National Committee for Quality Insurance (<www.ncqa.org>).

# APPENDIX C

# Pension and Benefits Agencies

The Pension and Welfare Benefits Administration (PWBA), part of the U.S. Department of Labor, is responsible for protecting your interests in employee benefit plans, whether you're a participant or beneficiary. PWBA covers plans run by for-profit and nonprofit organizations, not plans run by government agencies. Check the list below to find the regional office or district office near you; check the end of the Appendix for pension counseling agencies.

**For Tennessee, North Carolina, South Carolina, Georgia, Alabama, Puerto Rico, Mississippi, and Florida:**

Atlanta Regional Office
61 Forsyth St. SW, Suite 7B54
Atlanta, GA 30303
1-404-562-2156

Miami District Office
8040 Peters Rd.
Bldg. H, Suite 104
Plantation, FL 33324
1-954-424-4022

**For Rhode Island, Vermont, Maine, New Hampshire, Connecticut, Massachusetts, and upstate New York:**

Boston Regional Office
JFK Federal Building, Room 575
Boston, MA 02203
1-617-565-9600

**For northern Illinois, northern Indiana, and Wisconsin:**

Chicago Regional Office
200 W. Adams St., Suite 1600
Chicago, IL 60606
1-312-353-0900

**For Michigan, Kentucky, Ohio, and southern Indiana:**

Cincinnati Regional Office
1885 Dixie Highway, Suite 210
Ft. Wright, KY 41011
1-606-578-4680

Detroit District Office:
211 W. Fort St., Suite 1310
Detroit, MI 48226
1-313-226-7450

**For Arkansas, Louisiana, New Mexico, Oklahoma, and Texas:**

Dallas Regional Office
525 Griffin St., Room 707
Dallas, TX 75202
1-214-767-6831

For Colorado, southern Illinois, Iowa, Kansas, Minnesota, Missouri, Montana, Nebraska, North Dakota, South Dakota, and Wyoming:

Kansas City Regional Office
1100 Main St., Suite 1200
Kansas City, MO 64105
1-816-426-5131

St. Louis District Office
815 Olive St., Room 338
St. Louis, MO 63101
1-314-539-2691

For Delaware, Maryland, southern New Jersey, Pennsylvania, Virginia, West Virginia, and Washington, D.C.:

Philadelphia Regional Office
Gateway Bldg.
3535 Market St., Room 12400
Philadelphia, PA 19104
1-215-596-1134

Washington District Office
1730 K St. NW, Suite 556
Washington, DC 20006
1-202-254-7013

For American Samoa, Arizona, Guam, Hawaii, southern California, and Wake Island:

Los Angeles Regional Office
790 E. Colorado Blvd., Suite 514
Pasadena, CA 91101
1-626-583-7862

For eastern New York and northern New Jersey:

New York Regional Office
U.S. Dept. of Labor, PWBA
6 World Trade Center, Room 625
New York, NY 10048
1-212-637-0600

For Alaska, northern California, Idaho, Nevada, Oregon, Utah, and Washington:

San Francisco Regional Office
71 Stevenson St., Suite 915
San Francisco, CA 94119
1-415-975-4600

Seattle District Office
1111 Third Ave.
Suite 860
Seattle, WA 98101
1-206-553-4244

You may also contact PWBA headquarters:

U.S. Department of Labor
Pension and Welfare Benefits
    Administration
Division of Technical Assistance and
    Inquiries
Room N5625
200 Constitution Ave. NW
Washington, DC 20210
1-202-219-8776

COBRA coverage for employees of state and local governments is administered by the U.S. Public Health Service. For information, write to:

U.S. Public Health Service
Office of the Assistant Secretary for
    Health
5600 Fishers Ln.
Rockville, MD 20857

Health care continuation-of-coverage rules for federal employees fall under another law similar to COBRA. For information, contact your personnel office.

## Pension Counseling Projects

During the 1990s, several groups formed in separate parts of the country to offer free pension counseling services. The groups were given grants by the U.S. Administration on Aging, and are generally known as "pension counseling projects."

These groups specialize in difficult cases, situations that typically cannot be resolved through the usual channels. Finding lost pensions is one of their specialties. In some cases, these services can help you cut through red tape so you can get the benefits to which you're entitled.

Check this list to see if there's a pension counseling service near you:

### Alabama
Pension Clinic
University of Alabama School of Law
P.O. Box 870382
Tuscaloosa, AL 35487
1-205-348-1136

### Arizona
Pima Council on Aging Pension Project
5055 E. Broadway, Suite C104
Tucson, AZ 85711
1-520-790-7262

### California
Pension Rights Project
CANHR
1610 Bush St.
San Francisco, CA 94109
1-415-474-5171
1-800-474-1116

### Chicago, Illinois
Pension Information Effort
Chicago Department on Aging
30 N. LaSalle, Suite 2320
Chicago, IL 60602
1-312-744-4016
(This agency serves only people age 60 and over who live in Chicago.)

### Michigan
Michigan Pension Rights Project
Legal Hotline for Michigan Seniors
115 W. Allegan, Suite 720
Lansing, MI 48933
1-517-372-5959
1-800-347-5297

### Minnesota
Pension Rights Project
Minnesota Senior Federation
1885 University Ave. W, Suite 190
St. Paul, MN 55104
1-651-645-0261
1-877-645-0261

### Missouri, Southern Illinois
Older Women's League Pension
   Benefits Project
World Community Center
438 N. Skinker Blvd.
St. Louis, MO 63130
1-314-725-1516

### New England
New England Pension Assistance
   Project
Gerontology Institute
University of Massachusetts, Boston
100 Morrissey Blvd.
Boston, MA 02125
In Massachusetts: 1-617-287-7311
In the rest of New England:
   1-617-287-7332

### New York
New York Pension Hotline
Legal Services for the Elderly
130 W. 42nd St., 17th floor
New York, NY 10036
1-212-997-7714
1-800-355-7714

### Virginia
Mt. Empire Older Citizens Inc.
P.O. Box 888
Big Stone Gap, VA 24219
1-540-523-4202

# Bibliography

Allen, Everett T. Jr., et al. *Pension Planning.* Irwin, 1992.

Allstate Insurance Company. *Insurance Handbook for Reporters.* Allstate Insurance Company, 1985.

American Council of Life Insurance. *Life Insurance Fact Book.* American Council of Life Insurance, 1998.

Bamford, Janet. *Smarter Insurance Solutions.* Bloomberg, 1996.

Beam, Burton T. Jr., and John J. McFadden. *Employee Benefits.* Dearborn, 1996.

Bogosian, Wayne G., and Dee Lee. *The Complete Idiot's Guide to 401(k) Plans.* Alpha, 1998.

CCH Inc. *2000 U.S. Master Tax Guide.* CCH Inc., 1999.

Choate, Natalie B. *Life and Death Planning for Retirement Benefits.* Ataxplan, 1996.

Combe, Cynthia M., and Gerard J. Talbot. *Employee Benefits Answer Book.* Panel, 1998.

Employee Benefit Research Institute. *Fundamentals of Employee Benefit Programs.* Employee Benefit Research Institute, 1997.

Ferguson, Karen, and Kate Blackwell. *The Pension Book.* Arcade, 1995.

Garner, John C. *Health Insurance Answer Book.* Panel, 1998.

Goodman, Jordan E. *Everyone's Money Book.* 2d edition. Dearborn, 1998.

Graves, Edward E., ed. *McGill's Life Insurance.* The American College, 1994.

Jones, Harriett E., and Dani L. Long. *Principles of Insurance: Life, Health, and Annuities.* Life Office Management Association Inc., 1996.

Kaster, Nicholas, et al. *1999 U.S. Master Pension Guide.* CCH Inc., 1999.

Leimberg, Stephan R., and John J. McFadden. *The Tools & Techniques of Employee Benefit and Retirement Planning.* The National Underwriter Company, 1997.

Leimberg, Stephan R., et al. *The Tools & Techniques of Estate Planning.* The National Underwriter Company, 1992.

Lochray, Paul J. *Financial Planner's Guide to Estate Planning.* Prentice Hall, 1992.

McCormally, Kevin. *Kiplinger's Cut Your Taxes.* Kiplinger, 1999.

McDonnell, Ken, et al. *EBRI Databook on Employee Benefits.* Employee Benefit Research Institute, 1997.

National Center for Employee Ownership. *The Stock Options Book.* National Center for Employee Ownership, 1999.

Panszczyk, Linda. *1999 U.S. Master Employee Benefits Guide.* CCH Inc., 1998.

Rowland, Mary. *A Commonsense Guide to Your 401(k).* Bloomberg, 1998.

Sadler, Jeff, and Robert E. Parr. *The Managed Care and Group Health Handbook.* The National Underwriter Company, 1997.

Schurenberg, Eric. *401(k) Take Charge of Your Future.* Warner Books, 1996.

Tatara, Irene E. *Working with Cafeteria Plans.* CCH Inc., 1998.

Vaughan, Emmett. *Fundamentals of Risk and Insurance.* John Wiley & Sons Inc., 1992.

# Index